W9-BNJ-346

FROM THE LIBRARY OF

Trish Brown

THE
PASSIONS
_of_
M E N

THE
PASSIONS
— *of* —
M E N

Work and Love
in the Age of
Stress

MARK HUNTER

G. P. PUTNAM'S SONS · NEW YORK

This book is for Lise.

G. P. Putnam's Sons
Publishers Since 1838
200 Madison Avenue
New York, NY 10016

Copyright © 1988 by Mark Hunter
All rights reserved. This book, or parts thereof,
may not be reproduced in any form without permission.
Published simultaneously in Canada.

Library of Congress Cataloging-in-Publication Data

Hunter, Mark.
The passions of men: work and love in the age of stress

Mark Hunter.—1st American ed.
p.   cm.
1. Men—United States—Attitudes.   I. Title
HQ1090.3.H86   1988   87-32535 CIP
305.3′1′0973—dc19
ISBN 0-399-13322-4

Book design by The Sarabande Press
Printed in the United States of America
1   2   3   4   5   6   7   8   9   10

Acknowledgments

In writing this book I owe thanks to:

First and foremost, Lise Bloch-Morhange, who read the text in various drafts and added her insights, observations, and encouragement throughout the work.

My colleagues—Mark Schapiro, Rob Brezsny, Joey Simas, Richard Trainor, Suzanne Lowrey, Katherine Knorr—who discussed and/or provided documents for various ideas while the work was in progress.

The editors—Myra Appleton, Tracey Karstens Farrell, Hal Silverman, Nancy Friedman, Bonnie Blodgett, and Dave McGee—who commissioned articles that provided useful dossiers.

The archives staff, in particular Maggie Shapiro, Deborah Bouygues, and Dan Reasor, of the *International Herald Tribune.*

The staff of the Benjamin Franklin Library and the Government Printing Office of the American Embassy in Paris.

Raymond O'Kane of the United Brotherhood of Carpenters in New York; Naomi Spatz of the New York Federation of Teachers; and Al Mann of the Veterans Administration press bureau in New York.

My parents, Anita Hunter and Evan Hunter, whose support and encouragement in various ways is gratefully acknowledged.

My agents, Loretta Weingel-Fidel and Kathy Robbins, whose counsel and critiques were unfailingly excellent.

And my publishers, G. P. Putnam's Sons, with special thanks to E. Stacy Creamer, for backing the project in more ways than one.

Finally, thanks to the men and women who sat through long interviews, and who requested anonymity.

The author gratefully acknowledges the following publications, publishers, and authors for use of the following:

Academic Press: *Medical Psychology: Contributions in Behavioral Medicine.* Copyright © 1981 by Academic Press.

Alfred A. Knopf, Inc.: *Something Happened* by Joseph Heller. Copyright © 1974 by Scapegoat Productions Inc., and *Type A Behavior and Your Heart* by Meyer Friedman and Ray H. Rosenman. Copyright © 1974 by Meyer Friedman. Reprinted with Permission of Alfred A. Knopf, Inc., a Division of Random House, Inc.

Andrews and McMeel: *USA Today:* "Tracking Tomorrow's Trend." Copyright © 1986, Gannett News Media Services and Anthony M. Casale. Reprinted with permission of Andrews and McMeel. All rights reserved.

The Associated Press: "Family Sues in Murder-Suicide at State Office." Appeared in *The San Francisco Examiner*, January 30, 1987. Used by permission of The Associated Press. Copyright © 1987.

American Psychiatric Press Inc.: *The Trauma of War: Stress and Recovery in Viet Nam Veterans* by Stephen M. Sonnenberg, Arthur S. Blank Jr., and John A. Talbott. Copyright © 1985 by American Psychiatric Press Inc.

Bantam Doubleday Dell Publishing Group Inc: *Iacocca: An Autobiography* by Lee Iacocca. Copyright © 1984 by Bantam Books. Reprinted with permission of Bantam Books, a division of Bantam Doubleday Dell Publishing Group Inc.

Judith Bat-Ada: "Playboy Isn't Playing," and Interview with Judith Bat-Ada. From *Take Back the Night*, published by William Morrow & Company.

Mike Clary: *Daddy's Home* by Mike Clary. Copyright © 1982 by Mike Clary. Reprinted with permission of Mike Clary.

Condé Nast Inc.: "Must I Be Superwoman to Cope with Motherhood?" by Carole Suplina, *Vogue*, August 1978. Courtesy *Vogue*, Copyright © Condé Nast Publications Inc., and "Do You Have a Heart Attack Personality?" by Carole Tavris, *GQ*, January 1987, Courtesy *GQ*. Copyright © 1987, Condé Nast Publications Inc.

Doubleday: Excerpts from *How Men Feel* by Anthony Astrachan. Copyright © 1986 by Anthony Astrachan; *Sons* by Evan Hunter, copyright © 1969 by Evan Hunter; and *The Hearts of Men: American Dreams and the Flight from Commitment by* Barbara Ehrenreich. Copyright © 1983 by Barbara Ehrenreich. Reprinted by Permission of Doubleday, a Division of Bantam Doubleday Dell Publishing Group Inc.

Farrar, Straus, and Giroux, Inc.: Excerpt from "Memories of West Street and Lepke" from *Life Studies* by Robert Lowell. Copyright © 1956, 1959, by Robert Lowell. Reprinted by permission of Farrar, Straus, and Giroux, Inc.

Continued on page 308

Contents

CONTENTS

INTRODUCTION

BETWEEN A ROCK AND A HARD PLACE

> *A society which is clamoring for choice, which is filled with many articulate groups, each urging its own brand of salvation, its own variety of economic philosophy, will give each new generation no peace until all have chosen or gone under, unable to bear the conditions of choice. The stress is in our civilisation, not in the physical changes through which our children pass, but it is none the less real nor the less inevitable in twentieth-century America.*

> —Margaret Mead, *Coming of Age in Samoa*

Are men different from women? Choose one:
A. Yes, of course.
B. No, except women can have babies.
C. Maybe, but anything a man can do, a woman can do.
D. Yes, because women have babies.
Answer: All of the above.

I grew up seeing that men and women are different, and then I was taught that they are not.

What I saw was this: Men went away to work every day, and mothers were there when the kids called. Everyone was in a race, and men had to win it. Men talked and women listened unless, like my mother, they were strong-willed enough to take part in the conversation, and men didn't like that.

When women talked it was to each other, and what one knew, the rest knew. "Intuition" was what a man had in mind when he asked himself, "How does that woman know I'm lying?" You could not fool a woman, but she would sometimes let you off the hook; a man would not let you off the hook unless you fooled him.

Women and girls were cleaner than boys, and did most of the cleaning, which was a reason that men and boys needed them. Men made money. (At one point I literally believed that *making* money, the way I made plastic models of war planes, was what men did all day.) Some made more than others, but women rarely made as much as men, and that was a reason women needed *them*.

When boys grew older, they fought over girls. Girls wanted to have fun— according to rock singer Cyndi Lauper, that's all they want to do, even now—and to have fun you needed a car, so to have a girl you had to make money. To make money you needed a job, and to get a job you had to fight off other boys.

When I left school, for the rest of my life I would have a job. And I had to choose the job early—the question was posed to me formally, along with the rest of my sixth-grade class, by the elementary-school guidance counselor who made it clear that the longer I waited, the more other boys would be ahead of me. Once I had a job, for good and for keeps, I could choose a girl for good and for keeps, a girl who would know everything about me, and who would admire me for how well I did my job.

It was 1952 when I was born. It is 1987 now, as I write. From what I can see, and what men and women tell me, we have not changed greatly in those thirty-five years. *But we think we ought to have changed.* We do not know exactly *how,* though we know why: *because men and women are or ought to be equal.* Yet we are not sure what form this equality should assume.

For a good decade of my life, I lived among men and (mainly) women who reasoned that the sexes were not different, after all, except perhaps for "minor differences" related to the "act of reproduction," as Gloria Steinem said; and since reproduction was something we put aside, at least for a while, men and women were essentially alike. Women could have jobs to make money for their own sakes, and they did not need us to do it. And since they did not need us—men—for that, they would not bake our pies and clean and be silent. It was so simple a child could understand.

And we were the children who would not be like their parents.

We would work, not for money, but for pleasure. We would love, not for services rendered, but selflessly. We would not dominate each other, each a sort of bitter half-person; men would not be hollow kings, and women would not be "the power behind the power," as a man of twenty-six described his parents to me with evident disgust. No, we would deal with each other as self-fulfilled equals, and share equally in what life brought us. We would work and raise our children, not each in a separate corner of life, but together. What one could and would do, so would the other.

What we believed seems to have become part of what everyone believes. "Oh, sure," a man ten years younger than I agrees, "when I settle down with a woman it's got to be equal. Right down the line." It always has been like this in his relationships with women, he says—they have shared the cooking and cleaning, the needs and gifts, equally. It will be like that when he has children, he says in a tone that suggests the question needn't be raised; he wants to "share" equally in the childrearing too.

But that's for later. Right now he is fighting off competitors in the publishing business, trying to advance through the ranks of an independent company. His two main competitors in the office were women, but one of them left the industry, and the other left the company. The women have moved on, and he is still there; he will be there as long as it takes, by the hour (sixty a week at last count) or the year. It hasn't seemed to occur to him that the pattern of his life and the cut of his ideas—that someday he will abruptly put aside this career to raise children—do not point in the same direction.

I can see the direction he will ultimately take in a friend I'll call Peter. We entered college together; endured our parents' divorces together; shared the same roof often (including one night when my lover threw me out in the winter rain, and he found me wandering the streets as my wet sneakers froze, and took me to his home); began our careers at about the same time. I was best man at his wedding when we were thirty years old, he six years into his career in marketing, I five into mine as a journalist.

What we talked about a lot in those days was how much we worked. It is still our major topic of conversation, the one to which other considerations must ultimately bow. At the time his daughter was born, just after he was promoted to vice-president for international marketing of a Fortune 100 company, he was on the road half of every week, or in his office every weekday (counting the time it took to get there, on the subway and in his mind) from seven in the morning until nine at night. He'd never been sick, until the girl arrived. Then he stayed home from work for two weeks: the longest time he'd had off the job since starting his career.

Just imagine. *He had to get sick to stay home with his daughter for two weeks.*

He makes much more money than I, and doesn't always care for his job; I write, which is something he has always wanted to do but doesn't have the time for now. He dreams of returning to it someday. But in crucial respects our work lives are quite alike. Both of us worry over whether or not we spend enough or too much time on the job. Even times we've grown tired of it, we've each immersed ourselves in the long hours and seemingly endless days of jobs we know how to do. We did it naturally, without much of a second thought—the way Peter's wife devoted herself to their child, once he went back to work.

That is what we saw our parents doing, of course. It seems that we have traveled a long way to come back where we started. How did we become the parents we never wanted to be?

A man who was a student radical in the sixties, a public defender in the seventies, and a businessman these days, has an answer. Turning away from his pregnant wife, he tells me that "we're all getting more conservative these days." He hates Reagan conservatism, but when he laughs at it—he is indeed chuckling—he has to laugh at himself too. When push came to shove, he needed a house and a good—that is, well-paying—job, as much as ever his father did. "You gotta deal with reality sooner or later," he says. Reality is what a man has to face up to if he's going to be a man. Reality is the same as it always was.

Reality has not changed, not like we thought it should.

I'm no different from these men. The destiny I thought I would escape has turned out to be my own. I am like my father, like Peter: I work for a living, for my loved ones, in order to be someone—someone I know something about, who can at least say, "This is what I do, and I'm good at it." (More men, I have learned from a survey by Anthony M. Casale and associates, say that they are good at their jobs than at anything else they do, including parenting, by a wide margin.) I work to show my love for a woman, to have something to give her, and yet to have some life of my own that she doesn't know entirely—a life that is mine alone. I work for money, and I'd best never forget it.

And I do not have the time, or the energy, to enjoy the rewards of my labors as much as I would like, beginning with love and friendship.

You could say, *but that is not different from women's lives.* They now work, and for all of the reasons I've cited for why men do. Women earn money, wonder how best to divide their time between the job and their loved ones, and feel the need to say, "This is what I do, and do well." Yes, women do those things, all of them. Some women were doing all of them long before the Women's Liberation Movement (a term that already sounds oddly quaint) began in the early 1960s.

But since then two generations have matured, and it still remains the case that, in the main, men and women do different kinds of work, make different sums of money, and form different kinds of relationships with those around them.

And this leads to the contradiction between what we think reality should be and what it appears to be. We believe in gender equality, but we accept gender differences. We may not like them, and we certainly do not like to discuss them openly, man to woman—but we agree, if only covertly, that they exist.

What has changed is that we don't see these differences in the same way. We don't believe anymore that they are inevitable, immutable, ordained— by God or society. We think that men and women can be as similar, or as different, as they wish, and that neither has the right to say anything about it to the other. Men cannot tell their women how and when to have babies; women cannot tell their men to stop work and let the females take over. Such things do occur, but we would not consider them good or proper. We say that we have won the right, at least ideally, for each of us to live our lives where, how, and for what we please; perhaps some of us are exercising that agreed-upon right.

Yet many of us appear to be repeating our parents' lives; at least, so it seems. We have a choice in the matter—but it is not clear how, or how not, we are exercising that right of choice.

What is clear is that we're afraid to make the wrong choice, just as we are afraid not to choose.

The most central of these choices bear on the question of how to balance the demands of work, love, and money. The confusion I see in the men around me—a confusion that extends to every age group, every class— almost always comes down to this: *what must you give up to get what you want, and how do you know that you're making the right choice, one that won't blow up later in your face?*

The problem that men have now is not fundamentally different from the one Henry David Thoreau stated simply in *Walden*, published in 1854: "Where I Lived, and What I Lived For." How does one choose and defend a place to go, and a reason for being there? And what are the limits—economic, physical, and moral—within which those choices can be made?

We are trying desperately to answer these questions, and have been trying for three generations. I call the time in which those generations have lived "The Age of Stress," because since the end of World War II we have increasingly defined men's search for a place to be—in the home, on the job, and in the hearts of women—and a reason for being there, in terms of the "stress" this search creates.

When I began to think about this matter, some ten years ago, I took it for granted, along with everyone else, that "stress" is an objective condition, which can be defined and treated by doctors. I have since learned that it is not, for reasons I will discuss in Part II. On the contrary, "stress" is a way of talking around a deeper problem. *Blaming stress for the pain we feel in our current situation is a way of denying our power to choose a different way of life. And at the same time, it is a way of expressing the pain that comes from not choosing.*

We cannot choose everything that happens to us in life, and I am not about to tell you that we can. The real question is, how much choice do we have? Part of the answer, I think, is *more than we seem to believe*— once we have put aside the false choices, the ideals whose distance beyond our best efforts so oppresses us, and appears to make us sick with stress. We are walking a tightrope between the rock of our dreams and the hard place of reality; but there is a net below.

What is happening to us, I believe, closely resembles a phenomenon described by Michael Tierra in his book on traditional methods of healing, *The Way of Herbs:*

> It is essential to realize that every disease has a positive aspect. The ailment informs us of our resistance and of our imbalance, and it provides a focal point for discovering all the negative energies we have accumulated. *In the healing process, our lessons are learned and the body is brought naturally back to a reflection of total balance.* [My emphasis.]

What we are looking for—what we seem to have lost—is just such a "total balance" in our lives, between the need of making a living, for our own sakes and for the sake of those we love, and the love we hope to find in this life.

How we lost that balance, and what we can do about it—how men, in particular, can find the balance that now seems to elude us, with the aid and understanding of women—is what this book is about.

P A R T

——— I ———

MEN WHO WANT IT ALL

Man is an odd, sad creature as yet, intent on pilfering the earth, and heedless of the growths within himself. He cannot be bored about psychology. He leaves it to the specialist, which is as if he should leave his dinner to be eaten by a steam-engine.

—E. M. Forster, *Howards End*

. . . whosoever looketh into himself, and considereth what he doth, when he does think, *opine, reason, hope, feare, &c, and upon what grounds; he shall thereby read and know, what are the thoughts, and Passions of all other men, upon the like occasions . . .*

—Thomas Hobbes, *Leviathan*

CHAPTER

1

Maynard G. Krebs,
Where Are You?

The life of every citizen is becoming a business. This, it seems to me, is one of the worst interpretations of the meaning of human life history has ever seen. Man's life is not a business.

—Saul Bellow, *Herzog*

America doesn't eat its young, it forgets them. I realized this when I visited my maternal grandfather at a retirement colony in Fort Lauderdale ten years ago. Sitting in the brilliant sunlight with a group of people in their sixties and older, it struck me (and I mean *struck*, like a physical blow) that the music coming over the radio on the poolside loudspeakers consisted of current hits, none of which bore the slightest resemblance to the songs these people had heard in their childhood and youth. One day the songs I loved would likewise disappear, living only in record collections buried in attics and closets. And so it is; at thirty-five, a big part of me belongs already to the past, along with the Supremes and the Beatles.

And so does Maynard G. Krebs.

Maynard was one of the principal characters on a show called *The Many Loves of Dobie Gillis*, which was mandatory TV fare for kids of my generation. He was a skinny, scraggly, dark-haired guy with a little goatee beard; the last of the beatniks. Actually, he wasn't a beat at all—not like Jack Kerouac, Neal Casady, Allen Ginsberg, and those other American wanderers of the fifties, who lived on the edge of the working class, doing the oddest and dirtiest of jobs to earn the money that enabled them to write their books. Maynard was in a class of his own, a kind of suburban bad boy who couldn't be bothered to lift a finger in any cause, including his own. Even that level of physical effort smacked of work—and nothing could ever match the horror with which Maynard pronounced, in a voice rising to a scream, the hated term *Work!*

It was strange that Maynard should be the best friend of Dobie Gillis, a clean-cut, blond young man, not too good-looking or bad-looking, not too dumb or too smart, who told you flat out that all he ever wanted in life was one lousy girl. Having even one lousy girl, of course, meant that Dobie had to work—either that, or he'd have to beg for money along with the family car keys, an experience whose humiliations were well-known to the boys I grew up with. (We were living in an era when girls did not pay for their own movie tickets or hamburgers, let alone the gas and oil changes that made the wheels of love turn smoothly.)

Later I realized that the reason Dobie and Maynard got along was that each represented to the other a path not taken. Refusing to work meant that Maynard was free in a way Dobie could never be; but working meant that Dobie could taste pleasures that Maynard had no self-respecting choice, given his aversion to labor, but to disdain.

Now, this was a Manichean duality even a confused kid could appreciate. It confirmed what I saw in the grown-up world, and the world of teenagers ahead of me: males traded time for money, and money for the company of women. Women worked, of course—some of them, anyway—but unless they were poor, they worked for their own satisfaction. Men worked for women, and for their families, which women managed for them, as much as they worked because they liked to.

Other factors entered into this equation, certainly. No self-respecting woman would let herself be bought and sold, just like that; and boys talked with disgust about girls who cared for nothing except the newness and glamour of their dates' automobiles.

But even nice girls, like the cheerleader who lived next door to me, who dated the student-council vice-president and captain of the football team, would admit that "having a nice car counts, it *does*." When you got right down to it, a boy had an essential choice in life: he could be Maynard, or Dobie. He could have a nice car, a nice job, and a nice girl, or he could cultivate his goatee and walk alone.

At the time, I was ill-equipped to understand just how weighty the choice could be. An American teenage boy, which could be defined as a beast that never grows tired, doesn't think much about the energy wrapped up in the hours he sells. I never did through the first two and a half decades of my life, when physical exhaustion was nothing that a short night's sleep couldn't cure. (Let it be noted that being American means, for most of us, a well-nourished childhood, plus good health care, which adds up to a reservoir of physical strength that carries well into our adult years. A large part of the world cannot make the same boast.)

I still remember a shock that occurred in my twenty-sixth year, when I was working from nine in the morning until midnight six days a week, writing and editing a weekly newspaper. One morning I woke up more tired than I had ever been in my life, with another day's work ahead of me. The taste in my mouth was fear. It occurred to me right then that I could work myself to death, that I could become so tired that I would never be fresh again. And only then did I begin to reflect on the relation between my career and my love life.

YOU MADE YOUR BED—NOW MAKE LOVE IN IT

Work wasn't the only thing going on in my life at the time. Newly separated from the woman I'd lived with for six years, I was doing what surveys tell us is a marked tendency among divorced men: dating (and sleeping with, often enough) a number of different women. And I began to realize that when I was with these women, I was the same frazzled, harried, intense person who went to work and stayed there throughout the day and evening.

I still had energy enough to make love, often enough to reassure myself that I hadn't given myself over, soul and body, to my job; but making love and loving are not quite the same thing. The latter requires a sustained attention to the needs of another person, a certain emotional interest and presence, that is ultimately more demanding than producing an erection. And loving was something I avoided, precisely because of its greater demands.

In general, it is easier for a man to make love with a succession of different partners than to love the same partner over a stretch of time. This, at least, is what the men I know who have tried both approaches to the art of loving tell me, and it matches my own experience. A steady lover applies standards to a man that a casual partner does not; she is aware of what she needs from him, in ways that a one-night stand has neither the time nor, given our current sexual manners, the right to remark. The same applies to the way men view their partners. Once the novelty of an encounter with a new bedmate wears off, fresh efforts are continually required of both partners to renew their sexual and emotional interest in each other, and to resolve the inevitable conflicts and needs that arise.

Ideally, one can look at these efforts as a challenge; with luck and goodwill, they can be part of a process of unfolding discovery and delight. In any case, as a relationship deepens, its different aspects become intertwined: the discovery of a partner's character and sensuality progress together.

Or they do not progress. They reach a certain plane, and level off or decline. I am not at all convinced that when this occurs, it is because either or both partners are maladroit in bed, which is what men I know have a tendency to think (and to blame on their partners), along with not a few women. (One woman told me matter-of-factly that "after two years, it just isn't as good in bed," regardless of the partner. I think she was wrong; I have been with women who kept me interested longer than that, with whom I could have made love for the rest of my life, if other problems in the relationships hadn't got in the way.)

The real difficulty with sustaining a relationship, for working men and women, is that *a career demands a tremendous amount of energy and interest from a person*; and that, like an ongoing affair of the heart, *its demands do not lessen over time, but grow.*

This is true whether the demands of the job are professional, as in the case of a stockbroker who progresses to bigger, more complicated, and more time-consuming deals in the process of gaining his fortune, or repetitive, such as an ironworker's or secretary's work, which gets harder and harder to face at the start of every day. (If you don't understand this already, just look at the faces of the people on buses, subways, or in traffic at the start and finish of every day; they look like lemons caught in a squeezer.) If one has a career, sooner, not later, its requirements will conflict with the needs—not to mention the desires—of oneself and one's partner. And the conflict does not go away.

That is what 74,000 American women told the *Ladies' Home Journal* in a survey published in March 1985. "What makes a man attractive?" asked the survey's authors. "Sensitivity was the top choice at 41.3 percent." And what drew the married women in this sample to their husbands? "In order, the reasons women married their husbands are: mutual love, physical attraction, his income potential, his desire to be a father."

Two-thirds of these women—a figure comparable to Department of Labor statistics—were in the paid labor force, either full- or part-time. "Interestingly," noted the survey, "the women also continue to want their men to be the family breadwinner"—even the 35.6 percent of the women who said they were married to "new men" who did a fair share of household tasks and child care (with the notable exception of staying home to take care of a sick child), in addition to being the main economic support of the family in 73 percent of such couplings. Among women married to "traditional" husbands (who made up over half the sample), 58 percent thought that men "should" support the family, and that was how it worked out in 84 percent of the cases.

Among women in their twenties, a plurality of 42 percent cited a man's body as his main asset, in terms of physical attraction, and they preferred to see that body in jeans and T-shirts; but by their thirties and forties, a clear majority of women found men in suits the most attractive. Add up these preferences, and they suggest the following: young women are drawn to men who are sensitive and sexy and have good prospects. Ten years down the road, what these women find attractive is a man whose prospects have been realized, but who has kept his sensitivity. And, the survey showed, his sex drive.

The women married to "new men" and those whose husbands were "traditional" shared one thing in common with the unfortunate 8 percent who were married to "macho" men (a large majority of whom likewise earned the main family income): *they complained that their husbands didn't make love often enough (once or twice a week was typical), and that when they did, they didn't take enough time to satisfy their lovers.*

Why weren't the husbands of the women who reported to the *Ladies' Home Journal* more eager, patient lovers? Part of the answer is obvious. On average, according to the Quality of Employment Survey conducted by the University of Michigan Center for Social Research in 1977 (and backed by other studies), married men spend an average of seven hours every day—or 49 hours per week—on paid labor, more than working wives do, on average.

Given that 95 percent of married men between the ages of 25 and 45 in this country hold a job (a figure that has hardly varied since 1960), and that 70 percent of employed men work a full-time week, you have to suspect that much of the men's failure to satisfy their wives (to put it bluntly) was due to the fact that they were not often free to give rein to their amorous impulses. That would certainly be the case for those who had already given the flower of their vitality and passion to their jobs—which is what men who are going to grow out of their jeans and into gray flannels are expected by their employers to do.

If you are a woman who has likewise entertained ambitions of a successful career, of a job that demands and rewards (in terms of money and prestige) your best efforts, just ask yourself: how much did you feel like making love at the end of the day, day in and day out (or, for that matter, to engage in heartfelt, intimate discussion with your loved ones)? How relaxed did you feel before going to work—enough to talk or make love, spontaneously and at length?

Or have you ever felt like the pseudonymous Jon, whose marriage to "Cindy" was the subject of Lois Duncan's October 1984 column in the *Ladies' Home Journal*, "Can This Marriage Be Saved?" What the marriage needed to be saved from was Jon's impotence, which turned out to be due, among other things, to his resentment that Cindy thought that making love at prescheduled times was a less-than-natural activity. Unfortunately, Jon's career, which kept him on the road and at the office a great deal of the time, put him in just such an unromantic position.

I can only agree with Cindy's desire for heartfelt spontaneity, though I will confess that I have often engaged in such unnatural behavior as Jon proposed. It is either that, or give up lovemaking until fate hands you the first good chance, and everyone is in the right mood. The last time I was in a relationship which operated on that principle, it lasted eight months, during which my partner and I made love about once every two weeks. Some people are satisfied with that kind of sex life, but I wasn't. Nor was it the first time I had known that frustration.

When I stumbled into that affair, I was still bearing the scars of a relationship that had ended years before. It had taken three years to decline and die—years that coincided, I realized later, with the horrific beginning of my career in publishing, when I labored as a salesman of advertising space. After a day—and I mean from sunrise to sunset, daylight saving time—on the telephone and in the offices of hostile, skeptical clients, I would come home to the beautiful, strong woman with whom I had fallen in love, her face equally drawn, her muscles equally clenched, after an equally long day in the office where she directed an advertising account team. When the relationship began to sour, neither of us had the strength and clarity of mind, in those few hours available to us before we fell into bed, to grapple with the problems that rose between us.

So we ignored them, falling back on our good manners. But the problems remained, and grew, until a task that once might have amounted to squashing a bug assumed the proportions of strangling an angered elephant. Then we could no longer ignore them, and they were beyond the strength that remained to us. We struggled, but in the end were trampled. And when it was all over, we got back on our feet and walked toward the only refuges that remained to us: our jobs.

•   •   •

D. H. Lawrence, that much-maligned prophet, met this question of love versus work squarely in *Lady Chatterley's Lover*, a book considered so obscene on its first publication in 1928 that it was banned in England, Lawrence's native country, until 1960. By contemporary standards, the sexuality that drives this book is hardly racy—quite romanticized, in fact. One suspects that its allegedly pornographic qualities had to do mainly with the way Lawrence contrasted an impotent aristocrat and capitalist with a man who hated what work could do to him. Lawrence left no room for argument: the making of money is ultimately the death of pleasure. In our society, where work is the supreme good a man can do, that was—and still is—an obscene idea.

At the book's opening, Lord Chatterley "went back to Flanders" to fight in World War I just after marrying the beautiful Constance, and was "shipped over to England again" after six months in the trenches, "more or less in bits." The only thing Clifford Chatterley can still pleasurably use of his body is his head: he listens to the radio constantly, then throws himself into the scientific management of coal mines, dreaming of a day when sex will disappear entirely from the earth, and we will be exquisitely spiritual beings.

It is an anti-woman idea; Constance recognizes that, as she recognizes that the first lover she takes hates her pleasure. "But do you want me to go on, to get my own satisfaction?" she asks him. "I want to hang on with my teeth clenched, while you go for me!" is his sarcastic response. These men are afraid to make love to women; they are physically or morally incapable of it. "They were so tight, so scared of life!" she thinks.

But they could work. "Make money! Make it! Out of nowhere. Wring it out of the thin air! The last feat to be humanly proud of!" she reflects despairingly.

The gamekeeper, Mellors, who becomes the Lady's lover, is a different matter. He is virile, but has chosen to be celibate after three affairs, all of which were sexually unsatisfying, emotionally unsatisfying, or both. He has tried to take what he wanted from women, and tried to give women what they wanted, and neither has worked.

When he first makes love with Constance, he says three times, "I'm afraid." Not of her—she never feels that in him—but of "Things! Everybody! The lot of 'em!"

The threat Constance exposes him to, precisely, is not a failure of virility, but of reducing him to a common state: bringing him back into a world of relationships he cannot control, of promises that must be broken, of exhaustion without pleasure, of empty labor that denies his needs. When he realizes that he can trust her, he offers her a dream: "Let's not live ter make money, neither for us-selves nor for anybody else. . . . Bit by bit, let's stop it.

"Look at Tevershall!" he cries, the little town where Lord Chatterley's coal miners live. "It's horrible! That's because it was built while you were working for money!" The working men "can't properly be with a woman," can't "talk nor move nor live.

"Hark at yourselves!" he cries. "That's workin' for money!"

· My God, do those lines hit home when you are reading them after a day of doing work for the money, and not much else. When your body in the mirror seems soft, not in its bones and flesh, but in form, as if you had been pounded out of shape. When your sex lies dead between tired legs. When the radio talks for you, the TV gives your eyes a place to rest. It is indeed an obscene subject, this.

And not just for men. "[The] absence of sex," reported Anne Taylor Fleming in the *New York Times Magazine* (October 26, 1986), "is another one of the little secrets of young, upscale postliberation wives," who turn to their children for "an intimacy that is easier and often sweeter than sex," after coming home from work with the desire to "watch something really dumb on television"—can you hear Clifford's radio screaming in the background?—"and be left alone."

Is the only way out to live without money? Lady Chatterley's story ends before she and Mellors move to a farm, where they will live on the income from her inheritance and his farming, modestly but well. (Not that many of us marry money, however.) A nice fantasy, that; the kind that my generation tried to live out, on rural communes in the fat, waning years of the sixties. But in the hungry seventies, we arrived at a more pointed version of the question: how much money does it take to live well?

Depends on where you live. In the United States, it takes a lot, relative to other countries I have visited.

But what, precisely, is living well?

Depends on what you live for, doesn't it? On what pleasures you think most important, which efforts you find worth making.

I will tell you where I stand on this. I did not marry a woman just to talk with her on the phone while I was at work, or to make love with her when I was worn out, or to live off her money, or to let her cook for me when I came home from work. I can see why men do all of those things, and why women go along with it. I can see why we take different kinds of pleasure, and satisfy different kinds of needs in these arrangements, because I have lived in variants of them. I understand full well the necessity that guides our actions.

But that doesn't mean I have to like it. And it is no excuse for not imagining something better. Which, it seems, is what both men and women are yearning for.

THE RISING INTIMATE EXPECTATIONS OF MEN AND WOMEN

One of the things the *Ladies' Home Journal* survey confirmed is that women's expectations of their husbands have mounted since our parents' time— something we all sense intuitively, but rarely see in plain numbers. It would seem only logical that a woman who has her own career, or can have one if she feels the need, doesn't just want a breadwinner, she wants what the blues singer Bessie Smith called a "biscuit-roller," a man who can bake her over fresh every day.

If men weren't capable of seeing that, women have shown themselves capable of making it abundantly clear. "I want spontaneity, life in my relationship," the wife of the pseudonymous Albert Martin says in *One Man, Hurt: A Shattering Account of the End of a Happy Marriage* (so far as Albert was concerned). "Ours is dead, flat."

Though Martin's wife was hardly a card-carrying feminist, like him she was a regular churchgoer, both of them in congregations that made a proud point of discussing the new ideas about self-fulfillment in a changing world that were going around in the early 1970s, when this book was written. That is what makes their tale interesting: the Martins had not participated in the Women's Liberation Movement, but they had been touched by its precepts, all the same. Even women like "Jeanne Martin"—the model of a successful housewife, with three wonderful sons and a husband who loved and needed her—wanted men who were as sensitive as they were successful, as spontaneous as they were sensual; and they did not need a consciousness-raising group to tell them so.

In effect, *women had simply applied to men the standards that men had always applied to women*. Our fathers expected that their wives would be partners and allies whose affection, liveliness, and understanding would compensate and heal the wounds inflicted by men's competitors in the deadening routine of the workplace. The girl a man married would be there when and how she was needed, regardless of her mood at the moment.

Martin put it crudely on an evening when his wife refused to make love with him: "The religious sacrament, the legal document, the moral commitment is to marriage, not love," he told her. "You say we can't make love . . . because you're not 'in love' with me." As he saw it, that was a poor excuse: "An awful lot of people make love every day who aren't in love."

You could also state the converse, if 74,000 women can't be wrong: an awful lot of people who *are* in love aren't making love every day. And the women do not like it. They have come to expect better, and more, or they would not find what they are getting to be a cause for complaint.

Less apparent than the rise in women's expectations, perhaps, it that *the demand first put forward during the Second Wave of feminism—that men prove their love to their wives in ways more varied than bringing home a paycheck—has become a demand that men make on themselves, for motives both admirable and sad.*

Not for all men, certainly—but apparently quite a few of us. Remember that over one-third of the married survey respondents cited above called their husbands "new men"—meaning that he cooked, cleaned, did laundry, spent his free time with his family, remembered his wife's birthday and their wedding anniversary, and attended his children's births. In his massive study of feminism's effects on men, *How Men Feel*, Anthony Astrachan estimated that between 5 and 10 percent of us fit a far more stringent standard: "He works . . . for equal pay for equal or comparable work and equal chances for promotion for his female colleagues . . . he takes half the responsibility for house care and child work . . . he takes care of himself physically [and] emotionally."

If you apply Astrachan's high percentage to the male population between 25 and 65 years of age, you come up with some six and a half million men who fit what he calls "an ideal" of the new man; his minimum estimate still gives us three-million-plus. By the *Ladies' Home Journal* survey standards, about 12 million married men are "new men" (assuming that these survey results would hold up across the board for all 33 million currently married men, which is admittedly a big assumption). At any rate, it seems likely that this is a phenomenon being lived by more than a few million people. I would consider that admirable.

But of course men compete for women, as we compete in our careers. If you can't rock your baby, somebody else will. (I never forgot a scene from *The Many Loves of Dobie Gillis*, wherein our hero sneered to Tuesday Weld at the local malt shop, "Who would you go out with, if not me?" With a snap of her fingers, she brought three men to their table, all of them taller and handsomer than Dobie.) And these days our babies want the man who rocks them to be not only tough but also tender, not only tender but also ambitious. If you want to win the girl, and keep her, that is what you must be. So we think; so we worry.

But the demands of a career have not lessened since our fathers' generation; if anything, they have grown, in the same proportion that our economy has proven increasingly unable to guarantee even a minimum of job security at every level of employment (we will consider this problem in detail in Part VI).

At the same time, *our expectations of ourselves, as husbands and lovers and fathers, have not declined in proportion; they have likewise grown.* They have grown, in fact, far more quickly than our ability to meet those expectations. We have forgotten Maynard G. Krebs, but somewhere in TV heaven he is having a harsh last laugh at Dobie Gillis.

CHAPTER

2

Who Works in America?

L et us break a myth—the one which says that women and men are
making full and equal use of their right to take each other's places in
the work force. Some are, but they are by no means close to a majority.
That is something we could see every day, just by noticing the men and
women around us, how they are dressed, where they are going to and
coming from. But we have been seeing those daily events through blinders
of hope and fear. Men are worried about women taking their jobs (as
Astrachan discovered in detail), while women have been celebrating the
rise of their own kind in politics, business, and other highly publicized
domains. The fact is, *our career patterns have changed in degree, but not
in essence.*

True, in the past thirty years we have seen an epochal movement of
women into the work force. Much of the change was due to a doubling of
the percentage of married women who held jobs between 1960 and today.
Among these women, *the highest percentage of those who worked was
always found in age groups whose children had grown enough to be able
to take care of themselves* (at least until dinnertime); 36 percent of married
women between the ages of 35 and 44 had a job in 1960, more than for
any other age group, and they still led the pack in 1985, with an 80-percent
labor-force participation rate. In 1985, almost three out of four married
women still worked from 45 up to 65 years, about double the rate of 1960.
The working-woman rate likewise doubled for married women under 20
over this time, from one in four to one in two.

But *even in married couples, men were going to work in greater proportions.* While half of married women under 20 had jobs in 1985, the
figure for their men was 91 percent. In the 25–34 age group—which has
become, in the past decade, the prime childbearing years for American
women—three married men have jobs for every two married women. Even

between the ages of 35 and 44, the peak career years for working married women, married men hold a four-to-three lead in labor-force participation rates, and their lead grows with age.

Single men are also more likely to hold jobs than single women—twice as likely, past the age of 65. In absolute terms, *just under fourteen million more men are paid to work in our society than there are working women*; this in spite of the fact that there are more women than men among us, once you get past the age of 25 into career days. (We will look at the reasons for this mortality gap in "Where the Boys Are . . . Buried."

The gap between our belief that women now work for money as much as men do, and the fact of our careers, is even more apparent when you compare the percentages of men and women who work full-time. In the 16–24 age group, 37 percent of men with jobs work full-time, as opposed to 28 percent of women. But in the next decade of life, men's lead explodes: 80 percent of working men have full-time jobs, compared to 48 percent of women. By the age of 35, men have widened their lead by eight points. From the ages of 35 to 65, men's full-time work-force participation rates are twice those of women. *An employed man's chances of holding a full-time job, instead of working part-time, are better than four to one during his prime working years; for a woman, those odds drop to even.*

And there is more to it than that: women and men are still doing different kinds of jobs. There are now women miners and managers, lawyers and doctors, along with the secretaries and salesgirls. We have all read about them in various magazines. But there is a difference between novelties and trends. If a woman in a man's chair is a trend, it is still not anywhere near threatening men's domination of certain kinds of work. Except, that is, in principle; and we Americans do like to view things from a moral standpoint, as my French wife is fond of telling me. That is why we tend to get our ideals and our realities mixed up, for better and for worse.

In our economy, women hold a majority of jobs only in the categories of "technical, sales, and administrative support"—the pink-collar ghetto, where women have 64 percent of the positions—and "service occupations." "Service," in the sense used for these statistics, takes in everything from waitresses, teachers, and nurses to private household workers (which you could call the wet-knee ghetto, considering that 96 percent of domestic servants are women). This is something you can see anytime you walk into a corporate office, a hospital, a schoolhouse, a motor-vehicle bureau, or a rich man's home. In the pink-collar ghetto, women hold nearly half of the "supervisor" jobs—they are as likely as a man to be an office manager—and do a vast majority of the secretarial work. They also account for about nine out of ten nurses, and three out of four teachers (not counting college, where only one in three professors are women).

In the blue-collar world of unskilled factory labor, women hold a surprising two out of every five jobs—four out of five, in the apparel trades. But this is less surprising than it seems, when you realize that factory girls were a common feature of American life from the early nineteenth century up to the Great Depression, and again in World War II. Such labor has never been the employment of choice in our society for people who had that choice to make—and it is not a fast-growing sector of the economy, not where the action is.

At the top, women make up less than one-third of executive positions—and barely any of the chief executive officers (unless you count women who started their own small companies, somewhere near the bottom of the Fortune Infinitude). They are 3 percent of skilled, highly paid factory hands. They account for one in twelve architects, one in twenty-five engineers, one in seven lawyers and doctors.

When the Second Wave exploded, around 1970, most of those numbers were even smaller, by a factor of two or three. But let's face it: they are still small. Women's place in the most competitive jobs of our society as yet amounts to a beachhead, hardly a feminist version of the Normandy invasion. Some doors have opened to women—few remain entirely closed—but women are not flooding, only flowing slowly and steadily, through them.

We have not closed the employment gap between men and women so much as we like to think; that is what these numbers say. It seems that *while women are playing the game of careers, they are playing on a different schedule from men, for different stakes*. There are plenty of exceptions, but they have not fundamentally changed the overall pattern of the past twenty-five years. Our working lives are still, in the main, gender-segregated, and in more ways than one.

IS THIS WHAT YOU CALL A ROLE REVERSAL?

One of the reasons for the persistence of this pattern was implicit in the friendship of Dobie Gillis and Maynard G. Krebs. If Dobie could get along with Maynard, it was partly because he felt superior to his beatnik buddy. Maynard, after all, was even more a prisoner of circumstance than Dobie, though the circumstances were of his own choosing; his freedom depended on never wanting anything that money could buy, which is very little freedom in a money economy like ours.

I have felt a similar superiority, at different times, to men who earned

THE PASSIONS OF MEN

less than I, and I admit to being ashamed of it; I have seen a similar shame, directed toward me this time, in my richer friends. It is a complex emotion, this shame, compounded of envy toward those who have made choices in life that do not fatten the wallet, and of the childish need to be convinced that one has been a good, hardworking boy, after all, with a paycheck to prove it.

There is a double comfort in having that proof in hand: not only a certain security from financial need, but *a kind of self-respect that one cannot obtain only from a woman*. That is true even for the New Men among us. Take Mike Clary, a reporter for the *Miami Herald* and author of *Daddy's Home*, who took two years out of his career to care for his infant daughter while his wife brought home the bread. Clary documented as role-reversed a relationship as any of us could healthily imagine, and the reversal began early:

In the five years since Lillian and I had met in San Francisco [up to the birth of their daughter]...we had alternated the task of making our living. When she worked at counseling, I could write about the family of gorillas at the zoo, or spend the day in a darkroom developing pictures. When I worked for a newspaper, she could be a full-time student.

It was Lillian whose turn to work came first in this relationship, and that bothered Clary: "Although money had not caused any serious dissension between us," he writes, "neither Lillian nor I ever forgot that it was she who paid the bills." No wonder that when she wanted to go back to school, meaning that he would need to earn a salary for both of them, Clary found that "the image of me with a steady job, and a weekly paycheck in my name, rapidly grew in appeal." He wanted to pull his weight, to prove to her and to himself that he was capable and competent to earn a living—that he was a man, not a Maynard.

Most men, I think, resemble Clary; we like the sense of being self-sustaining, and of having the strength to sustain others, that work affords us. And if we do not share the repulsive and false idea I have heard from men at various times, that "a woman only cares how much money a guy has," we take it as a given that very few women will *not* care if a man has no money at all.

That is perhaps a main reason that over 85 percent of single men between the ages of 25 and 44—a figure that has not changed much since the days when Maynard and Dobie were roaming the airwaves, and which has remained about five points over the percentage of working single women at the same age—have a paying job. The rest, aside from the dwindling idle rich, are rarely prime targets of feminine interest.

In a conversation noted in my journal from 1985, a close friend put it plainly: "If you don't have the career, you don't have the girl." You don't, that is, have a girl worth having, as we define such girls these days: attractive, independent, intelligent, with a worthwhile career of her own. Such a woman is hardly likely to bind herself indefinitely to a man whose interests in life are confined to the news she can provide him, let alone one whose pocket money comes solely from her pocketbook.

Like so many words that come right from the heart, these were forgotten by my friend, who is engaged in the grueling rounds of advancing his career as a free-lance graphic artist. When I reminded him of them at a party, in front of his fiancée, a successful model—I apologize for using his words against him in getting her reaction, even with his permission (yet isn't it curious that the matter was such a dirty secret?)—she was evidently shocked. His declaration made her feel like an object to be bought and sold. But she could not tell him outright that he was wrong—and though she punched him on the arm in front of me, she did not—because the fact was that she had no intention of living with a man who had no career of his own, no means to match hers, no interest in life beyond what she could provide him.

Among the men I spoke with, there was little resentment of this prin-ciple—and that was merely fair in their eyes, because *not one man in my sample wanted his partner to be entirely dependent on him in these ways, without means of her own.* "I can't imagine living with someone who didn't have anything"—anything, that is, besides taking care of a house for a man—"going on in her life," said one, aged thirty and expecting his first child with his wife and partner in his business. "What would you talk about?"

And if it was him in that dependent role, what would he have to talk about—not only to his partner, but among other men?

Clary found out about that latter problem, too. One of the few pleasures he reserved for himself after his daughter was born and he took on full-time care of her was participation in a weekly basketball league. After the games the men would break for a beer, and on one occasion a man who had raised his first baby for nine months, but went back to work because his wife "was really into the kids," and kept his job when they divorced (she kept the kids), asked Clary what he was working on.

When he got the answer, "he looked surprised," recounts Clary. The man said, "I thought you were staying home to write a novel or something." No, said Clary, just bringing up baby. "He looked away," notes Clary. There was nothing more to talk about, it seemed—at least to Clary, who comments, "Without committing themselves to a term as househusband, perhaps no man *could* understand" the experience.

Or perhaps this man understood it only too well. Clary's friend had experienced child care, but for him it was associated with failure—with dependence and loss. He had given up his place in the world of work for nine months, and he had ended up losing his family. When the dust settled, he was back where he started, alone, working for a living. Between a job and a woman, he knew which would always be there.

Whether or not he has a woman, a man must work. That much is evident, cruelly so; just another fact of life. It is also evident that *just as men accept the necessity, not only for reasons of financial need, but for self-respect, of working, most have come to accept, if not expect, that their partners too will work.*

But the reasons for this expectation go way beyond our current conventional wisdom, which is that we all need the money a wife brings home. In their study of 1,225 Midwestern married couples conducted in 1974–75, *At Home and at Work*, Michael Geerken and Walter R. Cove found that, contrary to their own expectations, "the higher the husband's occupational status"—the more bacon he brought home—"the more likely the wife is to work." In other words, *the families that needed the money least were precisely those in which the highest percentage of wives were taking jobs.*

Geerken and Cove suggested that this was due, first, to the fact that a highly paid man would feel less threatened by a working wife than a man whose paycheck didn't top his partner's by a large margin, if at all. Moreover, since highly paid men tend to be college graduates, their attitudes might also have been more liberal than the average man's, who would presumably prefer a woman who knew her place. Where the women were concerned, the more education they had, and the greater their husbands' support for their ambitions, the more likely they were to work, and the more money they were likely to earn by working.

One might add that these days, all you need do is attend a middle-class cocktail party in any American city to know that a wife with an "interesting" career of her own, who can sympathize firsthand with her husband's workplace battles and those of his friends, is worth more in the status competition among men than a woman who keeps the house—an occupation we may regard as a kind of blissful escapism, even more so than in our fathers' time, when, as Barbara Ehrenreich noted in *The Hearts of Men, Playboy* magazine could talk with a straight face about "the easy, low-pressure, part-time job" awaiting the happy housewife.

In comparison to the lives of men and women in the paid labor force, being a housewife—as about one-third of American women still are—*is* a part-time job; various studies show that housewives have more time to sleep and relax, and about two hours per day less of total work (including unpaid tasks) than do employed husbands, four hours less than working wives. That is another reason we respect and value paid working women more than housewives: we think they have it tougher, and in that way, they do.

But there is another, as yet unspoken, impulse behind the high value men now place on working wives, I believe—one rooted in the fact than an enormous number of men in my generation, and the generation that follows mine, now in their early twenties, were young and to a large extent helpless witnesses to the phenomenon of divorce. *We came to regard divorce as a possible, if not probable, consequence of the kind of relationships our parents had—in most cases, a couple consisting of a working man and a housewife.*

One young man I interviewed, who disdained the possibility of marrying a woman who didn't work, was typical. His parents had divorced early in his adolescence, and both of them had suffered greatly. He had drawn the lesson that "when two people are dependent on each other, it's death."

But perhaps there was something besides lifelessness, the dead end of love, that made this dependence seem so horrifying to him. Part of what he was rejecting in his parents' example, I believe, was a certain possibility for shame in the failure of a marriage, of which I was terribly aware in my twenties, as I dealt with the implications of my parents' divorce, and the divorces of so many of my friends' parents, most of whom fit the man-at-work, woman-at-home pattern this young man had grown to loathe.

Anyone who has lived through this event can tell you that the hatred, fear, and guilt expressed by the separating partners is directly proportional to the financial dependence of one—as my generation experienced it, usually the woman, the mother—on the other. If young men now value independent, self-supporting women so highly, I am certain that it is partly because *we do not want to feel the guilt—deserved or not—that we saw in our fathers when they divorced our mothers.*

For example, when I separated from my lover of six years, it was a point of honor for me to wait until she had a job, an apartment she could afford, and a network of social and professional contacts in the city to which we had moved in the last, desperate year of our relationship. I did not want the panic I had seen in my mother, when my father divorced her, to be on my conscience. It would have been a failure I could neither gladly learn from nor repair.

I am well aware that the low percentage of men who honor child-support and alimony awards in the United States is a national disgrace (or, as a small minority of vocal men would have it, a justifiable revolt in an age when women can take care of themselves). But that does not disprove my point, which is that *men are well aware that divorce exists, and have learned to value female independence precisely because it promises them freedom from some of the more humiliating aspects of marital failure.*

All the same, in order to claim that freedom, men must guard their own independence—a job, and a living. Which brings us back to the larger point: *even at a time when half of American women work for money, the man who does not is still a rarity.* The bottom line of our intimate relationships, including stable but unmarried couples, has not changed here: most men act as though whatever their partners' preferences, they must work for a living.

WHY WOMEN LOVE LOSERS: THE MINORITY CASE

Let me tell you about a waking nightmare I have had: *I imagined that while I was pushing my career forward, out in the world on the job, another man came in through my back door and made love to my woman.* There I am, killing myself—for a woman, of course—and this lazy good-for-nothing-but-bed gets into mine.

I was hardly the first to have that idea. When Homer's Odysseus was struggling home from the Trojan War, a pack of hangers-on was clustered around his wife Penelope's loom, letting her know that her bed need not stay cold. The first thing Odysseus did when he got back was slaughter the bunch of them; a few died like cowards, but most fought to the end, which is Homer's way of letting us know that they were man enough to take his hero's place. And that, besides vengeance, was why Odysseus had to kill them; even a hero knows better than to leave a potent rival behind his back, to stab him and carry off the wife and the weaving.

Having remained single, because of my early unofficial marriage and divorce, past the age when most of my friends finally married, and being in a career that most Americans consider a little exotic, if not bohemian, I learned that a single man who appears to have time on his hands carries an aura of menace into polite society. He could come for dinner one night, and through the back door to seduce his hostess the next. (As I recall, a guy I took for a friend did exactly that to me when my un-wife and I were going through one of the rougher of the rough times; and he had the nerve to try it in front of my face. May someone pull the same trick on him.) He is Maynard with a knife aimed at your back.

His advantage, of course, is that you are on the job, and he is not. What makes him even scarier, I think, is the suspicion that, just as "no one is irreplaceable" in a job, no one is irreplaceable in our beds—especially if we suspect, deep down, that we are not giving our women enough of what they want.

Now, it is true, at least in my observation, that even if women like an occasional fling with Maynard, they are more likely to marry Dobie, and to stay with him long after they have forgotten his buddy's bearded, lazy charms. But it is also true that in some relationships, men have Maynard's cake, and eat it too: they live off their partners.

I am not speaking of men like Clary, who pull a certain weight, even if it isn't a sack of gold. I mean the ones I discovered when I researched an article about exploitive relationships for *Cosmopolitan* in 1985, who simply take, and all they can get.

The magazine wanted to know about the worst of the worst, and that is what I wrote about for them. I talked about Linda Lovelace, who was battered into making *Deep Throat*, about a woman who recounted to me the way in which her husband had drained the business they began together, beaten her, and stolen her children.

The striking thing in these and similar cases was that the women were not masochists, as psycho-gossip would have it: they were brave (they kept trying to break out), strong (they had to be, to survive), and, above all, traditional. They thought that if only they kept working on their relationships, proving their love, someday their exploiter would become a prince. It was the biggest thing the men had going for them—that, and their willingness to use physical brutality to retain control. We called these men "another kind of pimp," and that is what they were.

What was left out of the story was something far more subtle, of which I found numerous examples among the women I knew: a young woman with career ambitions meets a man who is likewise in a career or preparing one, and falls in love with him. Temporarily, she takes on support of the couple so that he can change careers or get the one he has off the ground. And then the arrangement becomes permanent. She is paying the bills, going off to work, and he is making excuses. Often enough, the excuses become denial: "I'm doing the best I can." Then he becomes righteous; she's pushing him, and it's not fair. And one day he pushes back: he hits her, or he hits her below the belt by finding another woman.

The women who put up with this situation weren't masochists either; they were catches, by any reasonable standards of beauty, intelligence, and self-awareness. They were investing themselves in men, and they had a lot to invest. And they were getting something back, at least at the start. They felt loved, in and out of bed. When it came to sex, they were having it as often as they made themselves available—after all, the men were there, with nothing to do but think about making love. More important, the men had the time to listen to their concerns and problems, especially about work—they knew how tough it could be on the job; they needed to know, or their own excuses would be worthless—and to offer the comfort that a working person needs.

"You know, for a while it was great," said one woman, who had not only supported a starving composer but also paid for the recording session that was supposed to revive his career, and might have if he hadn't puttered away the $120 an hour she spent by the day for the sake of the record, money she had earned. The main thing she found great was that "we had a lot of time for each other." Until, that is—after two years—she began insisting that he do more with his time than make love; then he withdrew his love from her.

And that was more or less what happened in all of these relationships. As the title of this section suggests, this is a minority case among us; and a far smaller minority of such cases last longer than a few years, at most.

Yet there is some deep rule at work here, one that American men apparently find it terribly hard to transgress: *we cannot love unless we also work.* We must have both; if we do not, *we will not succeed at loving alone.*

But that does not mean that we have balanced them. On the contrary, *as our working lives are constructed now, we cannot love as much as we wish.* We know it, and women know it.

And we both know why: we have a terrible sense of what Drs. Meyer Friedman and Ray Rosenman, the authors of *Type A Behavior and Your Heart*, have called "time urgency." We can be late to work, or late to love; but we cannot be late for both.

Time. It is what Dobie sold, in order to get a girl, and what Maynard held too precious to sell. Put them together, and they make one man, split down the middle.

CHAPTER

3

The New Man's Burden

On August 21, 1984, the *New York Times* ran an article on the front page of its "Living" section, under the headline "As Sex Roles Change, Men Turn to Therapy to Cope With Stress." Declared Daniel Goleman, who would thereafter regularly cover the subject of men under stress for the *Times*, "A growing number of American men who have embraced society's changing perception of manhood are finding that the change has brought on unexpected stress." That was due to the discovery that "their emotions do not coincide with their ideals."

"For example," wrote Goleman, "many men who want to be more involved with their children than were their fathers face doubts about their ability to do so." Sounding a theme that had become common in the press, he reported that these men were "troubled by the lack of a model for fatherhood." He quoted Joseph Pleck, director of the Male Role Program at the Center for Research on Women at Wellesley, and author of *The Myth of Masculinity*, that "in the 1950s, the secret was that, emotionally, Dad was not really part of the family." (In fact, it was not secret: in 1949 sociologist Talcott Parsons devised an influential model of family life in which it was assumed that women bore the "expressive" role, meaning they loved the children up, while Dad was at the job performing his rather brutally labeled "instrumental" role.) But in "trying to see the legacy their fathers left them," as Pleck put it, these men found it a pittance, compared to their desire to be better-than-ever fathers.

Goleman and Pleck were sounding a theme that had as yet been directly expressed, so far as Astrachan determined in *How Men Feel*, by "only a few thousands" of adherents to what had come to be known as the "men's movement." The theme was *the reclamation of fatherhood*, and it is essential to understanding the raised expectations of men. In fact, there is more and more evidence that something profound is stirring around this

THE PASSIONS OF MEN

idea—something so unbalancing in 1984, as Goleman showed, that it was making men feel sick with stress. So let's take a closer look at it.

Start with the men's movement, when the reclamation of fatherhood came into the open. It was a movement, according to Astrachan, that attempted to apply feminist principles, especially the logic of gender equality, to the particular situation of men—a task that feminism turned away from in the mid-1970s, when the so-called separatist movement (which I'll discuss in Part V, "Notes of a Feminist Consort") divided feminists over the question of whether it was worth the bother to coexist with men in the first place. The books that launched the men's movement—Warren Farrell's *The Liberated Man*, Pleck's essay on the "myth" of masculinity, and Marc Feigen Fasteau's *The Male Machine*—took off from the idea "that 'masculine values' and traditional sex roles damage men as well as women," as Astrachan rightly summed them up.

This was gender equality with a certain vengeance; it included the idea that *if women could do anything men could do, then men could do anything that women had always done—like mothering*. And was not this what feminists had argued—that biology was not destiny, if we would only break the chains in our minds?

On those grounds the reclamation of parenthood by men could be advanced without fear of attack from feminists—a fear that could, and did, make life rather hellish for American men during the span of a long decade. One lingering effect of that fear, I think, was that even the newest of New Men hesitated to blame their mothers for inoculating them with these almighty traditional values; instead, they turned their critical guns on their fathers, as Goleman's stressed-out sensitive types were doing. And along the way, they talked—God, did they talk—about whether and how they could become New Model fathers themselves.

Looking at ten years of "Men and Masculinity" conferences, Astrachan reported that every one of them had included workshops on "fathering." It was from such workshops that the current male buzzword "nurturing," which would be used to the point of nausea by New Men, emerged into current usage in the 1980s as a way of describing men whose human kindness toward their children and associates fully compensated for the milk they could not squeeze from their dry breasts. (If my tone here sounds cynical, that is perhaps because I have brushed up against many of these "nurturing" types, and read about their charms in Mark Gerzon's book, *A Choice of Heroes*, which offers the nurturing man as a new model of heroism. In my experience, and as they are described by Gerzon, most of these guys are quite as competitive as, and quite a bit more sanctimonious than, the rest of us; and most of the ones cited by Gerzon make a living out of selling their sensitivity to the rest of us, which might be considered as much a matter of minding the main chance as it is evidence of heroism.) The word was shorthand for a poignant and bold claim—that men could be mamas as well as anyone else, if they took the time to learn how.

In fact, a voice—only one, but a powerful and coherent voice indeed—in favor of full-time male parenting was heard from inside the feminist movement in 1976, when Dorothy Dinnerstein published *The Mermaid and the Minotaur: Sexual Arrrangements and Human Malaise*. Dinnerstein's impact on the aspirations of men—in particular men who wanted to make themselves over New—has been nothing less than astonishing.

The essence of Dinnerstein's argument was this:

> The deepest root of our acquiescence to the maiming and mutual imprisonment of men and women lies in a monolithic fact of human childhood: Under the arrangement that now prevails, a woman is the parental person who is every infant's first love, first witness, and first boss. . . . It is in the relation with her that the child experiences the earliest version of what will be a lifelong internal conflict: the conflict between our rootedness in the body's acute, narrow joys and vicissitudes and our commitment to larger-scale human concerns.

Note several features of this idea: first, that *both men and women are "maimed" and "imprisoned" by our first dependence on a woman* (in practice, argued Dinnerstein, this maiming took different forms); next, that *each of us is caught between the pleasures and pains of living, as a creature in a body, and our desire to escape that body and anyone who reminds us of it (usually a woman) by immersion into the world of work.*

Where a man is concerned, argued Dinnerstein, to stay by a woman is in some dimly felt but powerful sense to stay by mother (you know, to be a "mama's boy," a "teacher's pet," a "skirt-chaser," to name three of the ways we insult such men, or rather, insult ourselves). To enter the world of work may be a false escape, but it is an escape to a world in which the rules are clear, in which there is a job to do; and where, if you do it right, a man—a distant, powerful man, who enforces the rules sternly but fairly, like an ideal father—will recognize and reward you. At any rate, it is not like the home of dirty dishes, dirty underwear, and dirty needs over which Mother presided, in which even the strongest man was once a helpless baby.

Women, too, feel this conflict, but it is transformed by the fact of their femaleness. In rebelling against his mother's early power, Dinnerstein held,

a man could identify with his father. A girl could not, in the same way—
not a girl whose shame at distancing herself from her mother led her in
the direction of re-creating her mother's life, to make amends for her own
confusion and hatred: *"Her first fight for some personal autonomy,"* underlined Dinnerstein, *"fought against an authority so total that male authority seemed comfortingly limited by comparison, was in a sense fought
against herself."*

Here, said Dinnerstein, was the source of much of the virulence of the
Second Wave, of its denial that female anatomy was a significant fact: the
terrible foreboding of women that they could neither reject nor escape
their mothers' fate, even if they could escape or reject motherhood—because, like their mothers, they were women.

But in the end, men would be no better off: "When a man . . . takes some
measure of responsibility for his life into his own hands, and becomes to
some degree his own boss, his life is still in male hands and his new boss
is still a male boss." And this, she showed, was an element in the rage of
the young radicals of the 1960s against their fathers (a theme I will return
to in "Chameleons with a Cause"). The same fathers, not incidentally, who
had left Goleman's New Men such a lousy legacy, if you could believe what
they were saying about their stress.

Dinnerstein, more than any other writer, had helped to define the legacy
the New Men might hope to leave their own sons and daughters. If she was
absorbed so wholeheartedly by so many men, that may have been because
she held out not only a critique, but also compassion to men who were
struggling to treat their women right (and that is what most of us wish to
do, for motives good or weak).

She did not condemn men for the state of things (though she held, along
with the mainstream of feminist thinking, that disaster awaited us if men
kept running the world along present lines). You could sum up her argument
like this: men and women were locked in an uneasy, covert collaboration,
in which men made the world, and women raised their children. *If men
could accept the challenge of feminism—if they could get down and do
the dirty work of raising babies, which they had always left to women—
they would be playing an equal role in the most profound societal transformation imaginable.*

Of all the sometimes contradictory messages men received from feminism, this is one that was not canceled out. *Every man I interviewed in
researching this book declared that full and equal partnership in the
raising of his family was the standard he would, or did, try to conform
to.* Astrachan's larger sample of several hundred men, and his examination

of the men's movement, leads to the same conclusion: *this is a growing demand that men are making on their lives.* "I've learned more from my kids," a divorced man who had kept their custody burbled to Astrachan, "than I ever thought I'd learn from another human being." Having kids, for these men, may be a dirty job, but it gives back more than any other. It is an experience not to be missed, part of that elusive balance whose disturbance leads to stress.

Goleman was not the only one to discover how much men are disturbed about this. In a cover story published on February 16, 1987, *Fortune* revealed "THE NO. 1 CAUSE OF EXECUTIVE GUILT: Who's Taking Care of the Children—and How Will They Turn Out?" The magazine found, based on a survey of four hundred men and women executives, that "nearly 30 percent of the men . . . said that they had refused a new job, promotion, or transfer because it would have meant less family time," as opposed to 26 percent of the women (who already spend more time than men with their families, on average, and so might feel less worried about it). Though *Fortune*'s claim that "fathers are sharing . . . family responsibilities" was highly suspect, as I will show later in this chapter, the survey as a whole made it plain that they are indeed getting their share of "the worry, stress and guilt associated with leaving the child in someone else's care." In fact, "fathers were almost as likely as mothers to say that the job interferes with family life."

More ominously, one wing of the men's movement, whom Astrachan calls "the divorce reformers," have taken up the cause of gender equality to argue that when you get down to it, the children are just as well off, if not better, with their fathers than with their mothers—*because women are no better than men.*

You could see this principle at work in the recent case of "Baby M," a child born to what we call, by some twist of language, a "surrogate mother"— one Mary Beth Whitehead, a working-class woman who agreed, for a fee of $10,000, to bear an infant for an upper-middle-class couple in which the woman could not conceive. When the baby was born, Whitehead decided to keep it—and was thereupon sued for breach of contract.

At the trial, a procession of experts set out to prove that Mother Love does not a good mother make, at least where Whitehead was concerned. Hours of testimony were devoted to proving that the baby would be better off with the wealthier couple—the same argument that is being made in divorce cases across the country, where fathers are declaring that because they earn more than their wives, they can provide better homes. And in the Baby M case, the judge bought the argument—in fact, he harshly insulted Whitehead, calling her an inadequate parent in ruling that her contract should have been kept.

That was a sign of gender equality in the most negative sense: not an equality of the proud, but of the debased. *If feminism has pulled down the pants on masculinity, the same is now happening to the sanctity of motherhood.*

Dinnerstein had suggested—but only suggested—that we would arrive at this point, and that it would be a difficult passage for men and for women alike. In achieving gender equality, she thought, women would be forced to accept an "abdication of unilateral female rule over childhood"—in other words, *they would have to give up some of the joys, as well as the duties, of motherhood.* At the same time, men would have to give up the comfort and courage that they acquired in childhood, and get from their wives as adults, under an arrangement in which a woman "celebrates, stimulates, shelters . . . *the growth of the child's will*" (her emphasis).

Plainly, a number of men are determinedly, if clumsily, trying to celebrate, stimulate, and shelter their children in ways their fathers did not. Whether women are, on their side, willing to abdicate the joys and duties of motherhood is another matter, to which we will return after we finish our visit with the New Man.

WHO IS REALLY MINDING THE HOUSE?

Raising the kids wasn't the only thing that was giving the New Men stress: the second of the "key changes affecting men's lives," wrote Goleman, was "the increased housework they do." He cited studies showing that men's total time involvement in housework had increased 20 percent since 1965, while their share of child care had grown even more, by 30 percent.

But there was a downside to this creeping gender equality: "The notion that men and women should escape sexual stereotyping by sharing equally in household responsibilities can create problems," wrote Goleman. In defining those problems, he quoted "one prominent therapist, who declined to be identified," as saying that some men were facing "opportunists who pose as liberated women in order to get their husbands to help out around the house, but who don't pull their own weight in return."

Frankly, if I were talking so foolishly as that, I would not be eager to see my name behind the quote either. It may indeed be true that some women have taken advantage of our confusion about gender equality to pull a fast one on their husbands (it has happened to me, though not over housework). But these women are about as common as the black rhinoceros, according to the overwhelming mass of current evidence.

What this prominent therapist offered is called, in scientific terms, "anecdotal" evidence. So let me ask you for some anecdotal evidence of your own: how many men do *you* know who have taken gender equality to the point of assuming responsibility fully, or even *equally* in the strict sense of the word, for what were formerly considered female roles in family life?

Of the hundreds of men I know (besides Clary, through his book), I can think of exactly one satisfying and satisfied "househusband"—a very nice guy, who lacks the aggressive qualities necessary to success in his field (free-lance fashion photography), and who has elected to cook, clean, and make life more pleasant for his lover of many years, a very in-demand stylist, and her teenage children. He does a great job at it, and his friends have learned to stop demanding when he is going to get out in the world and start pushing his work. More important, it doesn't seem to be an issue between him and his lover, who deeply appreciates returning from her business trips to a well-kept home and well-cooked meals, not to mention a man who adores and needs her.

I could also cite a man whose artistic career never took off, because he simply wasn't willing to put in the bruising work required to advance in a competitive domain, and whose wife works as a secretary to support him and their child, while he handles the housework and child care. Far from having a mutually satisfying arrangement, both partners in this marriage are filled with a terrible sense of frustration. And I could mention a few men between jobs, with working wives, who took time to care for their kids and spouses—though on a temporary basis.

But these men are rare—not just in my experience (and yours, I would bet at steep odds), but according to the available numbers. *Almost every measure of men's participation in family life and housework tells us that in the main, men are not taking over women's role in the home, let alone the family.*

Start with housework. A wealth of studies from the early 1970s on shows that, while men are helping more around the house, women are doing an awful lot more. For example, Geerken and Cove found that *even in families where the wife worked, wives had 90 percent or more of the responsibility for housecleaning, child care, and cooking.*

Interestingly enough, women's estimate of their own responsibilities was 75 percent greater than what their husbands thought the wives were bearing. *Men apparently thought that they were sharing more than women believed to be the case.* But men did more than women only in yard and house maintenance; they were equal in paying bills; and they handled 3.2 percent of housecleaning, and 7.2 percent of child care.

If these researchers' figures were accurate, a 20 percent increase, like the one Goleman cited, in the husbands' responsibility for housework since this survey was conducted would bring the men up to—are you ready?— *less than 4 percent of the total.* For child care, after a 30 percent increase, it would be a bit less than 10 percent—and *10 percent happens to be the level of child care conducted by husbands of mothers employed full-time as recently as 1982*, according to the U.S. Department of Labor.

What these figures make blatantly clear is that while men help, and are indeed doing more than they used to, *women are still overwhelmingly in charge of these tasks.* In fact, in 4,500 interviews conducted in the course of three recent surveys, Anthony M. Casale and associates found that in the typical home, men are responsible for "deciding what to watch on television," and "virtually all other decisions are made jointly or made by the woman"—with child care, cooking, and managing the family budget in the latter category.

The portrait of men under stress that Goleman created, in other words, was less clear-cut than it seemed to be. He was taking it for granted that the problems men had with their ideals—initially women's ideals, since gender equality came through the Women's Liberation Movement—reflected a changed reality. But *reality had not changed that much*—not for men, anyway.

What had changed was what men thought reality should be. They thought they should be minding the kids and the house, but the fact was, they weren't. And though they thought they were doing a lot, even their inflated (as the women saw it) notions of their own contributions fall far short of halfway to the total. *The gap between their "emotions and their ideals," as Goleman put it, looks more like a gap between the equality they crave in the home, and the concrete fact that they are still, like their fathers, largely dependent on women to manage this domain.*

It was only recently that such a gap came to be regarded as a cause of stress. That this occurred can be credited in large part to Richard Totman, an English clinical psychologist whose book *Social Causes of Illness*, published in 1978, put forward an intriguing and coherent theory of the relationship between the values a person holds, the support and confirmation other people offer for those values, and the likelihood that this individual will become sick. After a comprehensive review of the scientific literature on the linkage of attitudes and illness, Totman concluded that

> Research has made it clear that many of the conditions intuitively believed to be "stressful," such as high noise levels, poor working conditions or a heavy work load, do not seem to entail anything like the threat to health that do changes calling for a reestablishment of a person's orientation to his social environment.

In other words, *hard work and hard places are not inherently stressful enough to make you sick*, at least so far as the evidence can prove. The stress most likely to make a person sick, if Totman's theory proves correct, is this stress of not knowing where one is living, and what for—of having, to continue the allusion to Thoreau, a life of "quiet desperation," always a day late and a dollar short, one long step behind the changes one has to absorb.

What made such changes healthy, Totman believed, was "involvement," by which he meant *being able to express one's attitudes about life to others, and to receive from others confirmation of the rightness of the way in which one faced life*. Totman wrote: "If an individual is healthiest and feels most alive when caught up in projects, or when there are others around with whom he can exchange opinions, the best of both worlds is had by those working with others toward the fulfillment of a shared objective." Conversely, *the worst of both worlds would be had by someone who could not express what he or she felt about life to others, and who felt that all his or her labor was going toward the fulfillment of objectives that mattered to no one else.*

Look at the new, sensitive man from this standpoint, bearing in mind that his wife is still cleaning up after him and the kids, for the most part. He thinks he's doing a lot—more than he ever did before, and more than his father did, certainly—of what only a generation ago was woman's work. But after all the extra time and labor he puts in, he senses, and statistics confirm, that his wife is still doing more. *In a crucial way, he is simply not her equal, not sharing the jobs that need to be done.* If he is at all aware, he knows it, and so does she; it is the simple fact of the matter. But apparently Goleman's overwrought New Men had no one to tell about their problems but their therapists. They were not, the story made plain, expressing their anguish to their wives and lovers.

As usual, this was blamed on men's unconscious adherence to the macho image of the strong, silent type, which made it "quite difficult for most men to shed their defensive layers and be as intimate as women say they want them to be," as one of Goleman's sources sagely commented. If only men would open up and show their feelings—something, of course, that their fathers were incapable of doing—why, everything would be fine.

Pardon my language, but: *like hell it would.*

If we are going to understand why men's ideals do not match their reality—and I believe very strongly that this is the case, for more and more men—then we had best stop blaming our fathers for teaching us to keep a stiff upper lip, and take a closer look at the realities. Aside from the shame we ought to feel for taking cheap shots at older men who did their best by us, so far as they could—which is what can be said, I think, for most of them—it is an enormous mistake for men and women alike not to realize that *men's silence is an effort to stave off a confrontation with cold facts that will not go away.*

There was a hint, but only a hint, of that confrontation far down in Goleman's story, where one learned from Robert E. Gould, a psychiatrist at New York Medical College, that "it's easy to share the dishes, but all bets are off when the kids come. Then they"—men and women both—"fall back into an old-fashioned pattern."

You could find another sign of that confrontation in the growing numbers of couples who were putting off having children—more of them, according to *Newsweek*, than at any time since the Depression. "In 1960," said the magazine, "only about 13 percent of married women between 25 and 29 were childless; last year [1985] 29 percent were." The magazine thought that, "faced with new options, many wives decide that motherhood is not an essential or even desirable role."

On the contrary, these wives were faced with *old* options. In the vast majority of cases, we do not have a choice—not as much of a choice as we have been busily telling each other we can have, for the past two-odd decades.

Gender equality had gone far enough for women to work, if they wanted, but it had gone nowhere near far enough for most men to stop working, even if they wanted to, with few exceptions to this hard rule. Which meant, where women were concerned, that having a baby would push them, more often than not, into the kind of dependent existence their mothers had had. Where men were concerned, it meant going off to work, and coming home at the end of the day, or the career, to a life they had missed.

If men were not spending as much time with their kids as they wished, it was because they had not yet mastered the technique of being in two places at the same time (which, perhaps not coincidentally, was one of the talents that made Carlos Castaneda's Indian sorcerer, Don Juan, a culture hero of the 1970s.) *They were still in the same place they had always been: the job. And they were there because it seemed that they had to be.*

WHO CAN STAY HOME WITH BABY?

One of the things that helped Goleman's article to get across to readers was that it seemed like a logical complement to an issue that was very much alive among women, and that was leading to a lot of debate in feminist circles. He had described an emergent male version of the postfeminist "Superwoman," who could do more in a day than her mother and her father combined—win the bread, bake it, clean the kitchen, feed the kids, and still be a lover to her man.

Though this woman was flatteringly portrayed in everything from TV ads to husbands' boasts as a prime specimen of modernity, in an important sense she was a throwback to the kind of working mother found in the United States from 1900 to World War II: *she had no time for anything but the tasks of life.*

For women in the pre–World War II era, to be a working mother was not a sign of liberation, but of the cruelest hardship. "As a rule, wives who worked in this era were poor women who needed to help support their families," wrote Lynn Y. Weiner in *From Working Girl to Working Mother.* "Jobs that were not sought after by single women because of oppressive conditions or odd hours were taken up by married women who had little choice." Though a half-century of struggle by organized labor had improved the conditions of work, for men as well as for women, it had not altered an essential fact in the life of the working mother: once she left the job, she was still responsible for taking care of home and children unless, as is rarely the case these days, her family was so large that older children could take over homemaking tasks.

One can hardly dispute, on the basis of current evidence, that even though men spend more time on paid labor than their working wives, *the working wife spends more hours on home and paid employment combined than anyone else in our society*, as I noted in Chapter 2—about eleven and a half hours per day, an hour more than the average husband, day in and day out. Not coincidentally, though the modern working wife is better paid and better respected than her grandmother, by the late 1970s she was beginning to realize that she was no more free. On the contrary, according to a popular social-science term of that decade, she was "overloaded."

Curiously, her first response to this situation was guilt. Or perhaps not so curiously—because her dual role was supposed to be a sign of a new freedom, that a new generation of experts, in tune with the logic of feminism, was urging on her. "What women have are options and choice now," one rather smug feminist therapist told the author of *Woman on a Seesaw*, Hilary Cosell. "I don't see a conflict in that, do you?"

But conflict there was. Beginning in the late 1970s, as young women of the Second Wave began to think about and start families, women's magazines ran numerous articles about the various guilts their working readers were feeling. They felt guilty toward their children, with whom they could spend only the rare "quality time" that became a buzzword at the end of the 1970s, and toward their careers, from which the kids sometimes kept them. And Superwoman felt guilty for her doubts about which came first, at a time when, as Cosell recounted, a women's conference might erupt into exultant cheers after an executive declared that she had gone to a business meeting instead of her daughter's school play.

"If your child is used to having you home, and you're suddenly not," wrote Carole Suplina for *Vogue* in 1978, ". . . I think you're going to create a certain lack of assurance in your child." You, a woman. But the fact was, "I just can't be everything all the time to everybody, including myself." Not only that, but "as much as I may be more interesting [to her husband]" because of having a job, "the day-to-day intimacy of marriage is very difficult to maintain when you're both absorbed, you're both tired, or you simply don't see each other." Once again, this was a woman's job, to be the one who was not worn out, who maintained the intimacy. In short, "In trying to play out this superwoman . . . I had made my life more chaotic than ever."

It was no wonder that by the mid-1980s, bestsellers with titles like *Enough Is Enough!*, which denounced the plausibility of a woman's doing it all, began to appear, hot on the heels of articles like one that appeared in *Mademoiselle* in 1983 under the headline "Do Superwomen Really Exist?" Women were wearing themselves out, shuttling between the labor force and their homework. Something had to give.

What seemed to be giving, more and more, was the idea that a woman *had* to prove that she could succeed in a man's world as well as (if not better than) any man. The odds and the data suggested clearly that she could not—not in financial terms, the simplest and most vital measurement of who is really ahead in the success race, the terms by which most men judge themselves and each other.

By the 1980s, women were earning, on average, about 60 cents for every dollar earned by men—less than in the 1960s. It was true that some seven million women earned more than their husbands, a not insignificant number.

But the vast majority of those families were at the bottom of the economic pile. When all families were averaged together in 1983, the income of one in which only the husband worked was just under $22,000; in families where both husband and wife worked, it was over $32,000; where only the wife worked, it was under $12,000.

In other words, where the typical family was concerned, *if the wife dropped out of the labor force, the family would lose one-third of its income. If the husband did the same thing, the family lost two-thirds of its living.*

Moreover, women were finding that the chief value they held for themselves—to be fully developed individuals, capable not only of working but also of caring for others—cut little slack in the money economy. "Does no writer on the subject of careers and motherhood have the temerity to tell a probable truth," wrote Willa L. Z. Armstrong to the *New York Times Magazine* in 1987,

> that . . . in business, virtue is not its own reward. It's not onward and upward just because you "deserve" it. Plenty of people, men and women, who probably should have succeeded, don't. Not everyone can.

Superwomen, and the "growing numbers" of idealistic men who lived with them, therefore had a "choice" to make—if not when they started living together, as soon as they began to have children.

Someone has to be with the kids. And given the realities of the labor market, that someone is probably going to be their mother.

THE BATTLE OF THE NURSERY DOOR

What was less obvious—and what the New Men hardly dared to say out loud—was that an awful lot of women preferred it that way. Not all, by any means; women still wanted the right to work, both for income and for personal satisfaction, at different stages of their lives. But in numbers at least as growing as Goleman's, they also wanted the right to stop working and be with their children. The chorus of their voices grew so loud, in fact, that it posed a real problem for the feminist movement.

In her 1982 book, *The Second Stage,* Betty Friedan talked of being "confronted" by a young working woman:

> "I know I'm lucky to have this job," she says, defensive and accusing, "but you people who fought for these things had your families. You had your men and children. What are we supposed to do?"

The question for these women, wrote Friedan, was, "If I don't have a baby . . . Will I be fulfilled as a woman?"

The answer, argued Deborah Fallows in her 1985 book, *A Mother's Work*, was a resounding "no." A career woman who elected finally to stay home and raise her children instead of staying on the job (which is, not incidentally, where her husband stayed), Fallows ended a long condemnation of Second Wave feminist hostility toward the homemaker with the words, "There is an honor and legitimacy about being home raising children that parents—mostly mothers—*know* exists." And this honor was both a woman's due and a woman's burden, she suggested: if we "put aside the ideal to talk about the real," then "the way most American families now function" could be seen in reality as Dad on the job, Mom with the kids—and that was where it would stay for the foreseeable future.

Fallows called for the professionalization of motherhood, *in the name of feminist ideals:*

> the parts of the feminist agenda most often directed at careerists—
> that they should strive to bring out the best in themselves, that they
> should be responsible for themselves, that they should be independent
> and strong—should also be issued, as challenges, to women at home.

Cosell took a harder tone. "Imagine my shock," wrote Cosell, a former producer for NBC Sports, "my near-trauma, when I realized that I wanted something else"—something besides "freedom from economic and emotional dependence on men," not to mention "the money that will buy a house and two cars, a condo and a boat . . . whatever is your pleasure and whatever makes you happy." (Indeed I can imagine. Nearly every man I know has experienced that shock sooner or later.)

Her answer to that problem was aimed solely at women: what she wanted now was "some kind of personal life that was more than casual, or occasional, unstable and rootless"; a life that would include—like her parents'—a partner, and a family. But given that child-care facilities in America remained dismally behind the need, and that corporations (run by men) were not going to help out, Cosell argued, women had not only the duty but also the *right* to stay home with the kids. Her program amounted to what Armstrong denounced in her letter to the *Times*: "leaving . . . husbands to face life's little economic realities."

What had happened here was both a profound rejection and a reaffirmation of the Second Wave, whose "dead end" Friedan had just announced. Women like Fallows and Cosell were arguing that the Second Wave's view of feminine "success" amounted to a wholesale acceptance of male ideas of what success might be—all work, good money, bye-bye love. The real meaning of feminism, they held, would lie in seeing through the masculine mystique of success, and in giving equal value to traditionally feminine concerns—to put people first, instead of a paycheck.

Instead of asking why women must be stuck with the children at home, as the leaders of the Second Wave had done, Fallows and Cosell, and the women who confronted Friedan, were asking what women got for giving up the experience of raising children, in order to compete with men *on a man's terms.*

And their answer was: *not enough.* Not enough to replace the "honor and legitimacy" that mothers knew; not enough to make Superwoman's burdens worth the stress. If women's liberation meant that a woman could choose her destiny, it had to make room for women who chose to be homemakers, either temporarily or permanently—and not grudgingly, but with honor.

But where did that leave Superdad? The New Man, who wanted so much to nurture and love, besides making money?

Right where his father had been: going out into the world to fight off the competition, coming home exhausted to do what he could to help, in his sweet but bumbling and distant way. And to wonder what he was missing, why he was turning out to be the guy who married the girl just like the girl who married dear old Dad. If he kept silent about that predicament, or complained vaguely about stress, perhaps it was because he had come to a conclusion—a most unsettling one.

What if the family has become more than a "new feminist frontier," as Friedan announced in *The Second Stage? What if it has the looming potential to be a postfeminist battleground, as both men and women, leery of the all-consuming demands of work, each try to reclaim the family for themselves?*

Men's eyes have been opened. They have seen the rewards of entering into domains previously consigned or left to women, and they want to taste those rewards. Like men, women are now committed, for reasons of self-interest as well as ideals, to equality between the genders. And like men, if you can judge by the cold-eyed finality with which Fallows and Cosell put their claims to the exclusive privileges of motherhood, they are becoming aware of the awful possibility—awful because it seems to point toward yet another round of intimate conflicts—that *beyond not having it all, what they can have will be at their partners' expense.*

The irony here, for men who have followed the evolution of feminism in these United States, is both absurd and cruel. Did not Gloria Steinem promise us in 1970 that "if women win," there would be a new era, in which men "will no longer be the only ones to support the family"? In a way, feminism has kept Steinem's promise; women are contributing more to family incomes, and the appreciation of traditionally feminine, "expressive" values has opened new doors for men. *But when it comes to the nursery, women are taking up positions in the doorways.*

I can understand why they would—just as the men of my father's generation did, in their way. They, too, regarded the experience of raising children, to an extent we have become fond of forgetting, as an essential part of life.

What we have rejected in their legacy is the idea that this experience can be meaningful, in some essential sense, if it remains vicarious—if it is experienced mainly or merely through the medium of a woman's reports about what Johnny or Suzy did all day. *And that is largely what the experience is going to be—vicarious—if a person spends the majority of the child-raising years going off to work in the morning and coming home at night.* Women don't want to lose the real experience, any more than the men who have been alerted to its rewards.

THE MALE SURRENDER

Yet if women are reclaiming the home for themselves, and for the most part succeeding, I believe that it is in large measure because *men are permitting them to do it—are, in effect, giving back the promise feminism made to us.*

We are doing so because we are uncertain, at best, as to how steep a price we must pay to claim that promise—just as the angry young women of the Second Wave were not fully aware of how difficult it would ultimately prove to reject the special experience and status of motherhood.

Once we get inside the doors of home to stay, where would we fit among the furniture women have always arranged for us? Would it be as comfortable, as much our own, as the traveler's motel room, the office chair? Would we be as much in charge of a baby as we are of a career?

That is the crux of the matter—we do not know. *We want a richer life, a life that has room in it for something besides a rat race. But the choices we have to make hold no certainties.*

Practically speaking, there aren't very attractive answers for a man. If he is working to win his family's love, and to prove his own, the job keeps him away from enjoying its fruits. If he stops working, he would probably not only be considered a lazy bum, he would most likely be a poor one; either that or his wife would have to take over support of the family, and of him.

Of course, that situation would offer him the chance to be with the kids. But it would bring other factors into play. What if he *liked* to work, and missed it?

The idea of giving up working had occurred to only one of the dozen-odd men of my sample who were not yet but hoped to be fathers. That one told me that when he was ready to have kids, "I'll find a rich woman who doesn't want to give up her career, and stop working awhile." Where would he find her? "They're around," he assured me. Indeed, I know precisely one woman who openly expressed such an ambition.

But this man and woman are striking exceptions. The thirty-year-old publisher of a profitable monthly journal in Manhattan was typical. Sitting on a couch with his pregnant wife, his partner in the business, he readily told me that when the baby arrived, he would do an equal part of caring for the baby. But he saw those forthcoming responsibilities quite as he saw running the business—as a job with clear responsibilities that could be rationally divided between him and his wife, like reading page proofs or returning phone calls—so many diapers, so many feedings, so much playtime. Just "like anything else," he said.

His wife was listening attentively, saying little. But her reaction was eloquent when he said, "I can't see just staying home and taking care of the kid. It's important, sure, but if that's all there is in your life, you gotta get bored."

At that moment the woman's eyes turned away, inward. She'd never raised a kid, but she was carrying one, and already she knew something about children that her husband could understand only by an act of sympathetic imagination. She couldn't put down what was growing inside her when she felt like it, and she wasn't yet done with the job; all this she knew, and he did not. How they would work out care of the baby, she didn't yet know, but she knew her husband was wrong. When the baby came along, the tasks and demands would be different.

But in one respect, he would not be. He would not give up his job. Doing so had at least occurred to his wife; it had not occurred to him.
Why hadn't it?

THE PASSIONS OF MEN

Maybe work could dull or snuff a man. But it just might be the most dependable thing he had going. It might be the hardest thing he could be called on to sacrifice. And he might resist that sacrifice as deeply as some women were rejecting their hard-won careers to go back to motherhood.

Among the young couples I spoke with who had small children, this pattern was repeated over and over: the man worked outside the home, or occasionally in a separate, isolated room, and the woman worked on raising the child. He helped, certainly, but he was neither the primary nor an equal partner in this respect. Their contributions may have been equal, in some sense of the word. *But they were not of the same kind.* And they were not fundamentally different from the contributions men and women made to family life in the 1950s. Men brought home most of the money, while women loved them for it and cared for the children most of the time.

I had met one of these men on a previous occasion, when I took a certain vengeful pleasure in remarking to myself that his talk about being an involved father with their two-year-old daughter didn't jibe with the fact that even on vacation, his wife was most concerned with the logistics of carrying and caring for the little girl. Another phony New Man, I thought. The kind whose grin tells you, "Be like me." The judgment was unfair, I learned.

On a later trip to this couple's home in New England, I was waiting in the house when he came home from his psychotherapeutic practice. His daughter loved him, had missed him during the day—that was plain; she practically flew to his arms and lap, begged him to read to her. At dinner she sat beside her mother, who simultaneously conversed, ate her dinner with one hand, and fed the girl with the other. She was so practiced at this "multi-phasic" behavior, as stress specialists call it, that she didn't even have to look at her daughter's plate while helping the child manipulate a fork. Daddy had not been there while these skills were being learned.

He was telling me that the main problem for his patients was that they were working terribly long hours, and getting little appreciation from their corporate employers. They felt as though a professional rule, to maintain an image of brilliance, was always in order—"especially in their intimate lives," he said. But they could not meet the same standards of performance when they left work. His typical male patient, he said, was "exhausted—he has minimal time for his wife." In some cases, and not uncommonly, they were obliged "to plan a vacation" every few weeks or so, "in order to have sex with their wives."

"It's a problem I have too," he admitted, referring to the constant battle to put in the time to earn the money, and then to be loving, attentive, healthy.

The guiding principle, he thought, was this: "The more successful you are, the more committed you feel to putting in more time to keep it going." His practice had become profitable only in the past year, and with that profit had come steeper demands on his time. He especially regretted the evening sessions, necessary because so many of his patients worked long office hours.

Hours as long as his own. I realized that part of his therapeutic function was symbolic: he had to prove to his patients that a man who worked just as hard as they did could have a full life. He had to offer some kind of success, to show them that failure was not inevitable. And to show them that to be "healthy and whole," as he described his patients' yearnings, was not beyond the price a man could pay.

He paid for his life, and his family's, in various ways: time, money, energy. "See this house?" he said. "Looks new, doesn't it? It was built in 1927, and we rebuilt it." Or rather, he did. During those eight months, he said, "simultaneously I was building my career"—building, like you build a house—"and I was here every day at eight in the morning, to supervise workers. Then I'd drive half an hour to the office at noon"—his voice on the tape trembles slightly—"work from one till eight, get home about nine, eat dinner, and get on the phone to organize things the next day."

There was a physical cost to all this work: he developed back and neck problems. "Stress becomes exhaustion," he said, explaining his illness. Or exhaustion, stress. He didn't have to be a psychoneurologist to diagnose his problem: he had worked beyond his reserves of strength and health. A man is, among other things, a beast that grows tired.

Wasn't it true, I asked him, that what he said his life was about—living with and for his family—and the way he lived were in conflict? In effect, I was asking him to admit the discrepancy between his rhetoric and his reality. He didn't dodge the question: "You have to feel guilty," he said, "either toward the work, your family, or both." He saw through himself. As most of us could, and would, if we cared to.

He was earning bread, but only once a day did he break it with the people he so evidently loved. But that alone would not make a man feel guilty, if he believed it could be no other way.

This man had made a choice, and he was ashamed, in some way, of his motivation for making it.

·　　　·　　　·

That shame is something our fathers could have told us about—if they had known how to tell us, and we had known how to listen. Like us, they came up against the awful conflict between work and love; and like us, they did not quite know how to express it, or what to do about it.

Faced with a choice between the devil they knew, the working life of a working man, and the devil they did not know, life in the realm that women made, they chose the former. But that choice gave them a sense of longing and pain so profound that—just like the sad sack New Man—it made them feel sick. And they were the first American men to call that sickness by the name of stress.

PART
—— II ——

THE AGE OF STRESS

CHAPTER

—— 4 ——

Doctor's Dis-Orders

On an average of once a year, starting around 1973, I would take a
test for my stress. No visit to the doctor was required, because the
tests were published regularly in the magazines my lover brought
home, under headlines that asked something like, "How Much Stress Do
You Have?" I did not know it then, because I hadn't yet formed the habit
of reading the fine print at the bottom of a page, but these tests were taken
more or less directly from a questionnaire developed by T. H. Holmes and
R. H. Rahe, and first published in 1967 in the *Journal of Psychosomatic
Research*.

Holmes and Rahe's "Social Adjustment Rating Scale" had been compiled
by asking a large number of individuals to name events in their lives that
had required them to "adjust"—in other words, that demanded an effort
to understand, accept, or simply to live with. When Holmes and Rahe had
finished listing these events, they assigned each a numerical score, which
represented the relative weight it carried in the experience of their subjects.
The middle of the scale was marked by marriage (50 points), because
nothing that happened to the people Holmes and Rahe interviewed was
more than twice as demanding an experience.

The top of the scale (100 points) was occupied by "death of spouse,"
followed by divorce (73 points) and marital separation (65). Of 43 items
on the list, 15 began with the word "change"—to another kind of work, in
one's financial condition, in residence, schools, recreation, church or social
activities, sleeping or eating habits, the number of family get-togethers, the
number of arguments with a spouse, responsibilities at work, work hours
or conditions, living conditions, or the health of a family member.

Whew.

On the basis of the *change* items alone, I usually went over the 300-point
total that, the magazines warned, indicated a real and present danger of

incipient mental or physical illness within the next two years, and a pressing need to visit a physician, who would presumably rescue me from my stress.

But I had even more to worry about: a "death of close family member" (my grandmother, in 1974—63 points), a "death of close friend" (three in 1972–73, for a total of 111 points), ending school (and thus being obliged to find a job, for a total of 52 points), "trouble with boss," an ongoing "revision of personal habits" . . .

In fact, about the only thing on the list that didn't happen to me between 1973 and 1978, when I left my lover and changed my life over again, was a "jail term," which saved a measly 63 points off my total. I knew other people who had similar experiences and stress scores; we would joke about our narrow escapes from whatever stress could do to us, with a mix of anxiety ("didn't know it was *that* bad") and pride ("didn't know I was *that* tough"). We thought we were lucky; we did not question the concept of "stress" that we were busy learning, along with the rest of America.

Holmes and Rahe never made the claim for the Social Adjustment Rating Scale that the popular press did—namely, that it was a surefire guide to determining whether you were headed for a psychological or physical break-down. They and other researchers indeed tried to discover a clear relation between scores on the scale and specific subsequent illnesses; but the connection was weak, of barely any statistical significance.

Nonetheless, during those years when I was half-jokingly, half-worriedly totting up my stress rating, physicians offered the public blanket assurances that the more "stress" in one's life, the more inevitable and swift would be the arrival of illness. "There are dozens of ailments that, in whole or in part, are caused or aggravated by stress—including heart disease, menstrual disorders, migraine headaches, asthma, skin ailments and all sorts of digestive troubles," Dr. William A. Nolen assured readers of *McCall's* in April 1975. "Whichever organ or system in your body is weakest by nature will be the one that gives you trouble when you're under stress." By the end of the decade, Los Angeles cardiologist Arnold Fox, M.D., was warning readers of his newsletter, *The New Health,* that "stress either causes, or excerbates [*sic*], or causes *and* excerbates every disease known to man. We know stress can seriously harm or kill us." In fact, according to Fox, stress was "the number-one killer in this country today."

But who was this killer? As Nolen told his readers, "we all know vaguely what stress is." But even after reading his and similar articles, I could not

say *precisely* what stress was. At the time these articles began coming out—
a stream that rose steadily, leveled off in the later seventies, and then began
a second climb that continues as I write in 1987—I thought that I was
simply ignorant. As a matter of fact, I was; but practically speaking, it would
not have mattered a great deal if I had known everything there was to know
about stress.

The fact is that, over thirty years after Hans Selye, M.D., published the
book that began our current obsession with stress, *The Stress of Life,* and
twenty years after Holmes and Rahe published their scale, no one has been
able to offer, nor scientists to agree on, a verifiable explanation of what
stress is, and what—if anything—it does to you.

Such disagreement is hardly unusual in science; scientists cannot agree
on the toxicity of various chemicals, on the origins and treatment of cancer,
on the chances that a nuclear plant will spring a leak. The best they can do
is try to construct experiments, in which a theory about a certain event or
idea can be tested, and which can then be repeated by other scientists as
a check on the results.

Stress does not lend itself easily to such experiments, because the number
of variables involved is huge—to start with, the fact that people may resemble each other, but are rarely exactly alike. How can one ensure that
the same experience will have the same meaning, or the same effect, among
different people at different times?

When you look at the items that Holmes and Rahe's test subjects offered
as examples of "stress," you see clearly that the events which most concerned them had to do with work, love, and money. Shifts in a relationship,
in a job, in financial means and obligations, appear throughout the Social
Adjustment Rating Scale in different forms. The same concerns run all the
way through the medical and popular literature of stress.

At the time that scale was compiled, "change" was a buzzword in American culture—an obligation for youth, who wanted to change themselves
and the world in one fell swoop, and a major annoyance to their parents.
"I'm *sick* of change," the mother of a girl I knew said one night in 1969,
while we kids were proclaiming the absolute necessity of it in her living
room. In 1987, even if we would still agree that change can be stressful,
we are probably not thinking about exactly the same changes Holmes and
Rahe's subjects had in mind.

In other words, stress was not merely an objective medical condition,
which is what people still seem to think it is. It was also a way of talking
about changes that kept on coming. The fact that we are still using this

nebulous word to describe our problems should tell us, among other things, that the changes are still coming, in unpredictable ways—even if at times they look suspiciously like no change at all.

WHAT IS THIS THING CALLED STRESS?

"Stress" entered our daily vocabulary in the 1950s, largely because of Hans Selye, who did a great deal to rescue the field of psychosomatic medicine from the oblivion into which it had fallen by the mid-twentieth century. Beginning in the 1920s, psychosomatic research, taking its lead from Sigmund Freud, had concentrated on looking for a direct relationship between neuroses and physical illness. This "specificity" theory bore a close resemblance to Freud's concept of "displacement," in which a neurotic conflict hides behind a physical symptom. But no one could demonstrate just how this process worked—why, say, an unresolved father fixation would give one man arthritis, and another hypertension. And the treatments based on this theory didn't work very well, except when practiced by doctors so talented that they might have achieved similar results with another method. By 1955 the specificity theory was all but dead.

And then came Selye.

Selye went at the psychosomatic problem from the opposite direction— he backed away from specificity and concentrated on the common. And when he went public with his results, he had a model of the link between feelings and the body, based on two decades of laboratory studies—on rats, not humans, but ours is a rat-race era, and his results were not seriously challenged on that basis. His ideas about stress marked an important turning point in the way we used a word that had been around since the time of Middle English.

From the fifteenth century on, "stress" was used to indicate conditions that caused a person difficulty—like poverty, physical menace, someone else's hostility. In the nineteenth century, the Industrial Age, the word took on a mechanical connotation; in physics and engineering, it stood for the pressure applied to an object, which could ultimately distort its shape, the way a high wind can bend and break the girders of a bridge. As in the earlier meaning, stress was something external to its object—if you are "under stress," the stress is over (and outside) you.

Perhaps the first person to think of stress in an entirely different way was not a doctor, but a novelist—none other than D. H. Lawrence. In *Women in Love,* published in 1920, he wrote of one of his principal male characters that there were only three things left that would rouse him, make him live. One was to drink or smoke hashish, the other was to be soothed by Birkin [another man], and the third was women. And there was no one for the moment to drink with. Nor was there a woman. And he knew Birkin was out. *So there was nothing to do but to bear the stress of his own emptiness.* [My emphasis.]

What Lawrence told us was that stress was something that happened *inside* a man, a result of his way of looking—or not looking—at life. It was an existential problem, not a mechanical one. The same theme peeked out from E. M. Forster's offhand comment, in *Howards End,* that a businessman who had "worked very hard all his life, and noticed nothing" had thereby become one of "the people who collapse when they do notice a thing." Man the doer had become his own hangman, and "the stress of his own emptiness" was the rope. The idea became a virtual cliché of literature before World War II, and science would not lag far behind.

Selye brought together mechanics and the existential, in a brilliant fashion. The core of his theory was something called the "general adaptative syndrome," GAS for short, which remains the foundation of the way most of us think of stress. Selye arrived at the discovery of the GAS by what some of us might consider torture of animals: he made rats sick through exposure to bacteria, turned up and down the heat on them, ran them to exhaustion, and so on. And he observed that such varied treatments aroused *the same response* from the animals' individual bodies. That is what made it "general." The response varied according to the intensity and duration of the "stressors" to which the rats were subjected; hence it was "adaptative." And it involved the interaction of various physiological systems, which meant it was a "syndrome."

Briefly, the response had three stages. First came *alarm,* in which the stressor aroused the hypothalamus region of the brain, the pituitary gland, and the adrenal cortex—"through pathways not yet fully identified," as Selye admitted in 1974, which remains the case. The body's lymphatic system became enlarged, and the hormone epinephrine was released into the bloodstream, causing a faster heartbeat, a rise in blood-sugar levels, and other symptoms of arousal. In this stage the animal was prepared to fight or flee—but at the cost of a heightened sensitivity to whatever caused the alarm, and the risk of death if the body's defenses were overwhelmed (as in the case of a serious burn trauma).

In the second stage, of *resistance,* the hormone levels remained high, but other systems, such as the lymph nodes, returned to normal; the animal was poised, no longer so susceptible to danger. But if the process was allowed or obliged to continue, the animal entered the third stage, of *exhaustion.* Its hormonal reserves were empty, its lymphatic system stretched past normal function, its ability to protect itself depleted. The alarm reaction reappeared, but now its signs were pointing to the victim's death.

One of the most innovative aspects of Selye's theory—once he applied it to human beings—was that this process did not necessarily result from hardship or external pressure, as in traditional views of stress. *"It is immaterial whether the agent or situation we face is pleasant or unpleasant,"* underlined Selye in 1974, trying to clarify a lingering confusion about his theory in the public mind. "All that counts is the intensity of the demand for readjustment or adaptation." Happy events—such as marriage—could evoke the same GAS response as sad ones (like divorce). Any and every variation in the flow of life could be a stimulus to stress. Like Holmes and Rahe, for whom he showed the path, Selye clearly implied that *change, in and of itself, was stressful.*

Another innovation was that although the syndrome Selye described was certainly "general"—it was built into our bodies, and everyone was subject to it—the way it worked itself out depended in practice on the way an individual coped with "stressors." Stress was everyone's problem, but a response to it could be determined only by the individual. And that response, Selye insisted, could be positive or negative: "Although, contrary to public opinion, we must not—and indeed cannot—avoid stress, we can meet it efficiently and enjoy it by learning more about its mechanism and adjusting our philosophy of life accordingly."

This, of course, is beyond the power of rats. Whether it is within the power of men, no matter how efficient and eager to learn they might be, is still an open question.

TYPE A BEHAVIOR AND YOUR HEAD

In 1959, San Francisco cardiologists Meyer Friedman and Ray Rosenman began publishing to the medical profession a theory that would quickly achieve general fame with the public. It was a fame that added a new phrase to the language, and a new, ambivalent image of masculinity. The phrase was "Type A," and it referred to a man who, like Hans Selye's rats, could not control what stress did to him.

In their 1974 book, *Type A Behavior and Your Heart,* Friedman and Rosenman rather disingenuously explained the beginning of their theory: in searching for a reason that their patients who worked in business were dying of heart attacks in their forties and fifties, ordinarily an age of health, they were struck by the remark of a woman: "It's the stress that's killing our husbands." In fact, Friedman and Rosenman's first scientific love, and one to which they remained faithful throughout their work, was the study of blood cholesterol levels. They wanted to use stress to prove that cholesterol kills, and vice versa. Their base concept was that emotions could alter cholesterol readings.

They were trying to test an "if"—*if,* as Selye said, certain emotions and tensions were associated with the physical signs of a stress reaction, then men who were prone to those emotions probably would reveal more signs of stress, among them high cholesterol, than men who were not. They would thus be more prone to heart attacks than men who felt less stress.

It was a logical idea, but there was a major question in it that has never been resolved by Friedman and Rosenman or anyone else—which comes first, the sickness or the way you feel? If your cholesterol is up, is that because you are angry, or are you angry because your cholesterol is up?

And there was another problem with their argument: one based on the fact that people tend to find what they are looking for. From the start, Friedman and Rosenman were looking for men who were obsessed with time ("If you make a DATE with someone . . . would you BE THERE on TIME?"), who felt they were bearing a load in life ("Does your job carry HEAVY responsibility?"), and who were afraid of losing even in jest ("When you play games with people YOUR OWN AGE, do you play for the FUN of it, or are you REALLY in there to WIN!"). They wanted to find guys who said "Yes!" when asked: "Is there any COMPETITION in your job?").

Not surprisingly—at least not to anyone who works for a living—they found such men. In fact, they found them all over the place. Friedman said, when I interviewed him in 1982, that 50 percent of American men fit the Type A profile to some extent. Type A was the enemy within Everyman.

The most universal Type A characteristic was *time urgency.* It was "the most overt factor, the one he is least likely to hide," Friedman told me. Of course, it is also built into the life of ordinary men.

The second important characteristic of the Type A, and the one he "certainly wants to hide," said Friedman, was *hostility,* verging on violence. If such a man found himself stuck in traffic, or on a cafeteria line, or at an airport, Friedman suggested, he would explode in rage at this unwanted stress: "The more trivial the stress," he told me, "the more severe the pattern."

As with Selye, a man's problem wasn't what happened to him in life, but what he made of it. If he made it out to be a threat—Type A's, said Friedman, tended to see the world as a conspiracy to rob their time and the success they deserved—he would trigger "the excess release of norepinephrine," one of the hormones Selye had identified as playing a part in stress reactions. Given that this man was likely to have such reactions on a constant basis, he would have "a hard time getting excess sugar out of the blood," said Friedman, and chronic high blood pressure, both of which would worsen his cholesterol readings.

And that was what Rosenman and Friedman found when they tested their subjects.

Case closed.

But, your Honor, there is new evidence.

The Type A theory sounded plausible—and still does, judging from articles with titles like "Do You Have a Heart Attack Personality?", which appeared in *Gentlemen's Quarterly* in 1987. But the theory, as time went on, had to take account of some facts that made it seem a lot less scary.

The numbers cannot be more clear. From 1960, when the Type A first became a cultural figure, through 1982, when we were still knee-deep in stress, *heart-attack rates for both men and women dropped steadily and dramatically.*

The fall took place in every age group, and every category of heart disease. For men aged between 25 and 44 years, the drop was over 50 percent. For men aged 55–64, it was 33 percent. Among women—despite frequent warnings throughout the 1970s that women's move into the stressful work force would rebound disastrously on their heart-disease rates—the decline in the death rolls was even more dramatic. For example, the death rate among women aged 45–54 from hypertensive heart disease—one of the categories that would seemingly be most responsive to stress—fell from 21.5 per 100,000 women in 1960 to 5.4 in 1980, and to 4.9 in 1982.

Sooner or later, reality catches up with hysteria, and there were far fewer men dropping dead than had been the case when heart attacks became a public worry in the 1950s. The reasons weren't mysterious. Men and women alike were watching their cholesterol, exercising more, making an effort to control their tobacco use. They knew what the health-risk factors were, and avoidance of them became a part of many people's behavior.

If 50 percent of men and growing numbers of women were Type A's, as Friedman claimed in 1982, either it wasn't enough to destroy their hearts, or heart failure wasn't really what they were risking. That was what the numbers suggested, in a country where people read lots of numbers. And as the numbers piled up, the lesson doctors drew from stress shifted: it was no longer merely that stress could kill you, but that you had never been alive.

WE HAVE WAYS OF MAKING YOU TALK: STRESS AND CANCER

Also in the late fifties, a group of cancer therapists and researchers was closing in on what would become popularly known as the Type C personality. This was the first model of how stress worked that made equal room for women, and the one that resided most firmly on the existential elements of the debate. Like Betty Friedan's housewife victims of *The Feminine Mystique,* who were introduced to the public at about the same time, the Type C had a "problem that has no name," or more exactly, a problem he or she was afraid to put a name to. The problem was not fear of death, but fear of life.

The most eloquent, influential, and just plain busy advocate of the idea that a patient's personality could have an influence on the growth and treatment of cancer—an idea that remains deeply controversial in the field of cancerology, despite widespread public acceptance—was Lawrence LeShan, a therapist at the Institute of Applied Biology in the media capital of New York. Beginning in the mid-fifties, LeShan collected the life histories of literally hundreds of cancer patients, and compared the resulting data with observations from psychotherapy sessions and structured interviews. What he found was a similar "pattern of development and relationships ... in 72 percent of the cancer patients and 10 percent" of the nonsufferers he used as a scientific control—a difference big enough to rule out chance from his results, if not to establish certainty that this pattern was among the causes of cancer.

LeShan argued that because of the loss in childhood of a loved one—a common experience in our parents' generation, which began their lives with shorter life expectancies than ours, then passed through poverty and war—the future cancer patient came to believe that "loneliness was his doom." He or she managed to conceal the wound, but "the orientation that social relationships were dangerous and that there was something very much wrong with him, persisted and colored his life. Little energy was invested in relationships." When a second shock of loss occurred, later in life, it was taken as the return of "the thing they had expected and feared all their lives—utter isolation and rejection," from which "the only way out was to cease existing." These people's dilemma, he rendingly declared, was that

> they need to be themselves, but they deeply believe that it is hopeless; that if they express this, attempt to be creative in this manner, they will be completely rejected . . . [hence] they tend either to provoke the rejection they fear or to perceive it where it does not exist.

They were, LeShan pointedly and ironically noted, " 'good,' decent, thoughtful, kindly people." Their key failing was an urge to please, to buy approval with self-sacrifice: "The wishes and needs of others were 'right' and theirs were wrong." What they gained in company, they lost in intimacy.

LeShan's picture was one that could apply equally to William H. Whyte's bestselling portrait of *The Organization Man*, who in giving in to the group had to "make a surrender that will later mock him," and to Friedan's housewife victim of *The Femine Mystique*, who "no longer has a private image to tell her who she is, or can be, or wants to be." Neither believed it possible any longer to express personal, individual needs; and both felt constrained to be decent and cooperative, on the job and in the home.

But the lesson of cancer—as it came through in David Kissen's study of male lung-cancer patients, who seemed to have "a significantly diminished outlet for emotional discharge," or in Arthur Schmale and Howard Iker's study of women with cervical cancer, who were characterized by an "overly . . . self-sacrificing approach to life"—was that suppressing your own needs for the sake of others was a self-imposed death sentence.

LeShan and his allies were severely criticized by other scientists, in part because their evidence was more subjective than was the norm in science, and in part because they couldn't account for the 30 or 40 percent of people who didn't fit their profiles, but still got cancer, or others who did fit the profile, but stayed healthy. Later researchers could not prove, except anecdotally, that working on cancer patients' attitudes toward life changed their survival rates—an approach so radical that the American Cancer Society felt compelled to issue a blanket denial of it in 1981.

But the ideas these researchers raised stuck, for at least one urgent reason: unlike coronary heart disease, there seemed to be no getting away from cancer. Overall death rates from cancer rose by 28 percent for men, and 23 percent for women, from 1960 to 1982.

The only exception—and an important one—was the 25–44-year-old age group, where *the death rate dropped by 27 percent for men and 37 percent for women over this period.* The cancer problem had a pronounced generation gap built into it.

It was therefore most significant that a generation gap figured prominently in the major studies, from both scientific and popular perspectives, of the effects of personality on cancer to be published in the 1970s. Those studies would seemingly confirm that one's relationships with others could affect one's health; and in so doing, they would, in a way their author had probably not intended, play into the anxiety Americans were feeling about their improvised intimate lives.

In the late 1940s, Caroline Bedell Thomas, M.D., had administered a series of psychological and biographical tests to 1,337 students of the Johns Hopkins Medical School. In 1973 she began to publish her correlations of the attitudes she had found in these students with their subsequent histories of disease. She wanted to see if the attitudes these men expressed had a "prospective" function—if the men who developed cancer, for example, had held certain feelings and ideas in common, to a greater extent than the overall group. The evidence suggested that they did.

In particular, the men she called the "Major Cancer" group had "checked proportionately fewer positive, or favorable attitudes, and more negative, or unfavorable attitudes, than did the Healthy Group," Thomas reported. But the finding that received even more attention was that 35 percent of the Major Cancer men characterized their relations with their fathers as "detached," their relations with their mothers as "reserved." The next closest group to express such attitudes were the men who developed coronary heart disease. Among the men of the Healthy Group, only 10 percent held these attitudes.

These findings were roughly consistent with LeShan's idea that disturbances in affective relationships early in life could later set the stage for cancer. Thomas would not declare that her figures were gospel—"All we have so far are *clues,*" she insisted when I called her in 1981 to discuss her studies—but her clues were discovered in a way that avoided the chicken-or-egg problem that plagued LeShan. The attitudes Thomas found in these men could not have been caused by their cancers, which didn't yet exist when she ran her tests on them, so far as we understand the etiology of cancer.

Aside from the care that went into her work, Thomas' public reception—her results were very widely reported—reflected a time when intergenerational conflicts, brought to a peak by the Vietnam war and the antiwar movement, were painfully fresh in American minds. Her work could be taken by Americans as confirming something that many of us already suspected: by attacking our fathers, we were inviting retribution. In fact, that was one of the first things that occurred to me when I read her study for the first time, in 1980—had I grown detached from my father? Had I always been?

In a broader sense, Thomas did much to confirm that an individual's health depended, in part at least, on that person's relationships with others. And this too was timely; in the mid-1970s it was becoming apparent that a broad shift was taking place in the demands we placed on relationships.

Across the cultural board, relationships were changing from the answer to the question "Who Do You Trust?"—as a fifties TV game show put it— to the proposition "Let's Make a Deal." On the latter show, a hit of the seventies, contestants bid for prizes that were hidden behind curtains, while the host tempted them to risk what they had already won for what was behind the next curtain. The contestants could win the deal, but they never knew what they were winning until they got it. It was all very honest, all very fair, whether the payoff was kind or cruel.

If the best you could do in the seventies was to make a deal—for the night, or the latest episode in your monogamous serial, or until the kids were grown and out of the house—well, then you'd want to see all the clauses spelled out in fine print. Not coincidentally, marriage counselors and psychologists were telling couples to "negotiate" their differences, instead of just being "mature" about them; to see their relationships as "transactions"; to make "concessions" in exchange for "rewards." Magazines compiled of pornographic letters spelled out in huge detail (sometimes actually provided by real correspondents, instead of editors on the magazine) the precise terms on which the writers made love. Making love meant being "up-front," instead of "uptight"—a word that white culture borrowed from black singer Stevie Wonder, for whom "uptight" meant "everything is all right," and turned on its head, to mean a nervous square. Being up-front meant being honest—about what you wanted, what you would give.

The demand spread from our intimate lives to our acquaintanceships. An eager convert would report to us that a young man had wet his pants in an est seminar, and then announced the news with the words, "It doesn't matter!" Barbara Grizzutti Harrison, in her report on est, found it evil; Tom Wolfe, in "The Me Decade," made it look silly. What was clear all around was that "sharing," which meant revealing one's deepest secrets to strangers, was becoming a social obligation, when only a few years before it had been an obscenity.

The obligation deepened, broadened: the price of making and keeping relationships—or of winning the White House, as Jimmy Carter understood in 1976—was complete honesty, "openness," "accessibility." In a decade when the personal became political, the same language described the relationship of one person to another, and of a leader to the electorate.

But there was a fatal flaw with our eagerness to deal, right up-front. The very fact that we needed to say anything and everything that came into our heads, in the name of honesty, showed that *we did not trust each other, no matter how honest we might be.*

In this context, the Type C researchers could be sensed as confirming that our inability to trust, to make relationships based on understanding and complicity, and on which we could unquestioningly rely, could make us sick. Isolation, loneliness, distance from others; a lack of trust in oneself, one's lover, one's boss and colleagues; a sense that people were what mattered in life, but that people were unapproachable or uncomprehending, if not dangerously dishonest: these themes would reappear again and again in the new models we constructed of men and women under stress. Thomas had found only clues, but she pointed to the right mystery.

The way a scientist is read by a given public often has more to do with the latter's needs than with the former's real message. Charles Darwin, for example, might well have turned in his grave when his theory of the evolution of species was employed by America's upper classes, under the heading of "Social Darwinism," to justify the brutal conditions of life among the working classes from the later nineteenth century until the Depression. Social Darwinism argued that the fittest do not just survive, they grow rich—that poverty is nature's way of improving the race. And people accepted that argument, until a Crash created by financiers not only risked the destruction of even the upper classes but also led to a lot of talk of revolution among poorer folks, which the wealthy took seriously, and which made it seem more delicate and sage for them to stop saying we all needed a good dose of poverty to keep us fit.

There was a similar detour taking place in the stress debate. In coming to see stress, and the fatal cancer it led to, not as something that happened to a person, but as the result of the way that person felt about what happened, it became implicit that stress was an individual's responsibility. If someone could not change his or her attitudes toward life, it was plain that no one else could be to blame—either for one's unhappiness or for one's cancer.

As Susan Sontag put it bluntly in *Illness as Metaphor,* "the cancer personality is regarded . . . simply, and with condescension, as one of life's losers."

What had the Type C lost? How had he or she failed?

A typical answer was given in 1976, in the popular magazine *Science Digest.* The headline asked its readers, "Do You Have a Cancer Personality?" The story then told them that "if you really want to protect yourself from cancer"—and who doesn't?—"you have to guard your psyche as well as your physique. You must modify your behavior patterns so as not to become a 'cancer personality.' "

The price of not changing one's behavior was shown by a married couple mentioned in the article, in a quote from Dr. Vivian Tenny, "a New York City gynecologist." Tenny told of a man who died of throat cancer, but not before revealing to her—why he went to a gynecologist for advice about his throat is not mentioned—that he felt "throttled by his wife." As for the wife, "she developed cancer of the breast within six months of her husband's death," her reward for having "treated her husband as an inept, not too bright child," instead of weaning him to manhood. Each got the cancer that expressed his or her emotions, to the letter.

What they got, they got for failing to act on their needs: "The psychological stress that seems to count," LeShan told me in 1981, "is an inability to sing your own song." Cancer was the "song"—in the gangster slang of Hollywood, the confession—you could not help singing. It was an honest disease; it would tell you how to change—or else. And it made you honest—or else.

There was a weird irony here. The stress obsession had turned full circle: psychosomatic medicine had gone right back to specificity, its favorite theory before Selye came along, and was looking at diseases as if they were fleshy metaphors for neurosis. "Much of the research done to show that the emotions can cause disease is credited to Hans Selye," said the *Science Digest* article, with a perfectly straight face.

And the emotion that mattered most, that created the most stress, seemed to be the *frustration* of men and women—at their inability to express how much they had come to hate their lives together, and over what they had to do in order to keep those lives going.

Stress had become both cause and effect, change and the inability to change, in the public mind no less than in the scientific community. It was a vague mirror image of the confusion men, and then women, began to express about the meaning of their lives, loves, and labors in the fifties and sixties—a confusion that outlasted the winding-down of the Vietnam war in the early seventies and the return of Americans to private concerns after a decade of foreign war and social upheaval.

No wonder that the idea of stress has never been so popular. In the past decade, we have subdivided it into separate types and effects of stress for men and women. Yet even as we struggled toward such specificity, the concept remained vague, as we groped to express our growing confusion over the pressures of making a living at the expense of making a life.

CHAPTER

5

The Misunderstood Man in the Gray Flannel Suit

I am not the first person to hit upon the idea that the way we talk about an illness can be an expression of other concerns. Sontag's book *Illness as Metaphor* showed how tuberculosis became a symbol of ethereal, poetic purity in the corrupt and dirty nineteenth century, and cuttingly attacked our current use of cancer as a sign of personal and societal decadence. In *The Hearts of Men,* Barbara Ehrenreich made a convincing case that for our parents' generation, stress was a way of dramatizing men's doubts about their dull and deadly working lives.

Ehrenreich found that in the fifties, that great era of contented togetherness in which fathers knew best, men were really bursting at the seams of their gray flannel suits. Like Maynard G. Krebs and Dobie Gillis, they were divided up by the experts of their time—especially psychologists, who in that decade enjoyed their first burst of popular glory—into "breadwinners and losers." Neither group got much pleasure out of life.

The breadwinners were "mature," writes Ehrenreich, and the losers were merely contemptible: "the man who failed to achieve this [breadwinning] role was either not fully adult or not fully masculine." And along with winning the bread went the daunting demands of togetherness:

Marriage was not only a proof of maturity, it was a chance to exercise one's maturity through countless new "tasks." Men as well as women were to build a "working relationship," overcome romance for "a realistic conception of marriage" and seek a mutual state of "emotional maturity."

Doesn't sound like fun, does it? It wasn't, Ehrenreich shows. Not only did *Playboy* and the beats take the immature way out, living for pleasure and finding it outside the confines of marriage (much to the horror of the rest of us, who set out to convince ourselves that beatnik fun was a bore); men who lived up to their "mature" duties got sick.

Beginning with Selye's discoveries, "stress entered the culture ... as if it were a powerful new paradigm for understanding the human condition," says Ehrenreich. Or at least, the male part of it; it took the Second Wave to win stress for women, as we will soon see.

The way that men interpreted stress, she found, was as proof that they were killing themselves to satisfy the greed of women. Asked how a woman could protect her man from a stress-induced heart attack, an expert cited by Ehrenreich responded, "Very simply, you can live within your husband's means." Apparently it took a fatal threat to make men feel they had the right to voice their rage over what they had to do to bring home the bread, and how much of it their demanding loved ones consumed.

Moreover, voicing it didn't make you any less a man. On the contrary, writes Ehrenreich, what stress "did explain, or at least justify,

> was the condition of the swelling number of white-collar corporate managerial employees. If they produced nothing—or nothing visible— and if they never exerted themselves in the tradition of "honest labor," still they experienced stress, and stress, like heavy manual labor, left its mark on the body.

In fact—or so far as we looked at the facts back then—stress could kill. It was proof that even a white-collar worker ran the manly risk of death for his loved ones, who would survive long after he had been replaced at a job that left nothing more tangible behind its holder than a paper trail.

Ehrenreich's purpose in drawing this portrait was partly polemical; she wanted to prove that the so-called "flight from commitment" of the seventies, when divorce rates doubled, was not the fault of feminist agitation, but resulted from men's realization that maturity was a dead end. (Leaving a dull, infantile, hardworking man is, however, a key theme of such Second Wave bestsellers as *Memoirs of an Ex-Prom Queen* by Alix Kates Shulman and *The Women's Room* by Marilyn French, so let us not rule women's wills entirely out of this matter.)

Consider Ehrenreich's point proved, at least in part; having watched numerous men divorce their wives, each doing the same thing for what he thought were his own personal reasons (often certified by psychoanalysts, a most expensive seal of approval), I can well believe it.

But in making her case, she had to admit that *"the surprising thing is that men have for so long, and on the whole, so reliably, adhered to what we might call the 'breadwinner ethic.'"*

Look again at what she says: being a breadwinner was a lousy situation, but men put up with it, even though both they and their wives (who went along with the stress fad) were convinced it was killing them. The men put up with it because otherwise they would be considered inadequate, and because they couldn't have a woman and family any other way.

At least, that's what experts told them, and what they believed. Not a family worth having, at any rate: a family that went further into the world, into comfort and security, instead of the squawling, shabby brats whom Jack Kerouac's hero in *On the Road,* Dean Moriarty, scattered as freely about as his woman-prized seed. Someone had to be mature, and pay for it.

And in general, men did it. They went about the business of being men, complaining of stress. They continued as before, though grumbling, like the young hero of the 1951 movie *Father's Little Dividend,* that they were killing themselves "for the sake of her and the baby."

You would think that the entry of millions of women into the work force in the 1970s would have changed this equation. But that was not the case.

On the contrary, the more that women went to work, the louder men complained about stress. By 1976, *McCall's* defined the popular image of the stress victim—"a red-faced, hard-drinking businessman, drumming his fingers with pent-up tension and gulping antacid to ease his ulcer"—in the single popular article of the decade which argued that "women suffer twice as much from stress as men." More typical was a piece that appeared in *Harper's Bazaar* in 1973, whose title said it all: "How to Help Him with Stress." As in the 1950s, stress was a killer that stalked men—men who worked.

But if work could give men stress—and everyone seemed to agree that it could—it also seemed to be the case that *not* working was equally dangerous. The personality profile that LeShan found in cancer patients, to take one prominent example, was also a *career* profile. His working patients were trapped in a stressful grind, but could stave off their deaths only while the grind continued:

In their daily existence, these people had functioned, continued the routine work of their lives, *gone on with their businesses* [my emphasis] and never believed that life could hold any satisfaction for them.

That in itself was not fatal, said LeShan, so long as they could find some compensation, such as "a job with a role for which they seemed particularly well adapted and which they enjoyed." But when "job retirement was forced on them," and "they tried to obtain new jobs . . . only to fail," the end was in sight: "They continued to function and went about their daily business, but there was no more hope or meaning to their lives." And then, "six months to eight years after the crucial cathexis was lost, the first symptoms of cancer appeared."

Men were damned if they did, and damned if they didn't; if the workplace held its hazards, the alternative was just as deadly.

Let's stop here and look back for a moment. From the first European settlements in North America through the mid-twentieth century, American literature had been practically a single, unbroken, healthy shout, a "barbaric yawp," as Walt Whitman put it, in celebration of the American man's limitless capacity to build, procreate, live, as no one ever had before. The difficult he did right away; the impossible took just a little longer. That was both a practical and a moral boast: work was good, and American men were the best workers in the world.

But they could no longer be so good—it was killing them. And moreover, they said so—indirectly, in the scientifically neutral language of stress, but no less clearly.

There was something historic in this confusion. *The complaint that work hurts men, and that this hurt is unfair and unnecessary, is simply extraordinary in a society where* not *working has always been regarded as the source of all evils.*

Something else was at stake here besides the physical symptoms that strike men who push themselves past their limits of strength and motivation. Men were wondering, with a fear too awful to express directly, what would happen to them if work lost its value as a way of defining a man's purpose in life.

In fact, they still are.

STOP ME BEFORE I WIN AGAIN

In the 1980s, as Gloria Emerson remarked in *Some American Men,* "No subject was quite as alluring as the perilous condition called stress, and stress-related symptoms," especially among "the powerful and the driven...."

For all that has changed, it is still a matter of life and death for some American men to lead impatient lives of immense exertion and then even more a matter of life and death to slow down and do less and behave with a sweetness they know nothing about.

You could see it coming in 1978, when *USA Today* reported that "Executive Stress" had become a "Million-Dollar Headache," for which "the price tag...has been estimated at $20–50,000,000 a year." Dr. William Hausmar, then director of the psychology department at the University of Minnesota, blamed the problem for "excessive anger, illness, and depression, along with a rise in accidents, heart disease, and absenteeism." *USA Today* chimed in that these were more highly marked among executives, because the poor old boss "must cope with frequent change, because of promotion and changing organizational goals." The most risk fell on executives "who are low in self-esteem," it added. Making money in exchange for the love of one's family, it seemed, was no longer enough of an incentive for a man to like himself.

Hausmar offered a prescription: "Healthy people have three sources of gratification—work, family, and outside interests—no matter how many hours they work. This despite the fact, duly noted by the newspaper, that "older executives"—that is, the men whose opinions of their subordinates have a direct effect on the latter's futures—"often consider [having interests outside the job] outrageous," which might well have a bearing on exactly how many hours a man had for his outside gratifications, not to mention his family.

"As a young M.B.A. who started a career on Wall Street," one Cathy Beekman told the *New York Times* in 1986—and wasn't it interesting that a woman, not a man, would bring the following matter up?—"I found that employers expected young employees to give up everything else for their jobs. Balanced life-styles, or even job flexibility, is [*sic*] not encouraged."

Success was a choice between giving your all and giving nothing at all, for men or women. But it was still a choice that men, in particular, felt to be illusionary.

That would explain—along with the vastly decreased physical dangers of white-collar labor—why the people who take the least sick time in our society, according to available statistics, are male executives and professionals, who are crying so loudly about stress, but are also among the most highly paid men among us. One reason for the paradox is evident: even a brilliant corporate lawyer, say, who calls in sick too often will be told, by his boss or his partners, to take a vacation—during which, even if he doesn't lose his job, someone else will be conniving to get it from him.

And the vacation had better restore him, fast. In a sample of 1,300 top and mid-level executives surveyed by Allan Cox in *Inside Corporate America*, one-fourth of the top executives and over one-third of the mid-level executives said that *short* vacations were encouraged by their companies (even an *average* vacation in America usually means two weeks at a time, instead of the four that are standard across Europe).

Back at the office, our lawyer must be capable of displaying the "fast pace of job" that three-fourths of all Cox's executives said were essential to their advancement. If he does not maintain this quality, he will fail the company— the company he works for, and the company of men, who will shrug over his absence ("no one is irreplaceable") and get on with the job.

A man who wants to move up the ladder of success, therefore, has to put some things—or someone—aside. The problem did not escape Daniel Goleman of the *Times*, who in 1986 reported that "For Some Executives, Success Has a Terrible Price." There was, for example, the 33-year-old executive with two Mercedes Benzes, a big house, a wife he cheated on, and a cocaine habit (just the thing for maintaining a "fast pace of job," until it wipes you out, as it usually does) who whined: "I was running through life so fast I didn't see that my role as husband and father was disintegrating, that my business abilities were crumbling." But that, said Goleman, was only "one of the perils of the success he had strived for since childhood. . . .

"Psychotherapists," reported Goleman, "say that many executives soon lose all sense of balance between work and the other aspects of their lives." As if it were a surprise, he announced that for these men, "money has become the main symbol of their human worth."

Whatever its symbolism in terms of human worth, money is indeed the measure of success in business, which is the work most of us are engaged in: "It's the way people keep score," as Joe Russell, vice-president of F Systems Inc., told the *Wall Street Journal* in 1987.

And men were scoring a different game from the one their wives were playing, the *Journal* reported: a study of "pay perceptions" by John Mirowsky of the University of Illinois found that "employed wives feel less underpaid the more their husbands earn, while husbands feel more under-paid the more their wives earn."

To be a man had come to mean not only making money, but *making more money than a woman.* "Perhaps the seductive quest for success in the business world can be likened to the quest for success in the bedroom," wrote Dr. Douglas E. Whitehead to the *Times.* "The psychodynamics in-volved in achieving these goals are probably similar." The man with the biggest "bulge" in his wallet was the man who was least like a woman, who could best satisfy her—at least in theory.

Whitehead added, smugly, "Professionals dealing with sexual dysfunction realize this; unfortunately, many success-oriented individuals do not."

Didn't they? As Beekman further wrote,

> it is difficult to break out of this trap because the life-style has become dependent on the high salary.... Once the employee becomes de-pendent on the employer for money, success, and prestige, it is very difficult to get off the treadmill.

Indeed it is: the love you make is equal to the bread you take. The work you do is equal to the time you have—all of it. The circle was plush, but everyone seemed to agree that it was mighty vicious.

Such considerations had not yet been raised in court, which is where some of America's best and brightest were finding themselves in the winter of 1986–87, as scandals rocked Wall Street. But it was coming: "How can people who earn more than $1 million a year need money so badly that they are prepared to break laws to get even more?" wrote Jay B. Rohrlich, a psychiatrist and partner in a consulting firm whose clients were on the Street. Rohrlich provided the *New York Times* with an explanation that a cynical person might suspect would be highly useful to stockbrokers facing criminal charges: the real problem, he said, was that these men were sick. They were " 'hooked' on money in the same way that others become ad-dicted to alcohol, cocaine and other drugs...."

> An injection of money can make people feel instantly secure, victo-rious, strong, loved, and sexually attractive. Money becomes the an-tidote to a feeling of insufficiency.... It is time to recognize it as a potentially desperate condition, and to develop treatments for it.

Such as, for instance, a hearty dose of the sweetness the victims of a money addiction knew nothing about, which is what the stress doctors were busily proposing.

Consider a pop medical book, *Is It Worth Dying For?,* published in 1984. Authors Robert S. Eliot, M.D., and Dennis L. Breo told their readers that "stress doesn't have to keep you from experiencing the pleasures of living." Eliot offered himself as a case in point: he had been caught up in "the blind pursuit of academic medicine"—in other words, career ambitions. Only after a heart attack did he "take time to rediscover my wife," and see how "surprisingly sensitive and loving" his children were. He urged men to realize that while "a career can be a source of genuine fulfillment ... it can also become an escape from other responsibilities, and a retreat from personal relationships."

And that, of course, was now a no-no, at least for those, like Eliot, who had seen the light at the end of the tunnel of love. If he was willing to confess that beneath the prestige and glamour of his career was just another poor, pitiful guy, he stopped short of condemning outright the attraction of wealth, which by any standards is part of the genuine fulfillment of work; and he was unable to say how one might become wealthy without retreating from personal relationships (though he did provide a how-to test to measure how far one was retreating).

Other stress experts made no bones about their contempt toward men who identified with the quest for success, instead of stopping to mix some sugar with their salty sweat. When psychotherapist Craig Brod's book *Technostress* was profiled for readers of *New Age* magazine in January 1985, Brod was quoted as saying that "25 percent of Silicon Valley's programmers and white collar workers"—at the time, over 80 percent male—suffered from this novel malady, which was defined as "overreliance on factual and logical thinking, emotional numbness, insistence on efficiency and speed, and little tolerability for ambiguity." Even worse, they took their wives for objects: "One patient Brod counseled," breathlessly reported *New Age,* "referred to his wife as a poor 'peripheral'—computer jargon for 'accessory.' "

Under his white-collar shirt and wimpy demeanor, Brod and *New Age* revealed, even the modern nerd is as macho as they come. These men were presented as an electronic version of the strong, silent type whom the Second Wave had taught us to view as a clown. But now men like Brod, armed with diplomas, had taken over the charge.

Once again, expectations put forward by feminists had become men's own. From a way in which men could get attention from their wives for the pain they suffered in the working world, stress had evolved into a means of attacking the impersonal values of that world.

But the attack failed entirely to take account of a crucial factor: a deep ambivalence among both men and women about what a person must do in order to get ahead in the rat race.

And ahead in the rat race is exactly where they wanted to be.

You can get an idea of that ambivalence by comparing the profile of a go-getter, compiled in the course of 10,000 interviews conducted by Srully Blotnick and associates between 1961 and 1986 (itemized in his book *Ambitious Men*), with the men the stress experts denounce:

First, he has to have a desire for more . . . money, prestige or power . . .

Second, in judging whether someone is ambitious the public doesn't care about "quality," they care only about "how much."

Third . . . the more of a rush he was in, the more ambitious they saw him as being.

Fourth . . . they felt the person had to be willing to strive virtually till the day he died.

And now, the clincher: "the person had to seem somewhat ruthless. *To the extent that he was concerned about other people's feelings, to that extent they downgraded the ambition they saw him as having"* (my emphasis).

In other words, if you worry about satisfying your wife or discovering your kids instead of getting ahead, you are not as ambitious as you might like to think. And we *do* like to think we are ambitious, Blotnick discovered: *"both men and women see themselves as somewhat defective if they can't comfortably claim to be ambitious."* (My emphasis.) In fact, "people look on the word more favorably now than at any time during the past quarter of a century." (If this suggests that our fathers were not so heartless as we have lately been claiming, wait: we will pick up this trail again.)

Obviously, a man couldn't have this cake and eat it too. The contradiction provided an opening for other stress experts, who were perfectly willing to propose that sweetness and light weren't necessarily the best choices he could make.

With perfect irony, *New Age* informed its readers, only thirteen months after Brod's blast, that "having a supportive family and friends is not necessarily a guarantee of health." Far better was pleasing the boss: "those who felt they had the backing of their bosses were ill half as often over the course of a year," the magazine summed up one study, "as those who said they received little support from their bosses." The same bosses, of course, who found it inconceivable that a man would put anything ahead of his work in *USA Today*'s 1978 report, and who urged young professionals like Beekman, a decade later, to forget about anything but making money. One does not need a degree in the helping professions to guess how one earned their approval. Either you pleased the boss, or your loved ones; you could not do both, even if both was exactly what you wanted to do.

So people kept talking around the problem: the root of stress wasn't work, argued *Gentlemen's Quarterly,* but disliking the people you worked with and against—a safe theme, at a time when American management was discovering that "the key to success . . . is people," as Lee Iacocca put it in his best-selling autobiography. And people did not like to be pushed around, threatened, or abused; they wanted to feel needed and appreciated, as management consultants were busily telling managers. Thus, there was nothing amazing in *GQ*'s suggestion that "hostility makes the difference between the kind of competitiveness and pressure that is hazardous to health and the kind that isn't."

It sounded simple. Unfortunately, the wrong kind of pressure is hardly uncommon in a system where, as Allan Cox reported, about one-fourth of both top and middle executives think that "driving competitors out of business" is *at least* fairly important in their companies' goals.

That same noxious pressure applies *within* companies: a study by the Cranfield School of Management in 1986 found, according to Sherry Buchanan of the *International Herald Tribune,* that managers who were fired from their jobs "were more intelligent, had good leadership scores, and were well-adjusted emotionally," compared to their peers who kept their positions. Unfortunately, "They scored low on being shrewd and cunning, high on being trusting, naive, natural and forthright."

But forget about that: the solution to stress was to be "ambitious and energetic but . . . motivated by challenge and intrinsic satisfactions instead of by external pressures and anger," as *GQ* declared.

It was, in other words, "to do extraordinary work—and love it!" as *New Age* advised its readers in a lusciously peppy tone early in 1986. (That this magazine, whose motto had just been changed to "Achievement–Commitment–Creative Living," should have been leading this charge was significant: in the mid-seventies, when I was its advertising manager, *New Age* had been the voice of the so-called Spiritual Movement, whose adherents were mainly dropouts from the rat race.) The year before, *New Age* approvingly quoted bestselling author John Naisbitt's latest opus, *Reinventing the Corporation:* "When you identify with your company's purpose . . . you find yourself doing your life's work instead of just doing time."

Some reinvention. "The most successful business people," wrote rent-a-car king Warren Avis in *Take a Chance to Be First,* "love business first, family second and sports and everything else third." He recommended that successful entrepreneurs develop "a severe case of monomania" for their work, along with "an unencumbered personal life." If one could not avoid being so encumbered, he said, "it is essential that your family and friends pull you toward and not away from your business goals."

Let us now sum up how well you have absorbed the wisdom of the experts, with a test. Answer true or false to each of the following statements:

1. An ambitious man can't afford to care about people, and not caring about people makes you sick.
2. A good manager trusts in people, and trusting people gets you fired.
3. Money is an addiction, and people who think only about making it are mentally ill; and making money is the best way of proving you are a man.

And you thought your problem was stress?

CHAPTER

―――― 6 ――――

Women and Stress

There had been a reaction to the implicit gender bias of the stress obsession, though a muffled one. There was, for example, a brief item in *McCall's* in 1976, "Stress: Why Women Suffer More," based on a survey showing that blue-collar women were greater victims of stress than other population samples. Other articles around this time were at least asking why women didn't have stress of their own. In fact, the writers generally concluded that women *did* suffer from stress, especially as they entered the work force in growing numbers.

But their emphasis was summed up by the title of a 1978 article in *Psychology Today:* "How Women Cope with Stress." This theme—that stress was something a woman could, and should, cope with—was a constant of the subject.

Psychologist Larry Furst, coauthor of what was promoted as "the first book to comprehensively cover stressors that particularly affect women," *Women Under Stress,* told the Knight News Service in 1982 that the experience gained through menstruation, sharing with friends, and crying provided women with mechanisms for coping with stress that men did not possess, because men were trying to protect the macho image of the strong, silent type. While *Dun's Review* was telling its mainly male executive readers about "Fighting Stress," Furst and his coauthor, dentist Donald Morse, noted that women simply dealt with it and got on with their lives.

Men fought stress, and often lost; women bled, complained, and cried, but they coped.

Not all women cope so well with stress—in fact, only recently have the mental-distress ratings of young women *fallen* to the same levels as men's, which might indicate that men either had a better grip on their emotions or could not afford to let go of them. One might just as well ask if women were portrayed as better copers because the consequences of their failure to cope were too frightening to consider—among them the loss of the stability and emotional support which, as feminists reminded us, marriage provided men.

In a world filled with Type A's, ruthless men who forced their competitors to keep a killing pace, there must be a place where a man could catch his breath, feel loved, feel satisfied with what he had, not what he would never get enough of. The person who had to provide it, of course, was his wife.

And the women did a good job. Survey after survey has shown that married men are more emotionally stable than their single counterparts.

If men made a big point of how much they suffered from stress for their wives' sakes, it could very well have been an indirect way of confessing how much they needed women's love, gratitude, and approval. I have often performed just such a maneuver—say, telling a woman how hard I've been working: *see, I could take care of you, I'm up to the job—so please, take me, and take care of me.*

If so, it would be no wonder that despite falling heart-attack rates, men talked more shrilly about stress than ever before—at precisely the time when women were saying, *I won't take care of you, if you can't or won't take care of me.* A message, of course, that depended on being able to add— as a new generation of working women was proclaiming—*I can take care of myself.*

BURNOUT: THE STRESS OF THE WOMAN WORKAHOLIC

But working women did indeed experience stress. In fact—and that is the strange thing—they have their very own kind of work stress. It was called "burnout," which meant complete emotional and physical fatigue resulting from overinvolvement in one's job. Though male experts were in at the birth of this particular blues, its subsequent evolution was proof that even if women were in the work force, their equality was still of a separate order.

When *U.S. News & World Report* interviewed "expert on job stress" Cary Cherniss, thirty-one, an assistant professor of psychology at the University of Michigan, in 1980, he dated his own interest in burnout from 1973. Asked for an example, he talked about "a young woman lawyer in her first year of practice, dealing with people at the poverty level. She . . .was very ideal- istic and felt that poverty law would be her life's work."

But "she was robbed at gunpoint a couple of times by clients," and her colleagues gave "little support." She thus began to show one of the "more subtle symptoms" of burnout, as Cherniss saw it: "losing one's idealism."

She was a victim of what Cherniss called "the professional mystique"—note the less-than-subtle allusion to Friedan's "feminine mystique"—which meant being "motivated by a strong need for autonomy," only to find that she "didn't have that much control" over her working environment and conditions.

In other words, Friedan's feminist daughters were in the world, full of fire and ideals—and the world was eating them for breakfast.

The ultimate solution, said Cherniss, would lie in "what employers can do to structure jobs and work settings to make them more meaningful to workers"—such as "having workers periodically fill out a survey in which they rate their supervisor's performance," to which "many supervisors respond positively," said Cherniss. People had to be given a meaningful reason to work themselves to the bone, especially if they were female; they had to be treated not just like machines, but like *persons*.

But with gender equality the rage, bosses—meaning men—claimed burnout for themselves, if only briefly. "Why," asked Herbert J. Freudenberger, Ph.D., in *Nation's Business* in 1980,

is the life you embarked on with such high expectations letting you down at every turn? Why does it seem you have gotten what you wanted only to find you don't want it?

Freudenberger's examples of burnout victims included "good old reliable Paul," who "suddenly tells a client to shove off," and "June, a successful career woman [who] starts coming back from lunch a little tipsy." Under their anatomies, both were rather alike: "still conscientious and hardworking, but they no longer are functioning as whole human beings."

Nothing really new there, so far as men were concerned; but however subtly it was put, the warning had been given: if women wanted to work, and beyond that, to succeed, *they would become as inhuman as men.*

And the target of the warning soon became clear. Within a year, the segments of the press that served mainly men had largely forgotten burnout. The magazines that continued to deal with the subject—such as *Educational Digest* (twice in 1982) and *Glamour* (in 1985)—were aimed at largely female readerships. The titles of articles that defined the problem—"Teacher Burnout," "Parent Burnout"—were code words for women's problems, because the majority of parenting and teaching was handled by women. And Freudenberger came out with a sequel entitled, of all things, *Women's Burnout.*

Obviously, the idea of burning out meant more to women than it did to men. But why?

You can get an idea of the reasons from a major study of the teaching profession conducted in 1985 by Louis Harris and Associates. A total of 1,846 teachers in elementary, junior high, and high schools was surveyed for their attitudes toward their jobs, and the conditions of their work. Just over seven out of ten of these teachers were women, which reflects their presence in the classroom (as opposed to the administrators' offices, where the majority of principals are men).

One of the survey's goals was to find out which teachers were considering leaving the profession, and why. Just over half (51 percent) had indeed considered giving up the job. But the men skewed that figure—two-thirds of them (67 percent) had thought of getting out, and only 45 percent of the women. The men's chief reason for wanting to get out, overwhelmingly, was their low salary—77 percent cited this reason, as opposed to 53 percent of the women.

Women, in contrast, hated their working conditions far more than did men (48 percent to 31 percent); and by a three-to-one margin over men, the women named paperwork as the thing they hated most about those conditions, followed by "nonteaching duties" and classroom "overcrowding."

Far more than the men, women expressed a sense of feeling overwhelmed by obstacles to doing their jobs—and they saw those jobs as dealing with individuals, instead of with paper or a faceless mob. Far more than women, men felt they weren't being paid enough to put up with the obstacles. The men who wanted to quit saw their jobs, more than the women, as a way of making money. So long as the paycheck was fat enough, they could put up with the rest. But the women could not. *The women needed to believe in the work they were doing, in a way most of the men did not.*

With all that, a far smaller percentage of women than of men were planning on getting out. If that sounds like a prescription for exhausted women, the survey backed it up. Slightly more women than men, by percentage, named "emotional aspects" of their job as reasons for leaving. Their chief reason was "boredom," followed by "stress" and "burnout"—and in each of these categories, more women than men were represented, as a percentage and in absolute numbers. When you concentrate on the absolute numbers, the gender differences are striking. Of 387 men who said they had "seriously considered leaving," 12 said it was because of burnout. Of the 598 women in this situation, 30 complained of burnout. *Two and a half times as many women as men in this survey said that their job was burning them out.*

Look at it this way: one of the reasons we all believed in the Type A man was that *we all know a man like that.* When it comes to teachers, according to the Harris study, you are two and a half times more likely to encounter a woman who says, "I'm burned out," than you are to hear the same words from a man.

And *don't you know a woman like that?* A woman who "loves too much," as the title of a 1986 bestseller puts it? Who gives too much and gets too little in return, who is being overwhelmed by what she has to do in order to hang on to the dream that got her into her situation in the first place?

It can happen to men, certainly, and it sometimes does. But men do not say they are burning out as much as women do. According to the Harris study, either they get out or they get better compensation, or both.

The women who burned out did neither. They had not made the same kind of deal with their work that men made—so much time for so much money, and you do the best you can under the conditions. Instead, the women hung on to jobs in which even their best could never be good enough. It was as though they were married, "for better or for worse," so long as they should live, to a man who refused to recognize the love they brought to the altar.

This was not the only domain in which all our newness made us old. I am thinking of something that happened when I took a job as editor of a weekly newspaper, at which the production staff—all women—was in the midst of a protracted labor struggle with the owner. They had organized a union, held a vote, and gone to the National Labor Relations Board, which called for negotiations on salary and benefit levels, which were appalling in that shop. The owner hired a lawyer and started negotiating.

The women did not hire a lawyer. Day after day, they represented themselves. It was a most significant fact.

I knew those women well—not only because we worked closely together but also because it was a small town and we were often in the same rooms after work. Several were feminists of the type that sees relations between men and women fundamentally as power struggles. Or so they said.

But that was not how the women treated their problem. One of them told me, with rage in her voice, that she was shocked that the owner would have hired a lawyer. It had not occurred to her that by doing so, he had recognized her union as a dangerous adversary, to be treated with the respect one shows an enemy, and confronted with all the means at his disposal. What she seemed to feel, along with other women in the union that I discussed the matter with, was that as soon as he had been told that he was not being a good boss—a good man—he should have given in. She felt that he should have treated the women *as women*—and recognized their moral standing as the ultimate authority in their dispute.

But *he was treating them the way he would have treated a man.* He had granted them a kind of gender equality, but they acted as though he had got his genders wrong.

And in the end, he won. He broke the union. Or rather, it broke itself: the women quit the paper, one by one. On the verge of victory, at the moment when they had achieved a real equality in their struggle, they gave up. *They did not want to win, if it meant becoming like their opponent.*

How many times did I see women caught in that same bind? Wanting a man to respect their power, the trouble they could cause, and the work they could do, yet all the same *to regard them first and foremost as women— as caring, concerned human beings?* It is not an unreasonable demand, but it is hardly the way that business—the realm of the impersonal, where anyone can be replaced by almost anyone else—functions, or is about to function.

Business, often enough, is men giving as little as they can to take as much as they can. But women, when they gave themselves—in work as in personal life—wanted more than what they could take; *they wanted to remain themselves,* in a way that men did not hope for, or even attempt.

And that was the message within the working woman's stress. If women were determined to prove that they could work as well as men, and determined to be paid as well for their work as men were paid, *they did not want to be treated like men.*

Good God, who would?

CHAPTER
7

The Pained and Silent Type

Most of the men in my sample were middle-class, and more or less ambitious. And most of them subscribed to the notion that the higher a man goes in our economy, the greater the stress he feels, like a young screenwriter who told me that the uncertainties of his free-lance work were a constant threat to his stability, and then added, "It's not like a nine-to-five, where you can just put down your tools at the end of the day and go home." As Gloria Emerson noted, the powerful and the driven among us likewise sing this refrain, to arouse our pity for the sacrifices involved in claiming the privileges of power.

This is simply false. If white-collar stress is seemingly rampant in our society, that is in part because men who do dirty and dangerous work have urgent reasons to stay strong and silent, which we'll look at in a moment. If we attach a higher value to the sufferings of the rich and the powerful, it is also because we have come to see those sufferings as a mark of status, as proof that a man is carrying a greater weight than others—and that he is therefore entitled to his greater compensation, morally and practically. It is another way of saying that grace and wealth are synonyms—as we so fervently wish they would be, more than ever, in an age when selfish greed seems to threaten our belief that we are all in this great democratic experiment together.

Those who were less powerful and driven were not free of stress by any means. In fact, in this decade they began using the concept of stress in order to protect themselves from their employers' demands, and making news in the process.

A psychiatric examination performed for the plaintiff in a workers' compensation case that was settled out of court in 1986 told how a dock crane worker developed symptoms of rectal bleeding over the course of eight years. The examiner noted that though the worker felt "worried" by the problem, he assumed that it went along with the job. Most importantly, he hid the problem because "he wanted to do a good job"—to prove that he was ready and able to work. And he continued to hide it when he was promoted to warehouse supervisor—at which point his symptoms became dramatically worse.

By the time the facility he worked at closed down, six years later, he was bleeding from his rectum at each of his dozen daily bowel movements, and was obliged to stay within short distance of the men's room, in case a spasm hit him. Meanwhile, he had been working fourteen- to sixteen-hour days, in the face of daily physical threats from truck drivers, and constant screaming telephone calls from his superiors and his clients.

That kind of pressure is not exceptional in blue-collar life, nor in the first-rung, frontline managerial posts to which this man had risen. Though factory owners may no longer claim the right to work their employees literally to death, as was the case throughout the first horrific century of the Industrial Revolution, there are still production quotas, and those quotas must be met. The supposed laziness of the American worker may have a basis in some individual cases, but it is hardly the rule: in most blue-collar jobs, if a man does not produce, he is fired, and the company can fire him in full knowledge that someone else can easily be hired to take his place. If that were not the case, it would hardly be possible for American corporations to force unions to make wage and benefit concessions, as has been the trend in labor negotiations throughout this decade.

In this particular case there is a scientific question that is not insignificant: did the man's stress cause his condition, or did his condition cause his stress? That question is at the heart of legal defenses against complaints such as this. It cannot be answered, on the basis of our current scientific knowledge.

But there seems to be a commonsense relation between this man's job and his illness: he was ignoring his pain in order to get on with his work. By the time he paid attention to his problem, it was quite out of control, and he was no longer fit to work.

He had worked like a man: bravely, refusing to give in to physical intimidation, physical pain, his own fear. And now he could no longer work.

He had been a man, and it had unmanned him.

. . .

"The family of a man who shot himself and his boss to death in a state employment office in Orange County last year," reported the *San Francisco Examiner* in January 1987, "is suing for $6 million." The family of Felix Gonzales charged that "the acts of [Louis H.] Zuniga," his boss, had "created a state of intolerable stress" in the worker, and was suing the state and Gonzales' union for "failing to challenge the poor working conditions" that allegedly drove him to his act, reported the paper. Among those conditions, the suit declared, was that Zuniga had been "expected and encouraged" to practice "oppression, humiliation and exploitation of his subordinates" by the state.

Dead men tell no tales, and the truth of this case may thus never be known in full. What is already known, by anyone who has worked for a living, is that oppression, humiliation, and exploitation of workers is hardly unknown, or, for that matter, unusual, in the course of a working day.

What is new is that these tactics have suddenly become unacceptable in our society, to the point where people think they have a fighting chance of winning a lawsuit over them. *Not only the victims of success, but the bedrock of our society, the working men, are saying that there are jobs no man should be asked to do, places no person should be asked to go.*

To get an idea of just how extraordinary it is for working men to voice this complaint, consider a basic fact: from 1970 through 1982, men had about three days of "disability" (a day when a person cuts down on his usual activities because of illness or injury) for every four claimed by women. This was in spite of the fact that this three-to-four ratio was *reversed* when it came to the number of persons injured in our society, to the point of needing medical attention—40 million men, in 1981, and 30 million women. *Men were more likely to get hurt (or hurt themselves), and women were more likely to take days off from work if they did so.*

Why this gap? Part of it is probably due to the same conditions that apply when couples have babies: if the man stops working, the income drops more sharply than if the woman does. An injured man is a man who cannot show up for work, a useless man, a breadwinner who will bring home no bread. If he is hurt, it is in his interest to conceal the injury, or to minimize it, to say, "It's nothin'," and get back to work. Otherwise he forfeits the paycheck on which his self-respect, and the respect of his family, depend.

Steelworker Mike Lefevre told Studs Terkel in *Working* that despite poor working conditions, which he hated, he kept at his job and bitched after the day was over, until a foreman who "thinks he's better than everybody else," and who had just cut Lefevre's paycheck in a gesture of malice, demanded that Lefevre "sir" him. And Lefevre snapped: "He was just about to say something and was pointing his finger." Lefevre "just reached up and . . . put it back in his pocket." And he added, "I grabbed his finger because I'm married. If I'd a been single, I'd a grabbed his hand. That's the difference."

And so men will grit their teeth, and grumble and sweat, before they will quit, even before they will stop to take care of themselves—except in extraordinary circumstances, when they can no longer bear what they are asked or expected to do. They stay within the limits of some kind of reason.

Those limits are determined not only by their responsibilities to their families, if they have families, but to their coworkers. One of them becomes most apparent, the further you go toward the dirtiest and most dangerous work: a man with serious psychological or physical problems is a risk to others in a job where mistakes can get people hurt. He therefore has potent reasons for hiding those problems or shrugging them off.

Would *you* want to work on a naked skyscraper frame, high over the street, beside a guy who said he couldn't handle his stress? If you were his crew foreman, responsible for getting the job done safely, on time, would you keep that guy on the site? You might not mind listening to him complain about his back, or his wife, or whatever else is bugging him, over a beer at the end of the day, but *you would not let him use it as an excuse to shirk his share of the work, or to botch it in a way that put other people at risk.*

You can see the extreme of this principle in Harold P. Leinbaugh and John D. Campbell's book, *The Men of Company K: The Autobiography of a World War II Rifle Company* (in which the authors served). This book was about combat, the most dirty and dangerous job anyone could have. And in that job, every soldier complained, but the good ones stopped complaining when they had to fight; the ones who didn't were thoroughly despised and hated. That harsh standard was normal, under the circumstances: "We were all in it together," recalled one soldier. "Each one's life depended on what the other one did." Said another, "That's when you found out that everybody was your brother." Everybody, that is, but the slackers who broke under the awful physical privations of infantry life, or the terror of combat. If a good soldier turned away to the rear with an honest wound, his comrades cheered for him; but they kept close watch on each other to make sure that men paid in blood for the right to leave the front, that *they did not leave until they could no longer do the job.*

In our daily, peacetime lives, ignoring pain in order to get on with the job for your own sake and everyone else's is likewise the rule (though the cost of breaking it is usually merely personal failure, rather than dragging another man to his death with you). And it is a rule that men seem to obey more than women. That is one reason why men still feel that their jobs are more risky and dangerous than the work performed by women—that working is a sign of courage in a man, in a way that it is not for a woman.

There is another, more basic reason: men still have the most dangerous jobs, in the main. Only 3 percent of truck drivers are women; only one out of six farm laborers; only one out of fifty construction workers, and about the same percentage of miners. The rate of death on the job was *five times* higher for those occupations than it was for all occupations averaged together. In other words, *the greater the chance that a given job is reserved for a man, the greater the chance you can get killed doing it.*

Men do dangerous work, more than women; therefore, if your job is dangerous, you are that much more likely to be a man. And the converse, according to some inner logic, likewise holds true—for men: because you are a man, your job carries more dangers than a woman's. "To say a woman is *just* a housewife is degrading, right?" said Lefevre to Terkel. "It's also degrading to say *just* a laborer. The difference is that a man goes out and maybe gets smashed."

That is his pride, and his pain. But neither, it seems, holds meaning enough for him any longer.

WHAT IS BEHIND THE WORKING MAN'S STRESS?

Is hard work enough to make a man sick? You would think that it would be—that a man who labored long enough would eventually drop, if not from exhaustion, then from misery. There is no disputing, either, that some kinds of work can make you very sick indeed: only the wealthiest stockholders in a power company could continue to argue that a man who breathes coal dust all day, while digging anthracite in West Virginia, has contracted black lung entirely by coincidence.

But most of us do not work so long, or so hard, under such hazardous conditions. Moreover, for all our complaints about the stress of work over the past thirty years, our mortality figures continue to decline. And there is another problem with the proposition that our work is making us sick: *studies of jobs that can be considered highly stressful show that men doing the same work do not always develop stress to the same degree, if at all.*

The most striking of these studies took three years (1973–76) and dealt with 435 air-traffic controllers, the kind of job in which a few minutes' lapse in concentration can produce a major tragedy. The study took in a wide range of "variables"—factors that could affect its findings—among them the kinds of environments where controllers work, their behavior patterns at the job, their physical status, and their psychological attitudes.

What the research team expected to find, in accord with the conventional view of stress, was that the men who expressed the greatest stress would also show changes in their blood chemistry, reflecting heightened activity in their endocrine (glandular) systems. But that is *not* what doctors Rose, Jenkins, Hurst, et al. found in air-traffic controllers.

The men in their study who showed the highest levels of stress-related hormones in their blood were not the ones who seemed to feel stress; on the contrary, the men who were running on adrenaline seemed *more* satisfied with work, *more* competent at it, and *more* contented with their lives outside their jobs than their colleagues who showed *lower* blood levels of stress hormones. And the contented controllers were also those who showed the *least* tendency toward physical illnesses over the period of the study.

This finding seems to support Totman's idea that *the way a person feels about a job, and the support that person finds in others for doing it, matters more in health terms than the nature of the work itself.*

Again, there are limits on this idea. An asbestos worker is exposed to illness in ways that people who do not breathe the stuff every day are not; and consciousness of that risk, or finding out that it has led to asbestosis, can be stressful indeed (as it has been for thousands of American asbestos workers). I want to make it plain that there is no excuse for subjecting people to such dangers on the grounds that they wouldn't get sick unless they had a personality problem; and I have heard just such claptrap mouthed all too often, not just in the press releases of asbestos companies, but by New Age therapists urging people to "take total responsibility for whatever happens" to them.

But if you subtract other risk factors from the equation, you have to conclude that *liking a job, and doing it well, whatever it may be, is pretty good protection against stress-related illness.*

This has been affirmed again and again by studies: for example, it "has . . . been found that a low risk of heart disease occurs in situations where stability, security, and support"—all factors that fit with Totman's theory—"were present among NASA professionals, industrial workers, and Japanese workers," as a Special Task Force reported to the Secretary of Health, Education and Welfare in 1970. The report, after surveying available evidence, concluded that "job satisfaction [is] perhaps one of the best ways of extending the length of life."

Now take this principle in reverse: given that a lot of us are claiming that work stress makes us sick unto death, and given that most of us agree that this is a valid complaint, you might well suspect that stress-talk is a handy way for people to say something that might otherwise get them fired, or make it impossible for them to go on with their jobs: *they hate their work, and they don't know why they are doing it.*

If stress made men sick, it was because their reasons for working—reasons for which men had already built, and were building, their lives—had stopped making sense.

The strong, silent approach wasn't working for men. It could only work while there was something worthwhile to keep quiet for.

What should really worry us about stress is not the symptoms, but the patient's refusal to hide them any longer.

THE END OF THE BARGAIN

Our society took its current shape in the crucible of the Depression, when men who wanted to work could find none to do, and in World War II, when the demands of the armed forces set American industry back on its feet. While the war lasted, as Peter Drucker wrote in his 1946 study of General Motors, *Concept of the Corporation,* it "supplied an emotional factor which made production meaningful—in marked contrast to peacetimes."

When we emerged from that war, we possessed a productive machine of astonishing power, dwarfing anything previously seen in the history of the world. But the men who came back from the war, to their places on the assembly line, no longer found meaning in their jobs, Drucker discovered:

> For the great majority of automobile workers, the only meaning of the job is in the pay check, not in anything connected with the work or the product. Work appears as something unnatural, a disagreeable, meaningless, and stultifying condition of getting the pay check, devoid of dignity as well as importance . . . a pay check is not enough to base one's self-respect on.

The problem didn't go away; it is still our problem. But in the 1950s, as our economy expanded (except for a brief recession) to unprecedented levels, it seemed less painful. The paychecks men brought home could buy an astonishing array of goods—not just TVs and giant refrigerators, but the homes to put them in. There was plenty of money to be made, and the money went far: at one point in the 1950s, the annual inflation figures turned *negative,* meaning that the dollar was gaining in value.

The government helped; GI Bill loans made homeowners of millions of returning veterans (many of them from families who had moved every thirteen months during the Depression, in order to profit from the free month's rent that desperate landlords were offering to anyone who could pay their bills for a year at a time). The same law put many veterans through college, from which they emerged to take white-collar jobs beyond their parents' dreams, as service industries sprang up on the shoulders of our revived industrial giants. And if blue-collar workers did not attend college themselves, they could more than hope that their children would rise in the world, through one of the universities into which federal aid poured, up through the days of the Great Society.

If work did not seem meaningful in itself, what a man could buy with the fruits of his labor was loaded with meaning. He could tell himself, and believe it, that his sacrifices were actually, tangibly making life better for those around him. It is difficult to overestimate the importance that achieve-ment held for the generation of our fathers, who had seen their own fathers ruined by the Depression, losing homes, farms, businesses in the ruinous Crash that opened the 1930s. I have heard my father, and my father's friends, say it so many times: "I wanted my kids to have what I couldn't have." And from the 1950s until the end of the 1960s, they were able to provide it.

It is not hard to see why that bargain broke down. "Give me a lever long enough, " said the philosopher, "and I will move the world." The lever that moved the world our fathers built for us, moved it so far from its foundation that it shattered, was the Vietnam war.

THE PRICE OF PEACE WITH HONOR

The cabdriver was nineteen years old, and he didn't have the grades or the desire to go to college. What he wanted to do, in the winter of 1986–87, was join the Army, serve in the military police, and then get a civilian job as a private detective. "You know," I said, "when I was your age, the Army was mainly made up of draftees." He hadn't known. "Oh yeah," I continued, "in fact, there were riots over the draft, because people didn't want to go into the military." He hadn't known that either.

I've met so many young men like him. They are unaware—at a time when the armed forces are selling themselves as an attractive career option to unemployed boys—that fighting in Vietnam was a job men had to be forced, in the main, to do. (In this Vietnam differed hugely from World War II, in which millions of men volunteered to fight, after the attack on Pearl Harbor in 1941.) After 1968, in particular, when the Tet offensive convinced the American people that the war might not be won, it became increasingly difficult for the government to convince young men that anyone at all should fight it. Not since the Civil War led to antidraft riots had American men refused, in such large numbers, to fight for their country. *It had become a job no longer worth doing.*

As the film *Platoon* showed, most of those who took on the job were men from the bottom of American society—the children of the poor, and of the working class. This was taken for granted, even at the time. When I entered Harvard in 1970, it was commonly said among my classmates that only one man from the entire Ivy League had died in combat in Vietnam; whether this was true or not, I don't know, but it certainly indicates how the privileged sons of Harvard viewed the draft.

And to a large extent the Harvard boys were right. A handout from the Veterans Administration, published in the *Congressional Record* of October 1, 1982, calls it a "fiction" that "America sent mostly its poor to fight in Vietnam." The "fact" used to deny this alleged error is that "76 percent of the men sent to Vietnam were from lower-middle/working-class backgrounds." If that is not poor in America, it is still relatively poor.

In the early and middle stages of the war, working-class men I spoke with were furious that going off to fight for America (which was how they saw it) was treated with contempt by their richer peers, who everyone knew would go to college and escape the draft. At my high school, a college-bound kid who refused to say the Pledge of Allegiance as a protest against the war was beaten black and blue by a working-class guy whose cousin had been killed in Vietnam. Working-class kids knew that this was a working-class war, just as much as the rich kids of Harvard did.

I would suggest that among the effects of the Vietnam war was this: In forcing poor men to do our fighting, *we put a curse on the American notion that doing the work you are asked to do for the sake of society—and by extension, for one's loved others—is an act of meaningful sacrifice, and a measure of a man's equality with other men.*

The first signs of this shift appeared in the mid-1970s, when doctors at the VA found themselves unable to treat the problems of the Vietnam veterans who came to see them, and when some of those veterans broke down in frightening ways.

At first the doctors refused to acknowledge that there was a problem. "For twelve years," wrote Arthur Blank in *The Trauma of War: Stress and Recovery in Viet Nam Veterans,* "most American psychiatrists . . . based their encounters with Viet Nam veteran patients on the official view that no such thing as PTSD [*post-traumatic stress disorder*, the specific stress that emerged in these veterans] existed." The reasons, he suggested, included fear on the part of the VA that recognizing the problem would help to bankrupt the Treasury, by opening the door to thousands of disability claims. Often, says Blank, therapists turned to the "poor soldier theory" to explain veterans' anguish—the idea that these men had simply not done a good job.

If therapists could get away with that, it was partly because the veterans shared that idea; it was intrinsic to their pain. They had, to start with, lost a war. (The claim, by the way, that this was the first war America had lost is false. Indians are Americans, and they lost the war against Europe; Southerners are Americans, and they lost the Civil War; all of us won nothing more in World War I than a dress rehearsal for World War II; and Korea was at best a bloody, exhausted draw.)

And even if American men had "really no feeling for the job" while they were doing it, as one veteran told therapist Robert S. Laufer in *The Trauma of War*, many of them saw themselves as having failed to stay within the limits, and to meet the demands, of their jobs in Vietnam. They feared becoming one of what therapist John Russell Smith identified as two distinct types of trauma victims: those who had turned "animal," reverting to the primitive abuse of violence; and those who went "wimp" ("These terms are actually mild in comparison to how the veterans actually view themselves," said Smith) and let a man die in their place. What both those identities have in common is this: *they are not quite men, not quite human.*

This, Smith believed, helped explain the notorious employment problems of some returned veterans; taking another job would expose them again to "a capacity for failure" like those they had felt in Vietnam. And it was behind the fear of *loss of control*—"the most significant issue" behind PTSD, thought Smith—that became the most frightening (for the rest of us) symptom of PTSD.

Magazines on the cultural left, like *Rolling Stone*, were the first to report on what became a well-known phenomenon in the U.S. by the beginning of the 1980s: a veteran under emotional stress, or under the shock of some environmental stimulus (a loud noise, a building that recalled one he had seen in Vietnam), went haywire. If he committed a crime during this incident, he came to trial. And by the hundreds, lawyers began to plead PTSD in defense of these men.

One of them was Charles Heads, "a scorned husband chasing a wife through the night from Houston to Shreveport," as *Newsweek* described him in 1981 when he came on trial for shooting his brother-in-law at the end of the chase. "I was on," Heads testified. "I could not have stopped." His lawyers, according to *Newsweek,* argued that "reliving combat" (the night was foggy, as it had been for Heads often enough in Vietnam) had "destroyed his ability to distinguish right from wrong." In October of the previous year, a Boston jury had acquitted a veteran pilot who said he had been turned into an "action junkie" by PTSD. Lewis Lowe III of Birmingham was acquitted of armed robbery in 1981 when a psychologist argued to the jury that he had been seeking a way out of his PTSD by actions "designed to put him in a situation in which he would be caught or shot." The experts, noted *Newsweek,* "said that Lowe was motivated by extreme guilt because he survived while his buddies died."

Such acting-out was hardly typical. Far more likely, said the authors of *The Trauma of War,* was that a man with such psychological wounds would remain silent, like any good working man (which, you will recall, is exactly what most of these men were). But in America, we tend to pay attention only to those who shout, which is why *Newsweek,* after sympathetic but sensational treatment of veterans with PTSD, felt compelled to add, "The idea that every Vietnam veteran is a ticking time bomb or a druggie is simply not true."

It was also not true, at least not entirely, that PTSD afflicted equally "all races, all income groups and all personality types," as *Newsweek* argued. The best and latest research, a study of 274 combat veterans of Vietnam, 275 noncombat vets, and 452 men who didn't serve during the war, conducted by Ghislaine Boulanger and included in *The Trauma of War,* found the contrary:

> Nonwhites (in our sample this included blacks and Chicanos) had a significantly higher proportion of stress reactions than did whites.... College graduates tended to be less stressed than were men at other levels of educational attainment, and nonwhites were considerably underrepresented in the college sample. Stable employment patterns were associated with recovery from acute stress reactions; [and] significantly more blacks are unstably employed both in this sample and nationally.

You get the idea. The poorer a man, the darker a man, the fewer signs he showed of belonging to the middle or upper classes, the more trouble he would have getting over the trauma that was Vietnam. Just as nonwhites get the dirtiest, most dangerous jobs at home, they had them overseas. *The working man's war led to a working man's stress.*

I would suggest that if we are finally acknowledging the trauma these men experienced, and only now—*The Trauma of War,* which represents a huge advance in official and medical thinking about PTSD, was published in 1985—it is because the message these veterans sent us, first through their silence, then through their acts, and now through their words, is one we are at last prepared to accept. We wasted them, asked them to do something that should never have been done, nor done as it was. When they came home, we didn't acknowledge their sacrifices—we blamed them for the worst that had happened, across the board. *We said they were inhuman for doing what had always been a man's job.*

In this way the Vietnam war helped destroy the idea of the value inherent in honest labor. That had been something a man who had a job could always claim, in America. The claim was weakened, in ways both direct and indirect, when Vietnam showed us that the working men who came forward to fight for us were not world-makers, but world-breakers.

And this gave women reinforcement in the new demands they made of men. The abuse of violence in Vietnam, broadcast and read about in American homes, was part of the context within which separatist feminists would warn women that all men are nothing but murderous beasts. The idea that serving in Vietnam involved a moral decision on the part of the draftee, that nice girls should "say yes [only] to boys who say no" to the draft, as a popular wall poster of the era put it, helped to set the stage for the turmoil that wracked our intimate relationships over the past decade, when the personal became political.

All of these were reasons that women had the moral ground to demand that men heed their needs and wishes in new ways—demands that came into the open, by no coincidence whatsoever, at the brutal peak of the Vietnam era. All of them helped create a social context in which men and women alike could ask if the sacrifices men made for women, or believed they made, were as false as they were futile. And the first and last of those sacrifices, in a man's life, is work.

PART

III

THE SECRET LIFE
OF WORK

*The mind believes naturally, and the will loves naturally;
so much that, lacking true objects, they must attach themselves to false ones.*

—Pascal, *Pensées*

CHAPTER

— 8 —

The Job That Makes the Man

It is one thing to say that trying to balance the demands of a job and those one loves is enough to make a man sick, as we have been saying for thirty years. It is another to ask yourself: If not work, what? If we had the strength to admit that something was wrong in our lives, we were still not at all sure that we could invent something that would make it right.

And while we were struggling to figure out what that something might be, we remained within a fundamental condition of masculine life: a boy grows up to be a man with a job.

In my sample of men, the youngest start at paid labor was eight years of age—a distinction shared by a farmboy and a working-class black man who picked cotton on his summer vacations—and the oldest was twenty-two, a rich white kid who got a job straight out of college. The average was thirteen years—about the time a boy enters high school, and is expected by his parents to start providing his own fun money. At the same time, he is expected by his peers to bear the same load they are carrying. One of the cruelest things a working boy could say to a rich kid, at the Westchester high school I attended, was: "I *work* for my money."

These are American questions—*what do you do, how much are you paid for it, what do you buy with the pay?* People in other countries might have these questions in mind when they meet you and size you up, but they do not pose them to your face on the presumption that you have an obligation to respond. Such matters are considered personal elsewhere; in the USA, they are public. An American—and especially, even today, an American man—must learn how to answer them.

Sooner or later a man gets a job, not just for the money, but because otherwise we do not consider him, in some essential way, a man. But that is only half of it: *in an even more essential way, he does not consider himself a man unless he works for money.*

That is not quite like what a woman feels, as one might gather from reading advocates of postfeminist motherhood. Certainly, women like the independence and self-fulfillment that paid work can bring, and the things that money can buy. But as Cosell said so plainly, they do not feel all right if they are not giving first rank in life to loving and being loved. If men feel the same way, it is not something they often say openly, and even when it is, they do not know what to do about it.

They have a relationship with work, a relationship as deep and satisfying, and in some ways unspeakably personal, as any other in their lives. In a real way, *that relationship is sacred for men—as sacred as motherhood is for women.*

In asking ourselves where we are living and what for, as we have lately been doing, we question that sacredness. It is an extraordinary thing for American men to attempt. And it is no wonder that even raising the question is enough to make us feel sick.

We are now beginning to explore the idea that relationships can take up part of the space occupied by work in a man's life. But we are making two big errors in doing so. The first is that *we are simultaneously taking for granted, and underestimating, just how big that space is.* The second is that we are not admitting a fundamental fact: when you get right down to it, *it is easier to be a success at a job than in one's human relationships.*

If our lives are to change to include new forms of complicity—that wonderful word we use so rarely, and then with a hint of malevolent conspiracy, unlike the French, for whom *complicité* is an ideal of intimate cooperation—men will have to change their relationship to work. The Second Wave recognized that fact, but we seem to be in the process of ignoring it, all over again, men and women both.

Before such a change can occur, we must first examine the aspects of our relationships to work that we refuse to recognize; then, how they are replicated and sustained in our intimate lives; and finally, why it is so very, very hard for us to let go of our respective jobs, and the prerogatives that go with them—and turn toward each other.

Studs Terkel's *Working* tells us where to start in thinking about the relationship of men to their work. Over and over, the men he interviewed said that *they worked in order to leave some sign of their presence and character in the world.* They said it in ways sometimes proud, sometimes perverse. "My work, I can see what I did the first day I started," said a stonemason. "It's something I can see the rest of my life.... Immortality so far as we're concerned." And Lefevre, the steelworker, said, "Sometimes, when I make something, I put a little dent in it. I like to do something to make it really unique."

For these men, work is a way of making the world their own. This is what Dinnerstein called the "world-making enterprise," which both men and women yearn to participate in, but which falls mainly to men in our society—even now. *It is a way that a man can feel part of something greater than himself, something that remains when he is gone or forgotten.*

Of course, women are not strangers to this motivation for working. Women, too, want to change the world, to leave it altered from the way they found it.

But the women in Terkel's book did not share that impulse in the same ways, or to the same degree. Their concerns were more here-and-now; at one extreme, an advertising writer and producer said that her job was "whorish," that it was simply a matter of making a good living for herself (and herself alone: she was single, no children). She didn't see a long future for herself in her business, nor that "what I do is necessary." She stood in sharp contrast to a male copy chief in the same industry, who said, "My career choice in advertising [is] connected with the fantasy of power"— the power "to do more," to "justify my life." And she was in even sharper contrast to his young colleagues in the office, who believed that "the advertising business owes them the right to create, to express themselves."

More typical in Terkel's sample was the cosmetics saleswoman who said, "When you wait on these lonely old women and they leave with a smile and you feel you've lifted their day, even a little, well, [the job] has its compensations." A nurse said, "you take care of the person, you can see the difference." A librarian said, "I can experiment with all kinds of things the kids might be interested in." Only one woman he spoke with, a nurse's aide, said that she hated to work with people; most said that the most important part of their jobs was their relationships with others, relationships in which they performed a service well.

Women more often found their satisfaction, their calling, in giving service, at least so far as Terkel discovered; men more often tried to find theirs in leaving something of permanence when the job was done.

I can only speculate as to why this is the case; maybe it is because, as human beings have remarked for centuries, men cannot bear children (though we certainly can take care of them, in ways different from those we are used to); and thus we long to create something else that will live after we are gone, something that will bear our names, or the mark of our labors.

Perhaps it is that, as some social-biological critics have asserted, men are more aggressive than women, and have been throughout our evolution; and like dogs, we must leave our scent on the neighborhood hydrants. Perhaps behind this aggression, as I will argue later, is a consciousness of violence and death that women do not share to the same degree, and that gives a man a certain awareness that at any moment, his feet could fall through a bottomless hole.

Maybe all this will change someday, as our opinions of what men and women can be have changed. But I don't think that it has yet changed as much as we presume. The men I spoke with, the men I have worked with, the men I see around me, still see work as the main way in which they can build a world: their families', and their own.

THE WORK THAT WASHES CLEANER THAN CLEAN

Among the men I interviewed, the editor of a newspaper financial page, when he came home from a ten- or twelve-hour day at the office, sat down to write fiction. The computer software tester at an insurance company carried a portable electronic piano keyboard on the hour-and-a-half bus ride to and from work, and composed music for a rock band. The fashion photographer sketched and painted, as soon as he had delivered his proofs to the magazines whose checks paid his bills. Others had "hobbies"—that curiously American word for the work one does for pleasure, with as much discipline and attention to detail as the most demanding task you can think of.

When their jobs were over, they did what they called their "real" work— the work that counted most to them, that defined them more clearly than any other side of their lives. Meanwhile, their wives and lovers were in touch with family and friends, performing the tasks that go into loving and caring for others—writing the thank-you notes, making the follow-up calls, planning the time together, inviting friends for dinner, asking the children what had happened during the day and passing on the news to their men.

There was, for example, a surgeon in his late thirties, whose working life had begun at the age of eight in the packing shed on his father's farm in the Midwest. "I'd lift hundreds of fifty-pound packages of cabbage in a day," he said. "By the time I was in high school, I had a seventeen-inch neck." He was proud of that statistic—"in my high school," he said, "the only guy shorter than me was a dwarf"—proud that work brought him into the company of big, strong men. But he realized early on "that I had to make something of my life, or I'd be lifting cabbage for the rest of my days. I decided right then that I was gonna make the most of my education."

Not quite right then, as it turned out; first he had to give up what he most wanted to do, which happened to be playing football. At the end of his freshman year in college, when he starred on the football team, "My father sat me down," he recalled, "and said, 'You a good ballplayer? Good enough to make a living at it? Then you better sit down and think about what you can do that you can make a business at.'

"As a premed, I studied *hard,*" he continued. "You had to be goal-oriented. If you didn't get the right grades, the right doors wouldn't open. I looked at education as opening the right doors." Once he stopped wasting time, he developed a solid discipline: "I went out on dates Saturday night, but Sunday morning I was studying. Coming from a small town, I had an awful background." And he was determined to overcome it: "Whatever it took"— he shrugged, as we talked in a restaurant one night from eleven till one in the morning, at the end of his normal working day, which had begun at eight that morning with hospital rounds—"that's what it would take."

His wife worked in the premed department at his university; he married her at the end of med school, and their first child was born "when we got to Cambridge. Harvard Med Center," where he served his internship, "was one of the doors I wanted to open, and it opened." His salary as an intern was $10,000 a year, "and my parents gave no financial support, so I moonlighted as the night-call doctor at a drug rehabilitation center." After that came a residency at a major medical center in the Southwest, another of the doors he'd wanted to open; and a second child; and then a third, when he entered a private practice.

"After two years in practice, we were making ends meet," he said. "More than anything else it involves getting a patient population." Plus serving them: at the end of office hours, every day, he still spends two to four hours on the phone, returning his clients' calls. And between attending to patients, he wrote research papers, plus a highly regarded book in his field.

He had developed what he called "little tricks" to maintain his health and motivation. There were his twice-weekly judo lessons, and workouts with his partner in the practice (which had the added benefit of helping to compensate his short stature; with glowing eyes, he recounted how he'd flattened a bully in an argument over a parking space). He had a gun collection (he discoursed expertly on the difference between Soviet and Chinese submachine guns). He refused to work weekends (except for his writing, an important exception, but one that kept him in the house if something came up), and took weekend trips with the family. He had organized his life into a single, tightly woven discipline, a series of jobs that he loved to do.

The chief difference he saw between himself and his patients, men either en route to or coming back from heart attacks, was that "they do primarily what they think will make them financially successful, whether they like it or not. They go into the *shmatta* business—whatever it is, it's dull. They're paying the same price that I do, to do something I love—and they *don't* love it.

"People are *dumb* about themselves when it comes to stress," he said. "All stress translates as dissatisfaction—not enough success, say. Or they say their kids are important, the key to their happiness—but it's an indirect relationship. They're not there for the daily things."

But mixed with his pleasure in the daily things were small nodules of discomfort: "I hate to leave work undone," he said, and repeated himself twice. Work undone was a door that would close in his face someday, the last door he wanted to walk through: he wanted to retire early, no later than fifty. "I see myself sitting on a beach," he said, "writing about medicine, my experiences, my insights."

And there was another discomfort, one that made his voice drop suddenly when he said, "My wife knows me as well as anyone—but there's some things she ignores about me." He didn't tell me what they were, but he was worried about them: "My wife's got me cross-haired," he said; in her sights, like a target. She knew something about him that made him vulnerable, something that his work was designed in some way to compensate.

He had arrived at a moral balance, agreed with himself that he was doing the best he could, in his work and with those he loved. "You can't do both," he said—can't, that is, give equal time to the work and the kids and the wife. "My value system on that is, to the extent that I can make her comfortable, and provide her with help—a full-time maid—I feel that I'm all right."

And just barely: "I've gone from a C− to a D−," he said, on his own husband- and father-grading system. Not really much of a grade—unless you count the work he did for the sake of his family and patients, the prizes he won for them when he walked through the doors of labor.

His wife's part of the bargain was thoroughly traditional: "I expect her to be there for breakfast and dinner," he said. "If I cannot support my wife and kids"—to the point where "she would have to work," where she would not be available to him as he needed her to be—"I'd consider that to be my responsibility," his failure. "She's happy raising the kids," he said, and I believed him. And he seemed happy enough: like his clients' dreams, of which he said, "what most of them want [in a relationship] is something stable, that mothering thing, that security," *he had found an arrangement that gave him what he needed, on terms that he could comfortably afford: hard work, and plenty of it.*

He could not be further in social status, wealth, or life-style from a man I met in the office of a macrobiotic foundation in Boston a few years before, whose life was dedicated to furthering the esoteric doctrine that the consumption of brown rice could save the world. But the surgeon's philosophy of relationships was not fundamentally different from the whole-foods crusader's: "The man dreams," the latter told me, "and the woman cooks for his dream." Like the activist, the surgeon lived for a dream; the dream infused his working day, gave it meaning and continuity.

The dream changed throughout his life; from time to time it moved behind another door. But a woman was cooking to keep it alive. A man was working to make it real: to flesh it out in terms of comfort and security, to prove that the promises he made were the promises he would keep. And that work pardoned whatever he could not accept about himself—whatever he imagined that his wife had chosen to ignore about him.

In ten years in the journalism business I have interviewed hundreds of men—rock stars, prosecutors, corporate executives, organic farmers, marketing aces, carpenters, film directors. At the center of 99 percent of those interviews was their work, and not by coincidence. When you talk about men, their work is the main thing that makes them interesting, that leads them to riches and fame, power, and the love of women (or so we think). And that is how we think it ought to be.

Men who succeed are careful, when they come into the public eye, to make sure everyone knows they worked hard for what they got, just like the high-school boys who hate rich kids. We despise an idle man, when we do not envy his idleness (as we have all envied happy bums like Kerouac); but we will grant all sorts of grace to men who seem to be working hard.

If you critique them in print, for example, you can't get "personal" about it—that's libelous—unless you can prove that their personal foibles have made or could make them louse up their jobs. Unless you can do that, in any case, no one would care. People knew, for example, that Ronald Reagan had a most wayward attitude toward the facts of any remotely complicated matter, even before he was elected President, but as long as he seemed to be doing all right at the White House, few of us cared.

What shows up in the ground rules of journalism is something much like the masculine characteristic I mentioned in Chapter 1: our sense that while a man is doing his job right, *everything* is all right. (In this way we do not judge our stars more harshly than we judge ourselves.) *If a man is doing a good job, whatever the job may be, we will forgive him almost anything else.*

David McClintick documented that principle in business life in his book *Indecent Exposure*, where he showed how the board of directors of Columbia Pictures Industries, upon learning that its president, David Begelman, had forged three checks against the company accounts, became bitterly divided about how to handle the problem. There was no disputing that Begelman was a forger—he admitted as much in court—but he had helped Columbia back into the front rank of the movie industry, and key board members thought that without him the company would fail. And they kept him, despite the doubts of chief executive officer Alan Hirschfield, until massive hostile publicity made it impossible for Begelman to function at his post.

We take this idea even further sometimes. When I was in high school it was not uncommon to hear some guy say, "Hitler was a genius, he just went too far." What this meant was that if only he had done a better job— God only knows at what—everything would have turned out for the better.

There is a double standard here, one that makes it relatively easy for a man to leave his home, and the penetrating regard of his intimate partner, and go into the world of work. Ours is a business society; and *as long as his business dealings are reasonably fair and honest, and profitable for all concerned, others will do business with a man they dislike.* If not, business would come to a dead halt, because it is inconceivable that everyone engaged in business is or can be likable, any more than that you will like every person you run across in life.

This is a rule of social intercourse in which any person who wishes to succeed must be trained, and which Second Wave women I have known in business frequently had a hard time learning; at a time when the personal was political, it was extremely difficult for idealistic women to accept the essential impersonality of business. Doing so, of course, involves nothing more or less than a certain polite hypocrisy, a willingness to ignore the fact that you may neither like nor respect the person you are working with. That operation is doubly difficult for someone who insists on seeing through the roles one enacts in business, to the person behind the friendly smile.

But the fundamental impersonality of business relationships, our focus on what a man *does* instead of on what he *is,* provides the opportunity for a real pleasure, and one less risky than intimacy.

When I sold advertising space, the majority of my clients were nice guys, in every sense—fair, friendly, honest about what they needed. My feelings toward them are still warm; we worked together as colleagues in a common situation, accepting each other's idiosyncrasies *without asking what rested behind them,* as matters of amusement (of which a working person can never have enough). We were of quite different philosophies, my clients and I; only one of them had read Franz Kafka's nightmare novels, for example, and he read them as if they were guidebooks. All the same, we got our work done, made money, and had some fun with each other—and that is the best business has to offer, for the vast majority of us.

This camaraderie hardly ever becomes more than casual friendship—it disappears when a man moves out of the circle of work. But it has its points, not the least of which is that *it compensates, to some extent, for other kinds of intimacy that work would otherwise make us miss even more than we do.* And it demands less vulnerability than one would feel toward a mate, precisely because less is known about the people involved, and nobody is pushing hard to find out. My clients and I kept a distance from each other—we had to, because that is business—and that was what made our friendships so easy, when the work went well.

But when the work is over, and a man goes home, that space disappears—and once again, he is on his own, face-to-face with someone who cares less about what he did during the day than who he is in the present moment.

That person—usually the woman he loves—poses questions to a man, even in her silences: Who are you? And why are you here? They are reasonable questions; but they are questions he has not had to pose to himself, either in the same way or to the same degree, while he was at work.

We are judged by our work, for better and for worse. We are granted privileges—pay and perquisites—according to how well we do it; we are excused (or excuse ourselves) from other tasks, even loving, because we have been elsewhere, doing a job.

And while we are doing our jobs, *we know who we are.* We are account executives, truckers, cops, CEOs, whatever. *And we know where we are:* "out in the world," "on the job," "in the trenches."

There is a place for us—not the heavenly place lovers yearn for, but a place all the same, a place that is a man's own—so long as we get up and go there, to work.

CHAPTER

9

The Job That Never Ends

Sooner or later, as we all learn at work, a job ends—when the day is over, when the sale is made, when the task is finished—and then begins again, almost of its own volition. It is a burden, but a familiar one.

There is never enough time to get *all* the work done, but *enough* of it gets done, all the time. And at a job—even the better-paid executive jobs in our society—"enough" is plenty. One of the findings of Allan Cox's survey of 1,100 executives in thirteen corporations was that a majority of both top- and mid-level executives believed that their companies "harbor average or mediocre executives." Cox summed up: "there is no denying that in many corporations marginal performance is tolerated."

When you put this beside Cox's finding that the vast majority of these corporations likewise expected long working hours from their executives— 70 hours per week was common among men at the top, and one-third of both middle and top executives said that 60-hour workweeks were "strongly encouraged" by their companies—you have to conclude that *presence* counts nearly as much as *performance* in the contemporary American corporation. *If a guy is where he is supposed to be during working hours, doing enough to get by, that is fine.* He won't reach the top, but he will probably keep his job.

Some people give more than an acceptable or healthy minimum to their work, of course. Those who do are, sometimes, the most successful among us, when they have the talent and energy to sustain the jobs they take on. But they are not the majority case. *What most of us do, most of the time, is get through the working day, so that we can come back for the next.* It is a survival strategy, and a practical one; we can get away with it, and no one will be the angrier.

It is an acceptable and useful (if not really efficient) way to work; but it is a poor, poor way to love. And we know it.

. . .

In our current ideals of intimacy, there is no "enough" between lovers (even if in practice we all accept, at one time or another, an acceptable minimum of attention and affection from our partners). Our longing for the "return of romance," which has sold reams of lingerie and vacation packages, and the calls of experts to keep our relationships "fresh" are ways of saying as much. When we get up in the morning we want more than another body in the room; we want another person, whose concern and interest encourages and rewards our own.

And we don't stop expecting that the relationship will "grow," or "deepen," or "renew itself," to cite three of our current buzzwords. We think that "a relationship takes work," and that *the work of a relationship never stops.*

That is not like any other job you can think of. (Certainly not like the "executive" jobs the best and brightest among us aspire to, which amount to seeing that other people finish their own tasks.) *A relationship is never finished, and no one else can finish it for you.* One cannot delegate the demands of love, the way one can delegate the various tasks that make up a piece of work. And *one cannot put aside the needs of a lover the way one can put off the majority of tasks that go into a job,* without putting the relationship at risk.

If you are not a woman, imagine that you are. Imagine that a man who wants to be your lover says, "I will give you the best of me." And then gives you what is left when his work is over. Imagine that he treats you the way he treats people at work—half-distracted, listening for the tasks he must do (and no more), thinking ahead to the next part of the job.

I don't have to imagine, because I have treated women that way. I can't recall one who liked it. But I had to learn not to like it myself, alone, after the women walked out. And I found that I did *not* like being alone more than I liked being able *just to do my job.*

The job was simpler; I did not have to question myself in performing it, the way a lover can make you question yourself. And doing it well, becoming known for my work, seemed to me a way of impressing women (to some extent, it was—at least until they knew me better), of having the cake of doing something that satisfied me more than anyone else, and then handing a slice of it over to a woman when I had had enough. But the women were not fooled. They knew that I was giving them second place, and they wanted a man who put them first.

What women will not stand for, men who need women will not insist on. Even at a time when some 10 percent of our population is homosexual, most men do need women—to care for them, as we saw in Part I, to raise their families, and to love them. That was women's main job in our society before the Second Wave—and still is.

In exchange for doing it, until recently—within the lives of the middle-aged—women did not insist that men put their partners before a job, in ways beyond the symbolic toast to the sanctity of the family. How could they, in all decency? The working day in the America of the nineteenth century was twelve hours, six days a week (it remains at that level for the most ambitious among us); the twelve dropped to ten by World War I (though not in every industry), and to ten hours, five days a week (counting the time required to get to the job and home again) only at mid-century. Until then, it was enough if a man worked—for the wife and children who depended on him, and to earn him the comfort of knowing someone cared for him.

But it is no longer enough. We now, apparently, have the energy to reconsider our intimate lives beyond work, if not always to do something about it—that is, to take the hard path of relationships, instead of the relatively easy (though difficult enough in its own right) road that leads to a job.

The difference between what we say we want, and our behavior—which hasn't changed all that much—demands an explanation. I would suggest that placing relationships above a job requires a sacrifice—of freedom, and of power—on the part of a man. It requires that he live on a woman's terms, as much as on his own. And it requires him to reject the solution to his dilemma that he sees practiced by the vast majority of men around him— to doubt, for the first time in his life, that work will make everything turn out right, in more ways than one.

I WANT TO BE GOOD WITH MONEY: THE MORAL ECONOMY OF WORK

The therapist I introduced in Chapter 3, who felt guilty toward his family, deeply loved his work, and said so; but he was less explicit about the pride he felt over the money he was finally earning from his labors. That pride showed in his excitement over his still-small art collection, his pleasure in how well his table was set, the richness of the food his wife had prepared— in short, in how well he was providing.

Yet he could hardly believe he had earned these pleasures, this satisfaction—earned, in the sense of having made a sacrifice equivalent, in some inner economy, to the money he was given in exchange for it. This showed when, without waiting to be asked, he brought up the subject of his fees, which he had recently raised. They had been $70 an hour, and he had planned to raise them to $75 (in keeping with the ethics of his profession, he charged patients what they could bear, to a floor of around $15 an hour; I still am grateful to a therapist who was likewise generous with me, one year when I badly needed his care). But one of his patients had written him a check for $80 an hour, telling him that $5 "isn't even a 15 percent raise."

At that point the therapist said, like a worried man would say to a woman at certain moments, when their relationship grows serious, "I've never been good with money." The other man, a top executive in his field, replied: "Neither have I."

Never been good with money—never handled it well, he meant.

Or perhaps "good" in another way: he had never been worthy of money. He felt ashamed in some way to have it; something, perhaps, like the rich kids I knew growing up, who were embarrassed by the toys their friends did not likewise possess. He had never been a rich kid, but he had been head of a chapter of Students for a Democratic Society in his college days, and fought for "a qualitative transformation of life, a workers' democracy." That transformation had not come, and he was now dealing with people who had, he said, "a certain amount of success and freedom"—that is, a wealthy clientele. He had been lucky to do something he liked doing, and be paid for it; *why him, and not someone else?* (That kind of question comes naturally to a man raised in a society where we like to think that all of us are created equal; and where the rich and famous nearly always tell interviewers who ask for the secrets of their success, "I was lucky." If they worked hard, they would still not dream of saying, "I'm better than the next guy.")

I was reminded, listening to his story, of the Prosperity Consciousness workshops that sprang up within the New Age movement in the 1970s, and which laid the groundwork for our current national obsession with "positive thinking." In these workshops, several of which I attended, participants were always told to look each other in the eyes and say something like, "I deserve to be rich."

As the evening progressed in a rose-colored room at one prosperity seminar, we paired off, sat on the floor, and literally gave each other permission to realize our wildest dreams—you know, stuff like real jewelry, a German sedan, "your perfect soul flame." The theory was that to get it, you had best not be ashamed of wanting it, like a man who worries if he's worth a raise. You might say, for example, "I want to own the World Trade Center," and your partner would reply, "You may have the World Trade Center, and Trump Tower to boot."

At this point my partner went so far as to tell me he wanted to sell more records "of my music" worldwide than Stevie Wonder—*why someone else, and not him?*—and I replied, "You can sell more records than Wonder and Led Zeppelin together." Then he wanted a palace, so I told him he could have the Taj Mahal. It was getting hard to offer him stuff he hadn't already thought of.

Then he went in reverse: now he merely wanted a house. Then he wanted a place to stay that night. When I missed the hint, he asked me if he could go home with me, because he had no other place to go. (No, I did not say, "You may stay with me for the next five years, and never contribute to the rent.")

He was a funny, sad New Age bum. But he had some things in common with the prosperous young therapist. *Each had an essential sense of his own unworthiness. And they both prescribed the same cure for themselves: to be rich.* The difference is that the bum thought that it was enough of a job merely to say that he wanted to be rich, while the therapist was ready to work for his wealth.

The most important thing they had in common, and a deeply rooted American trait, was *to need the permission of someone else*—for the therapist that someone was his wife, while for the bum it was a mere stranger—*in order to obtain wealth for themselves.*

It is quite American to think that money, honestly gotten and nobly spent, can go a long way toward resolving just how deserving, how worthy, one might be. The Pilgrim Fathers, for example, chose their leaders from among the parties to the Covenant, membership in which was reserved (through the first American-born Puritan generation) mainly for the prosperous. Honest-gotten wealth was considered a sign of grace in this world.

But only under certain conditions. Most important, the Puritans argued that work must benefit others, or it would destroy the community and its Covenant with a protecting God. The injunction was laid down by John Winthrop on board the *Arabella* in 1630. "The only way to avoid [a] shipwreck," in America, he told his Puritan shipmates,

> is to . . . be knit together in this work as one man, we must entertain each other in brotherly affection, we must be willing to abridge ourselves of our superfluities, for the supply of others' necessities . . .

Either that, or "we [will] be consumed out of the good land whither we are going."

I have modernized the spelling; the message Winthrop put across remains current, and not only because we are consuming ourselves into the hands of foreign manufacturers of automobiles, computers, and hi-fis. *Deep down we feel that we must do good with our money, or we are bad.*

The earnings of labor are sinful when they serve no one but yourself; when they reflect not love, or even a general social welfare, but mere greed. Even a corporate raider like T. Boone Pickens feels constrained to claim that his immense profits amount to a service to stockholders in the companies he harries (and which are thus obliged to put aside other tasks, like actually producing something), because he makes the price of their shares rise when he moves in.

The pleasure of gain, in the American moral economy, must be matched (at least symbolically) by the service and sacrifice one provides with the profits. *In order to enjoy our wealth, one way or another, we need someone else's permission.*

But work requires no such permission. (On the contrary, one needs permission *not* to work.) If you happen to enjoy your work—and let us say, once and for all, that when work goes well, and one likes the doing of it, it is as great a pleasure in itself as nearly anything else you can name, and *one which is not dependent on the cooperation of another person to the same extent that intimacy is*—you will get away, more or less, with taking on as much of it as you want, assuming that you bring home the money to prove that you were indeed working.

To whom? If you are a man, the answer is: the one you love—who, 90 percent of the time, is a woman.

To work is the first promise a man makes a woman, and for Albert Martin it was his last defense: when his wife gave up keeping house (it became and stayed filthy) and told him, "This is the way it's going to be," all he could say in answer was, "Yes, but I wind up paying for it!"

In working for a woman—in winning the bread she eats—a man reclaims something that he would otherwise not believe he held the right to demand: moral equality in a relationship.

It is not only to win her that he works, but to win over her—*to be able to face her on some kind of equal terms,* this woman who gives so much when she loves, as women (God bless them) do, who gives us the care we have not the time (or all too often, the interest) to provide ourselves, and who therefore holds a power over us.

The Second Wave equated that power with slavery; exercising it certainly requires drudgery, and the helplessness of financial dependence, if that is all a woman does. But only a minority of women are solely housekeepers these days. In this, I think, women's power, while not yet the equal of men's in financial terms, has grown in relative terms. And it remains far stronger than men's, when it comes to the capacity to care for oneself and others.

Money is, when you get down to it, the main thing many of us can provide for a woman, that can compare in some sense with what she provides us. I am not talking merely about the domestic services that women still perform in the main, like housework and child care, nor about sexual favors. I am talking about what Lee Iacocca, the CEO of the Chrysler Corporation who "became a hero" (in his own words) when he saved the company from bankruptcy, revealed in his autobiography: a painful *inequality of emotional support* in his marriage.

"All through my career at Ford and later at Chrysler, my wife, Mary, was my greatest fan and cheerleader," said Iacocca. "We were very close, and she was always at my side." It took enormous courage on her part to be there, he said, because she had diabetes, and "a person with diabetes has to avoid stress." (It is true, as it happens, that emotional extremes have an effect on blood-sugar levels, and diabetes works its havoc along the same route.) "Unfortunately," he continued, "with the path I had chosen to follow, this was often impossible."

When Iacocca was fired from the presidency of Ford, and was offered the job of saving Chrysler, his wife's reaction was, "I love you, and know you can do anything you set your mind to. But... there's no disgrace in walking away from an impossible task." Not a word about the risks she would run, which Iacocca spells out: "On each of [the] occasions when her health failed her, it was following a period of great stress at Ford or at Chrysler."

He continues: "One evening two weeks before her death, Mary called me in Toronto to tell me how proud she was of me.... *Yet during those last few difficult years, I never once told her how proud I was of her.*"

I have underlined one of the most devastating confessions a prominent American has ever made in public. Iacocca went on the record not only with his success as an executive but also with his failure to thank the person who held his life together during his greatest crisis ("Mary sustained me," he said). It took courage to do that, for which we owe him thanks. We should also ask why he was unable—as so many of us are—to express gratitude to the most important person in his life, for sacrifices that ulti-mately included her own.

We come back to this curious thing, the "strong, silent image" men should supposedly conform to. Indeed, Iacocca did keep his silence; he never told his wife or family "how bad things really were" at Chrysler. (The knight may fight for the fair lady's honor, but it is bad form to boast of his wounds until after he has won.) And how could he have kept silent, if in acknowl-edging how badly he needed his wife's aid and support, he showed her the truth of their situation? *He could share with her, or spare her—he could not do both.* (The awful irony, of course, is that in the end he could do neither.)

I have heard similar reasoning from many men: if you let on how bad things are, at best, if you win in the end, you'll have inflicted worry on your loved ones for nothing. At worst, if you fail, you'll have started their suffering sooner. And in any case, you'll have made a mockery of the sacrifice you undertook for them—the sacrifice that gives a sense of moral satisfaction to what would otherwise be merely naked ambition, or brutal drudgery—which was precisely to *get the job done, whatever it is, whatever it takes, for their sakes.*

So a man does what he has to do, for the sake of his loved ones—as did Iacocca, whose devotion to his family would be questioned only by someone more cynical than myself. Yet when he is done with the job, as for Iacocca, there may still remain the terrible sense that all he accomplished was in some fundamental sense not enough.

That, however, is hindsight. While the job goes on, another kind of moral balance is in place—a balance that combines a real satisfaction with a real guilt, one driving the other.

Having flaunted our earnings, the fruits of our virtuous labors—God, do we like to complain and brag in the same breath, about how hard we work—we may claim the right to balance it with a sin. Like Alan Hirschfield, who took time out from his struggles at Columbia Pictures to buy himself a Ferrari, we may offer ourselves a reward, with the happy sense of fully deserving it.

But sometimes the pleasures we offer ourselves, with a sense of bitter justice, are quite simply perverse.

When I was working as a salesman—my best boss from those days tells me he is still working the hours we had together then, seven in the morning till eight or nine at night, road trips every week—I developed a little analysis of what was going on in the part of my mind that wanted pleasure. Of course, there were little bits of fun scattered through the working day. But the fun wasn't enough to satisfy me, nor most of the people I worked with. How could it? A shot of amusement is hardly as satisfying as eating well, sleeping, dreaming, and making love.

As time went on, I wondered if this was making me weird, in as yet small ways. For one thing, as hellish as my days were, I passed my moments of free time in daydreaming about making love; and not with the woman I lived with, as good a lover as anyone could want, but with the women I saw during the working day, when I still had energy to flirt and fantasize.

The perverse element was in hiding this secret dream life from my lover; if I had confided it, the pleasure would have been lost, at home ("you don't know what I'm thinking") and at work (where if the dreams had been acknowledged I would have felt guilty, and guilty flirting is just *so* pathetic). I liked that hiding. It gave me a sense of control that I did not enjoy at the job. While I was at work, and when I came home, I flattered myself that no one knew my mind, even if they had a claim to my body.

I began to realize that my case of job madness was mild, compared to one of my clients'. His first meeting with me in his office was as sadistic an encounter as ever I care to experience. He regarded me the way a frog regards a succulent fly. He insulted me in a manner so gratuitously crude, so salaciously intoned, and with such naive bluster, that I could only gape: I had told him that he and I were in the same business (making money, by selling the same product), and he replied, "You're pulling my wang."

That line was the tip-off: he had sex on his little brain, and he wasn't about to hide it, only disguise it a little. He was going to use me, the way a man uses an unwilling partner. (What men do to women, I have also noticed, they will do to men.) When I recovered from that shock, I was watching him warily, the way you watch an angry or frightened dog.

Thus I noticed when his manner shifted suddenly, from hostility to pleading. "I need money," he said, or he couldn't buy advertising space in my newspaper. He said he wanted to run promotions in the paper, with giveaway prizes. He had already taken away the prize my company had provided for a previous promotion (and he was not the only one who did so, though the other one paid back when enough time had elapsed to fool his companies' bookkeepers. Such skimming practices are endemic in the film and other industries, another of the little strange pleasures of work). I got the strong impression that he was saying, "Buy me." He had gone from whoremaster to whore in two minutes flat.

It is not that work makes you this way. But work does afford the opportunity to behave like this: to mistreat other people for the sake of one's own pleasure, *with the feeling that one has the right to do so.*

Sometimes the righteousness can create disaster—as seemed to be the case at Hyatt Clark, a roller-bearing firm whose employees and managers came together to buy the company in 1981, when its owners wanted to close it down. For the first three years, all went well, as a labor-management coalition brought the company back to profitability. Productivity and morale were up, from the shop floor to the executive suite.

Then the managers did two things, backed by the board of directors. They held back bonuses and raises for the line workers, and reinvested the profits in new equipment. And then they gave *themselves* bonuses. At that point, the workers staged a slowdown—in effect, they struck against themselves, in order to get back at the managers.

And that killed the company.

"The problem," commented Hyatt Clark board member Douglas Fraser, former president of the United Auto Workers, to the *New York Times,* "was an unwillingness to share power." True enough; but beyond that, there was a sense of moral righteousness on both sides of the labor-management divide, carried to a perverse extreme. The managers thought they deserved their bonuses, and the workers felt they had been just as deserving. If the workers couldn't have the money that makes you good, neither would their bosses; and in the end, they combined forces and killed the goose that laid the only eggs they had.

When we go to work, we give up something that we cannot get back: our time. In exchange, we get something we cannot honestly obtain any other way, short of having it dropped in our laps: money. And with the money go various little pleasures that help to compensate for the loss of the love our work is designed to earn for us—love, the most time-consuming activity known to human beings.

But this exchange is not evenly balanced like the swings of a pendulum. Its tilts toward work are deeper, longer, more time-consuming, than its tilts toward the relationships to which we return when the work is done.

It is indisputable that the way our economy is now structured, people who have to work do not have control, in the short term, over how much of their time they wish to sell in exchange for a comfortable living. Figure it out for yourself: the average American manufacturing wage is $9 per hour, which adds up to $360 over a forty-hour week, $18,000 over a fifty-week year—at a time when, according to one recent survey, it costs over $20,000 to have a decent life-style for oneself and one's family.

But in the long term, one has to ask if there is something at work in this uneven equation besides material necessity—if *the hours we spend at our jobs reflect not only the need to provide for ourselves and others, but an escape from other needs*—especially among men who *can* control the hours they give to working.

The pleasures of work are real enough. But in taking them we give up others—whatever pleasures are available in the eyes, smiles, and beds of our lovers. It therefore seems possible to me that the balance we have presently made in our lives, between work and love, is also a balance between needing love and wanting not to need it. And that latter balance, I believe, is precisely what we have in mind when we speak of "success."

CHAPTER

—— 10 ——

Hopalong Henry and Other Self-Made Men

In Michael Korda's laughably self-serious bestseller, *Power! How to Get It, How to Use It,* published in 1975, the reader is told that "power— 'the ability to bring about our desires'—is all that we have left." A novel twist, that, on the idea that the personal is political.

We discover that "half the reason for working at all is the hold it gives us over other people." We learn that to become powerful, we must develop "absolute control" over our bladders, and that "constipation is often the price of power." The point is so important that Korda must repeat it: "a good many of the powerful people I know not only suffer from constipation, but discuss it quite openly"—ah, the life-styles of the rich and famous— "as if it were proof of their success, a form of self-imposed suffering." Along with emotional constipation; most of Korda's heroes, he remarks in passing, are lonely.

But this sop to our hunger for the dirty secrets of the mighty pales beside an unanswerable achievement: Korda's heroes no longer need love like the rest of us do, to give them self-respect. And they expect to be pitied for that, too: "When a man really makes a success of his life," whined publisher Bob Guccione, "ninety-nine percent of his friends vanish." (Yes, but it must be worth it; to carry Korda's gossipy confidences to their logical conclusion, who needs a surrogate mother, when he runs no risk whatsoever of soiling his pants?)

There is a perverse pleasure in playing the poor little rich and powerful kid, as Korda shows so abundantly: the pleasure of fooling others, while assuring priority for one's own needs and desires. The hustle depends on hiding the obvious—that no one can possibly have a fully intimate emotional life when he is engaged in working all the time—while simultaneously making use of that fact to arouse the sympathy of others.

Look at what happened when Oriana Fallaci cracked Henry Kissinger wide open, in the course of a famous interview at the peak of Kissinger's fame as Richard Nixon's Secretary of State. Fallaci did to Kissinger what you might see a high-school girl pull on the captain of the football team: she asked him over and over, in a teasing, mocking tone, what magic secret of success he possessed. *Gee, Henry, you do great work.* Finally, Kissinger blurted out:

> Well, yes, I'll tell you. What do I care? The main point [is] that I've always acted alone. Americans like that immensely. Americans like the cowboy who leads the wagon train by riding ahead alone on his horse. . . . All he needs is to be alone, to show others that he rides into town *and does everything by himself.* [My emphasis.]

Now, of course, even Henry Kissinger needs a little help from time to time (when President Nixon let his displeasure with Kissinger's boastful claim be known, Henry was forced to declare that Fallaci's tape recorder had heard him wrong). But he was right about what Americans like— especially men, and especially in the press, business, and government circles on whom his legend depended.

We like to see a guy who can do everything himself. We would, even if only in fantasy, like to feel that way ourselves. It would mean a free, independent position in life—and yet one in which we were admired by others, where we could profit from their goodwill without feeling reliant on it.

More specifically—and Kissinger let that cat out of Fallaci's bag, too—*if only a man can succeed enough, then he will not need women.* As Henry said so bluntly, "For me women are only a diversion, a hobby. Nobody spends too much time with his hobbies." (Nor would a man like Henry worry overmuch about his kids: "The fact of not living with my children doesn't give me any guilt complexes.")

What counted for this man was being able to do what made him feel (and look, so far as the rest of us consider him) complete: his work. And that was enough, in his own and the public's eyes.

But it is a false pose. Kissinger admitted as much. For one thing, he used women—in particular, in order to prove to others that he was a man. "I think that my playboy reputation has been and still is useful," he opined to

Fallaci, "because it served and still serves to reassure people. To show them that I'm not a museum piece."

And perhaps to distract attention from an incapacity for intimacy: "To live with someone else and survive that living together is very difficult," he admitted. "The relationship between a woman and a fellow like me is inevitably so complex."

Did you hear the self-pity?

How do men get away with this? How do powerful, successful men fool us into taking them for lonesome, aching studs who do it all for our sakes?

The only possible answer is that *we need to be fooled.* And we do—at least, men do. Otherwise we could not convince ourselves that we were fooling anyone else, starting with the women in our lives, about a matter that women would otherwise find mortally offensive: by going to work, into a world where men still call the shots in the main (and where even successful women call the shots according to criteria laid down by men), *we enter a realm where what women know about us is less important than what we accomplish on our own.*

THE SECRETS OF SUCCESS

The extremely successful men I have met held different standards—values, if you will—in life from my own, and different from the men in my sample (who were, in the main, middle-class like myself). *They recognized quite clearly that they could not have both success in prominent, and therefore highly competitive, fields, and close, time-consuming personal relationships—and they were not about to try.* They saw that there was a choice to make, and they made it. They decided to engage in relationships when they felt the need, and no longer; others' needs would attend on their own.

The big men follow fashions; the guy who was a swinging stud one year would be a devoted father the next, depending on what the public expected (this year, the fashion in 1988 presidential hopefuls is for men who cry, just as it was the fashion in male movie stars of the 1950s, like Montgomery Clift and James Dean). But year in, year out, *they put their careers ahead of their relationships; and they get rid of the partners who hold back their careers.*

For example, when I interviewed a corporate president who spent a total of two weeks in every year with his wife and children (during which he spent four hours every day on the phone to his corporate affiliates around the world), and passed the rest of his time at the office or on the road, he said with a weary smile, "This is my universe, and I'm its slave."

A slave? He could have sold the company and walked out with his millions anytime he wanted to. *He didn't want to, not ever.* He was perfectly contented that his wife kept her own apartment in another city, that his closest relations were with employees who put a "Mister" in front of his first name when they addressed him. He would have been ill-at-ease anywhere but in his own private universe, where he made the rules.

A couple of years ago I interviewed Mick Jagger. Jagger makes no bones about the fact that he is one of the most competitive people on earth; told that hitmaker David Bowie had backhanded him in another interview, he said, "Well, David and I are very much in competition," and then dropped a bomb of his own on Bowie. He is hardly the type to tell a stranger with a tape recorder his deeper feelings about any subject you might mention, so I asked him to talk about the work of singing and writing songs, and then started asking him how his relationships with other people—musicians, hangers-on, friends who failed, "the girl who's had ten years of looking at your pictures," as he put it—affected his work.

What I wanted to know, without blurting it to his watchful face, was how a man who works nearly all the time—and by studying his career before the interview, I knew that Jagger worked an awful lot, that he has rarely left anything in his career to hazard—makes his own balance between work and love.

From the start of the interview, Jagger had been bragging about how busy he always was; he had even written the songs for his first solo album "on a *vacation*," he stressed. Even when he went out dancing, he was listening for beats he could use on his own records; like Andy Warhol, he apparently thought that the reason for playing all the time is to work all the time. But certain kinds of work and women did not mix (at least not at that point in his career). "One of the great things about [working in] the studio," he said, was that there were no women around. He had nothing but contempt for guys who left a recording session to be with "the old lady."

Surely, I hinted, he must have some time for his own pleasure. How did he unwind? He collected cars, he said, "but I never have the time to drive them. It's like, when you're on the road, the whole time you're away, you know that little thing is there."

There was something in his tone on the words "little thing," something dreamy, sexy. Sometimes men call women sexy little things. I wondered if the whole time he was on the road, during the years when the road was his life, he had counted on knowing that a woman was there, whoever she might be.

And I remembered how another rock star's wife, Mrs. Roger Daltrey, when asked what she thought about her husband's affairs on the road, had said, "I'm his security," that he needed her to come back to.

And I thought about how whenever my work has taken me away from home, I longed to be back with my lover, yet longed to enjoy my time alone as long as I could.

In all these cases, I saw a similar pattern in a man: *he needed work to take him away from a woman, so that he could come back to her; and he needed to come back to her, so that when he left again, his work would seem not a chore, but an escape.* If she was the reward of his labors, the prize at the end of the road, she was still the trap he must escape.

And that, I saw, is part of what we mean by success—to be able to make use of those escape hatches, when and how one chooses.

It is in part to be free of dependence on a particular woman, to control the terms of our exchange with a needed other, that we give the best of ourselves to our work.

This is what gives the lie to our working man's honor, that makes women distrust us when we say, "I gotta go to work, honey." We do not just *have* to go—we *want* to go, for the pleasure of coming back, and the pleasure of *not* coming back *until we feel like it.*

It may be, in some respects, a lesser pleasure than uninterrupted intimacy—but it is also an easier pleasure to attain, assuming that one doesn't mind doing the work required to earn it.

Look at it this way: is it tougher to deal with people from the standpoint of wealth and fame, power and position—or from the standpoint of one man, looking one woman in the face, a woman who knows everything about you that never gets into the newspapers?

I have never been as famous as Mick Jagger, but I think I know the answer. And so did he: the title of his solo album was, *She's the Boss.*

THE GREAT ESCAPE

At some point in every one of my interviews, I asked the man in front of me: "Which is harder—to do a good job at your work, or to have a good relationship with your lover?"

Every one of the men, without exception, said that the relationship was more difficult—more "demanding," more "complicated," were the words they most often used. And those who had a choice to make—whose occupations gave them a certain control over their hours and conditions of work, such as a doctor, a lawyer, or a musician—went on to admit that the hours they spent on their jobs provided, in some way, an escape from the hard, hard work of intimacy.

One of these men had in the past two years reached an important turning point, in both his career and his relationship. From being an untenured assistant professor of environmental studies, he had moved to an executive job with an international ecology-watch organization. The pay wasn't terrific, but the work itself gave him a sense of accomplishing a vital task in an urgent policy domain, in sharp contrast to the days when he was obliged to cajole students to turn in their papers on time.

And along with that satisfaction went the perquisites of prestige and travel. He was in demand for legislative conferences, for lectures, for international colloquia, all of which kept him on the road a minimum of ten days each month.

The year before he took that job, he had met a woman who taught creative writing at a university in the city where he worked. She was, he admitted to me, crucial in helping him to cope with the bad days at his former job, and in encouraging him to take the next step in his career. I met the woman; a smart, well-mannered, kind person, a few years his senior, who wanted to start a family with him. She had a certain stake in his career, besides the fact that her salary alone wouldn't have sufficed to support a family: she had realized that without work that mattered to him, he wouldn't be happy, and that their relationship was bound to suffer.

She was, in short, the kind of woman who cares about her lover as much as she cares about herself, which is certainly no small thing. That was a main reason behind her tolerance of his schedule, as he was well aware; when duty called, she shrugged and helped him pack. And he went on the road with the confidence that she would be waiting for him when he came home, untouched by another man's hands.

But he was betraying her, in more ways than one; counting on her to be better, in some way, than himself. Not only because he liked to get away from her, to enjoy the bittersweet solitude of a hotel room that someone else would clean when he had turned in the key, to travel light and fast in a world he had always dreamed of seeing.

He was betraying her in the most basic way: when he traveled, he was on the lookout for other women. What he said was, "I get an affirmation from these women that I can't get any other way." He used that word, "affirmation," several times in the course of a half-hour spent in discussing this subject with me. It was affirming to know that he was desirable, he said; he had always doubted his appeal to women, fantasized about the beauties who passed him in the street, on their busy ways, ever since the grinding days when he had been pursuing his doctorate and working nights to pay his living expenses.

Was it not affirming, I asked, to know that he could get another woman, if his relationship broke up? "Well, yeah." And if he became more successful, might he not trade up, to a higher grade of female (assuming that such a thing exists, which I doubt)? Right again.

Was it not, then, a way of holding power over his lover? And wasn't this one of the reasons he liked his job?

"Yes."

I had told him that I was neither different nor better. I had looked forward to business traveling myself, and like him, one of the reasons was that from time to time—not always, but often enough—somewhere along the road was a woman who would take me, and then let me go, back to the woman who waited for me at home. A woman, here and there, who did not have the right to prevent me from going off to do my job—was I not working to provide some woman, someday, with a future?—or from going home when the job was done.

The man I told this to, I later learned, was not fooling his partner; she had written a letter in which she discussed, without embarrassment or self-pity, his desire to escape from her. I was shocked when I read it, because she knew everything that he had never told her: the letter was written from *his* perspective, in terms that he hadn't dared to use with her, and followed his logic to ends he couldn't express, even in trying to explain himself to me. *She knew him better than he knew himself.*

That was why she knew that his career offered him a role—the self-assured, confident, rising young man of excellent prospects—that he could not always sustain when they were alone together. He was trying to withhold from her, and avoid facing in himself, the knowledge she discovered on her own—that he did not love her as she loved him. And she knew that in making his business trips, *in sacrificing their time together in order to make his way in the world, he was providing himself with a power base that would survive the failure of their relationship.*

This, I think, suggests another reason that even at a time when our women—at least in theory—are just as capable of earning their livings and having careers as we are, and even when we are no longer obliged to work all our waking hours, we keep our noses to our grindstones.

Our women's earning powers are real enough—enough to relieve them of the sheer terror of drudging survival that an unmarried woman once faced. So are their powers to choose another man, for their own pleasure, or for a better relationship than a given man might provide. This was a lesson that men of my generation drew during the 1970s, watching relationships and marriages split up, each partner going his or her separate but equal way. *We know that it could happen to us; and if it happens, we do not want to be the one who can be replaced, but who cannot find a replacement.*

I have seen time and again how even good men feel themselves drawn toward work, to an environment where they can take care of business (if not always of themselves). Not only for the "affirmation," whatever form it may take, that work can provide—doing a good job, getting paid more or less well for it, earning the recognition and approval of others for how well you do it—but because work is where a man will always have a place, if only he will earn it; and because it is the easier place that a man can earn, compared to earning and keeping a place in a woman's heart.

And thus *we are caught between doing the job that makes us feel virtuous, and taking vengeance on those whose approval confirms our virtue; between making a sacrifice, and hating those in whose name the sacrifice is made; between the guilty pleasure that goes along with working, and the work that makes it right.*

CHAPTER

—— 11 ——

The Failure
Men Fear Most

If knowledge is power, then women tend to be more powerful in relationships. The image that comes to mind is of Jack Nicholson in the Mike Nichols film *Carnal Knowledge,* screaming up a staircase at Candice Bergen, "Tell me my thoughts!" A man doesn't know what he thinks, what he really wants, how to tell it to a woman he loves; he needs her to tell him.

And that is only natural. While he has been paying attention to his work, she has been paying attention to *him.*

Such an imbalance of intimate power played a large role in the divorces I witnessed growing up. Those divorces took place around the time a man enters his mid-life, when he starts to see the distance between what he dreamed of achieving and what he has actually attained. When he came to that crisis, the last thing he wanted was a witness, someone who could (and did, often in spite of herself) remind him of that gap.

Not surprisingly, that witness often turned out to be his wife. And not coincidentally, many of these men later married younger women—women who looked up to them for the success they had achieved already, instead of the dreams the men believed they had failed to achieve.

These men still had years of productive, procreative energy in them—enough to start out on a "new life," in the awful phrase of the time. They may have agonized and given in to self-pity in front of their old wives. But they had not given up. *They had not yet admitted failure.*

And that was the strange paradox: *they treated their wives like witnesses to failures they could not admit to themselves.* That was why, I think, throughout the divorce process such men displayed a rising hostility toward their former partners—to prove that someone else, and not them, had failed.

But usually, even the women who were left alone, who did not remarry, at first, but went on with their lives, seemed to emerge from these traumas in better shape than their ex-husbands. The women kept their relationships with the children, more than did the men, who were out working on their new lives (as if any human being gets such a thing, short of reincarnation—which, by the way, is seen by the Hindus as a punishment for the old life). The women stayed within the circle of the broken couple's friends, while the men more often sought new contacts, with all the risks and disappointments such a search implies. Rarely did the women have the problems with alcohol or drugs that racked the men who left them.

In short, the women coped better. They emerged stronger from their experience, if terribly saddened by it, often enough, while the men were weakened in numerous ways. I believe that this is explained by the observation that *the women understood why the men had left them, better than the men understood why they had left.* The wives understood that the men were unhappy and confused, and needed someone to blame besides themselves; and the women could see, eventually, that no matter how much they had given their men, it would not have been enough.

The men would say, "I gotta be me," as a hit song of the seventies put it. They would say that they wanted to discover their own "human potential," in the dumb (to be blunt) phrase, "I have to be free to find myself."

But they did not know who, or what, they were looking for. And their new lives turned out, in the cases I had the chance to witness, to be an awful lot like the old ones.

How could it have been otherwise? They had never known how to live, really; that much of what they said was true. *What they knew was what they had always known: how to work.*

Which is, when you think about it, what men still know.

If these men were afraid of what their ex-wives knew about them, that would not be strange. Nor would it be strange if they refused themselves the knowledge that they saw in their wives' eyes. It would simply be the continuation of a lifelong habit of ignoring what hurts—a lesson that applies not only to a man's body but also to his mind. It is why he says, "What you don't know won't hurt you"—even what you don't know about yourself. If you don't know it, no one else can. So one feels; so a man hopes.

If he wants to feel that way, it is largely because the price of self-revelation for a man—if the revelation is of a weakness, a doubt, an anguish that will not go away—is quite high. Other men, even your friends, cannot be counted on to keep secrets; some will use your secrets against you, because we are all still in a race, where all is fair. Moreover, women—despite our current fashion for "openness"—do not at all enjoy hearing that a man on whom they depend (and we do depend on each other in many ways, even now, and probably always will) is ambivalent at best, and hostile at worst, toward the demands life and love make on him. At least, that is my experience, and the experience of most men I know.

And because we are, after all, American, we do not like to pose ourselves problems for which we have no practical solutions. "Don't just stand there," we have heard throughout our lives, *do something."* We are men, doers. We are not supposed to be trembling with confusion about what to do next. And when we take on a job, a woman, a family, we are more than anything else supposed to do supremely well. "Winning isn't everything," read a sign in my high-school locker room, "but it's way ahead of whatever comes second."

What comes second is failure.

We are pursuers of happiness; we cannot admit to unhappiness without failing. A high-school friend of mine, at the age of twenty-two, told me one night, "I'm a failure." He confided that he had a pistol, bought on a trip through the South, and was considering whether or not to put it in his mouth and pull the trigger. I couldn't understand why he had failed (I was terrified that he would kill himself, and I would lose his friendship, not to mention be partly responsible for his death—couldn't I have helped more? His failure would be mine). Why did he think so?

Only this: he could see that he might never become a successful record producer, his dream. And he didn't. He moved into business, and is now vice-president of a major corporation. Over dinner, flanked by his wife and child, he volunteers the information that he never had the taste to tell a good song from a bad one. He is wrong; I worked on the sessions he produced, and he picked good songs and good players. But he was afraid to fail in the record business, because most people do. He did not want to live with that fear, because it made him want to kill himself.

So he sidestepped it; he became a success at something else. To guard his present happiness, he denies a talent that was part of himself, and with it the pain of the choice he once had to make. Perhaps that is one reason our relationship became so distant, in the years after he gave out his fear to me: I remind him of that fear, that choice. And I pushed it away when he showed it to me, told him simply and brutally, "Cut the crap," as I would have pushed away fear of my own. It was, I told myself, the best thing I could do. Failure would be crueler than I had been, and even lonelier.

Of course, he would succeed. That was what I told him, and myself. But in doing so, I merely reaffirmed what he already knew—that failure was simply, horribly unthinkable.

The fear I saw in my friend, and which I have felt often enough in myself, reflected a hierarchy of failure. At the top of the list was failure in the work that makes a man's world. There is a paradox here, too. Nothing, it seems to me, is more devastating than to fail in love, to be incapable of satisfying a woman, of keeping her faith and affection.

But in some sense, *such a failure is less to be feared than failing in work.* If work is the easier channel for a man's energies, at a fundamental level it is also the more essential. The reasons, I think, go way beyond the necessity of providing for oneself and others, real enough in a man's life.

One of those reasons is that without work, a man's identity seems truncated, first and foremost to himself. *If working is the way he leaves his mark in the world, then the work he cannot accomplish diminishes his sense of his own presence, breaks the mirror in which he reads the proof of his own existence.* This is not only an abstract principle, but a practical one. You can see it at work in men's lives.

Failure cuts a man off: from his woman, who will take care of herself if he can't take care of her, or find another man who will (I am speaking of a fear I have felt myself); his colleagues, who will go on with their jobs after he has been replaced ("no one is irreplaceable," remember); and the men in whom he trusted.

"I speak with the authority of failure," wrote F. Scott Fitzgerald, who knew early success and fell from it, adding that Ernest Hemingway, once his friend, spoke "with the authority of success. We can never sit across the same table again." He had learned that "friends . . . won't save us any more than love did." Not when you fail.

Fitzgerald displayed his failure for everyone to see, in an essay called *The Crack-Up.* "One should," he wrote, "be able to see that things are hopeless and yet be determined to make them otherwise. . . . Life was something you dominated if you were any good."

But he could no longer dominate; he was "inhuman and undernourished," filled with "too much anger and too many tears." His books no longer sold as much, he no longer cared to write them, the woman he loved was in an asylum. ("When she went down that road," he said, "my life went with her.") All of his success had not sufficed. Life had dominated him.

When the essay was published, Fitzgerald's friend John Dos Passos exploded to him in a letter, "Christ, man, how do you find time in the middle of the general conflagration to worry about all that stuff?" Dos Passos suggested that Fitzgerald, only ten years earlier the most famous novelist of his day, "get a reporting job somewhere." *Do something—anything.*

"Here you've gone and spent forty years in perfecting an elegant and complicated piece of machinery," said Dos Passos, "and the next forty years is the time to use it." *Use it or lose it—all of it.* He told Fitzgerald all about what he, Dos Passos, was working on, presumably to inspire his shattered friend to get back into the game—or perhaps to ward off his own fear, the way I had with my friend. And the last thing Dos Passos said, with peculiar embarrassment, was: "Forgive the locker-room pep talk." *Winning isn't everything, but it's way ahead of whatever comes second.*

The only problem was, Fitzgerald no longer cared for the game. He would rather fail than keep on trying to win. *"Everybody works,"* he underlined in his notebooks, *"and I'm the guy"*—but no more. For those, unlike him, who preferred to stay in the game, nothing could be more repulsive than "a man giving up the idea of himself as a hero," and well he knew it. He was repulsive to himself, a bright piece of porcelain that had "cracked like an old plate." And was thereupon "snubbed when he dramatizes himself as [a] victim of American failure."

He could fail—that was his own affair. It was his dramatizing that seemed frightening and disgusting to others, as much as it was to himself.

Only success and happiness, the rewards of productivity, have the right to be heard in polite company; a man who breaks this rule, in Fitzgerald's day and now, is not to be excused. The feminist movement has not changed our customs in this domain as much as we once hoped, it seems to me. A woman who gives up her career to raise a child would be considered as having a good excuse, if she cared to use it; a woman who failed to achieve her ambitions—say, to be a CEO—could blame the way the world of men treats women, and that also would be a valid (though lately weaker) excuse; but a man who did the same would be considered, even in our postfeminist days of liberation, as eccentric at best, weak at worst. In any case, he would see himself, and be seen, as not quite a man.

Every man I know has been unhappy from time to time, because that is the nature of life. But when I am unhappy, and someone asks me how things are going, I say, "Fine." I often add—and so, oddly, do many men I know, without waiting to be specifically asked—"I'm workin' a lot." If I can still work, still have work to do—not like poor Fitzgerald, but like peppy Dos Passos—I'm fine. I haven't failed, not yet. Work will cure what ails you; the idea is as American as Mom's apple pie.

The desire to avoid failure, and the way I usually deal with it—by going to work, and staying there—is one of the things that tie me to my father, to our fathers. I am like him, like them. When a doctor told my wife and me that she was pregnant, my first thought was: I'd better get to work. I had to make money for my family; I could not fail them.

But there is a new element in this equation: it seems that the failure which most worries me and my peers is less a matter of careers than of the heart—or rather, of both at once, and equally—which is why simply going to work no longer works.

We do not want to love a woman and leave her behind (we need women more than ever, in ways I will discuss later), to have a long road between us and her; and yet we do not want to give up the work that matters so much to us, either, because by doing so we will fail in the end just as certainly. We do not want to be gruff strangers to our children; nor bitter servants to men who live only for their work, with whom we must compete.

In a word, we do not want to live merely for the pursuit of happiness, we want to be happy, *now*. But *we are not certain that we can achieve this success without failing elsewhere—that a job and a woman (let alone a family), ambition and friendship, wealth and love, can peacefully and equally coexist in one man's life.*

And that, strangely, is why we do not question the "success" of men who are willing to give up the love that the rest of us need—why, at the very moment when we most need a new path to follow, we stare longingly at the well-worn route behind us.

Someday, we suspect deep down, we will have to make a choice between the one and the other, the job and the woman. Like any smart fellow, we want to keep our options open. And in the absence of new options, we cling harder than ever to the old ones.

But what we end up doing, in effect, is closing our options off.

You have the right—if you will claim it—not to tell anyone more about yourself than you want him to know, *once you go out to work*. (You do not, if your partner has any self-respect and wit about her, possess that right when you go home at the end of the day.)

You can, in the meanwhile, become a success. You will be heartily approved by those who share your fortunes, detested by those who do not. *What do you care?* You can pay people to work with you; you can even pay a woman off, one way or the other, if and when the marriage goes bad. And nobody can say a thing about it that you cannot laugh off. That's the way it is, for some men.

Just one thing. If that's the way you want it to be, *you'd best not fail, because if you do, no one will care.* You will be gone, and people will be indifferent to the fact. In other words, once you get up, you'd better stay there.

Failure, of course, does occur. It is essential to our mystique of success; if failure is not frightening, how can triumph be heroic? Who would go to NFL games if every one ended in a tie? We *like* to watch failure, as long as it is not our own, or that of someone we care about. (That is another reason that successful men hide their private lives. They know how many enemies they have.)

We can live with someone else's failure—even look at it, when we need a fearful burst of adrenaline. We can be happy when it happens to someone we hate. We may even long for it ourselves—I have met men who did so, and David Begelman's legal defense in the Columbia scandal was predicated on the argument that he secretly wished to fail, because of unconscious feelings of self-hatred—if only because we could use a nice, long rest from trying to succeed.

Failure is the threat we hold over our stars, our heroes: we can ignore them, laugh them out of existence, once they make a fatal error. We can thus get back at them, for compelling the rest of us, if only for reasons of self-defense, to struggle that much harder for our own successes.

But holding to that threat means that we must accept the ideal of success that they represent—the gathering of fame, money, power.

If they gain those, and keep them, we have nothing to say. They have done the job they set out to do—which is nothing more or less than the rest of us hope for.

Thus we find ourselves trying to make new lives on an old base: if a woman will be judged for what she is, a man will be judged by what he does; and what he does, by how far it takes him in the world, how much of a mark he leaves on it.

So he feels. And the feeling goes deeper than we often recognize: not just deep enough to live for, but deep enough to die for.

PART
IV

THE MARRIAGE OF WORK AND DEATH

Her room and board
he can afford, he has made friends
of common pains
and meets his ends.

Oh god, decry
such common finery as puts the need
before the bed, makes true what is
the lie indeed.

—Robert Creeley, *The Bed*

CHAPTER
12

The Sidney Carton Complex

I cannot count how many times I have fantasized dying gloriously, in front of a woman, for her sake. It is ridiculous, I know; the stuff of supermarket romances, nothing at all like the normal course of my life. But the feelings behind it are no less real.

The fantasy combines nobility and relief—a final heroic effort that wins the prize, and simultaneously relieves one from carrying it through life. I felt it working in me one night when I was walking with a woman I loved, and a big, mean man blocked our path and demanded money. The thought and the action were simultaneous in me; I pulled the woman around my back, and kept my face to the man as we moved around him. If someone would be beaten, it would have to be me—or I would not be worthy of this woman. Or any woman. And if I have not always been so brave, morally or physically, I can recall those moments only in shame.

Like our parents, we are the inheritors of a certain code of honor—which we can trace back to the (much-abused, in practice) ideals of chivalry in the later Middle Ages. Part of that code was to protect the weak. (A man must therefore be strong.) Part of it was to keep one's pledge, to fight for the name of a woman. (The most curious modern specimen of this commandment I ever met was a guy who spent every night in Manhattan until three A.M. with his drinking buddies and mistress, then drove across the George Washington Bridge so his kids would see him at breakfast with his wife. He didn't love her anymore, but he kept it private, kept some shred of his pledge to love, honor, obey.) And part of it was to be ready to die for the sake of an ideal—in the chivalric code, represented by "pure" womanhood, from the Virgin Mary to the virgin lady, the good wife.

"Women and children first" is one saying we have about such sacrifices. The saying comes from the law and customs of the sea; in one known case, a British regiment went down with the ship off the coast of Africa, while their wives and kids took the lifeboats to safety. Men are not always so noble; the rich men who shoved aside poor women and children in their haste to leave the *Titanic* are one example. But their brutality was balanced by the fact that the all-male orchestra played calming music till the ship sank, with them on it. The exception here turns out to confirm the rule: *a man is expected, and expects himself, to value women and children more highly than he values himself, to the point of giving up his life for them.*

Such a death, in literature, is almost universally represented as more meaningful to a man (and the witnesses to his act) than dying for his own sake. It has been portrayed, time and again, as a way of joining something greater than himself. Even Ernest Hemingway, that self-consciously hardboiled realist, fell back on it at the end of *For Whom the Bell Tolls,* when his hero dies in combat after sending off his lover to bear his memory, and thus to grant him eternal glory. *It is the act of love that creates a world, instead of the making of a world that kills love.*

I am fully aware that the male sense of moral inferiority to a woman—and *that is exactly what is at work behind this fantasy, and what is redeemed through it*—has hardly been the sole theme of relations between the sexes, now or in history. But it has nonetheless been a constant and powerful theme of Western culture for at least a century; and I believe that *it still plays an active role in persuading men to give the greater part of their lives to a job.*

Look at how the fantasy runs through Charles Dickens' novel *A Tale of Two Cities,* in which a beautiful and pure woman is pursued by two men. The men are mirror visions of each other—so alike that in a courtroom, a witness is unable to tell the difference between their faces. But their souls are a different matter. One of them is an alcoholic, who earns his pitiful living writing legal briefs for cases of dubious merit; the other is a man of such high principle that he will later risk his life in Revolutionary France for the sake of a loyal servant whom he has not seen in years. The woman they both love chooses the man of principle for her husband, of course; even the disappointed suitor, Sidney Carton, realizes that it could not be otherwise. But before vanishing from her life, he tells her that if ever she has need of him, no matter how terrible the task, she need only raise her voice, and he will hear.

When Carton learns that his rival, the man who claimed the woman he loves, has been imprisoned in France, he goes there without waiting to be asked, to join his beloved and offer what comfort he can. Using the kind of connections only a man familiar with criminals could have, he arranges to smuggle the good husband out of prison—and to take his place on the guillotine. In the famous closing scene, he comforts a terrified girl about to mount the scaffold, facing death with as calm a courage as any man could claim. And amidst the carnage, he thinks ahead, to the child his rival and his beloved will name after him, the eternal love his sacrifice has earned him.

Carton's resemblance to the man who lives in his place is not merely a clever plot device: as with Maynard G. Krebs and Dobie Gillis, it is a way of representing a divide in the soul of a man, between honor and baseness. Carton does not have what it takes to live for a woman—but he has what it takes to die for her. And only in that way can he become a man. *Only then can he be equal to the woman he loves.*

You can sometimes read certain attitudes on men's faces, when those faces are trained on women; something like the desperate longing of Sidney Carton for the prize he could never capture, combined with a smiling, covert resentment (not unlike what you see on the face of the secretary whose boss would be out of a job without her to do his dirty work). The feeling behind those faces is: I can never be good enough for this broad. How we want her—her beauty, her liveliness, her love. How we resent her, not only because she can withhold it but also because she has the right to do so. The legal right—boys who insist on "yes" to girls who say "no" are called rapists—and the moral right. *In some way, she is our better.*

That attitude gives the punch to Cary Grant's line in *Mr. Lucky,* a film made during World War II, when as a lowlife gangster he snarls at a rich girl, "You're so *very, very good.* And everyone else is *bad.*"

In this film, he is bad indeed—yet she needs him, for the services and excitement he can provide. And what makes Grant good, finally, is that he quits gangstering and takes a dirty, dangerous job in the wartime Merchant Marine, from which he finally returns to claim the girl.

Change the ending—a torpedo hits his ship, he drowns, she gets the telegram from the Department of War (as it was then honestly called)—and it is the story of a Sidney Carton, who took his only chance for redemption in the eyes of the woman he loved.

.   .   .

When a man finds "The Girl," as Fitzgerald called her with such poignant awe—this woman whose love redeems whatever secret evil or shortcoming resides in him; who for Fitzgerald was the emblem of a rich heaven ("gleaming like silver, safe and proud above the hot struggles of the poor," was how he described that clean but careless flower, Daisy, in *The Great Gatsby*)— he remains unsure that he deserves her. He must earn her love, every day. And that is, in the main, what men do, or try to do.

But whatever his sacrifice, short of a final, heroic one, he is still "not worthy of her," as the quaint English nineteenth-century phrase put it. And he can never be. *Even a good man, if the men I have known were any good, has felt this.* She is his "better half," as she always was. She is what gives meaning to his life, as he cannot give meaning to hers.

But he would lay down his coat, his dollars, his life for her.

He would even get a job for her.

And when he does, in some sense, he will be purified. The bad in him will fall away, as he stands to meet his maker—and his mate. In her gratitude, her approval, he will find a respect, a cleanliness he cannot provide himself. "My wife is happy," a garbage-truck driver—talk about dirty work— told Terkel in *Working.* "This is the big thing. She doesn't look down on me."

At work among men, and when he comes home to the woman who depends on him, he can find a pardon from unworthiness—in the eyes of colleagues, who approve the way he does his job, and in the eyes of a woman who, for all her powers, depends on him, and for whom he sacrifices his life in labor.

If we have started to see working as a sin that demands pardon, it is also still the main way a man buys pardon for his sins. Unlike Sidney Carton, we will not be called on to die for a woman. *We will be called on, and call on ourselves, to live for one;* and the way we meet that demand, most often, is to tell ourselves that we are working for her.

But why do we yearn for such proofs of our worthiness? *Why can't we be good enough, just as we are?*

THE SUPERIOR SEX

One of the dicta of feminism that I found most confusing was the idea that men consider themselves superior to women. My perception was always quite the opposite. It seemed to me, long before men started running around taking seminars on "intuition" and other previously feminine traits, that neither men nor women believed that males constitute the better sex.

Perhaps men are still superior in "upper body strength," as the male cadets of West Point argued so proudly and pathetically to Friedan when she asked them to account for their hostility to female cadets. Perhaps men could get away with claiming that they were more "rational," less "emotional," than women—as they did, before we started to think of the world as a model of cold rationality gone mad.

But lately—in fact, over the past century—it has been more and more difficult to argue the case that men are the moral betters of women. On the contrary, *we take it for granted that in terms of their humanity, women are better than men.* (Which, not incidentally, is one reason that the jeremiads of the feminist movement created such anguished guilt in men who listened to its message. If a woman said we were pigs, we were already partly inclined to believe it.) And we recognize that fact in numerous ways.

Instead of simply portraying Woman as the root of all evil—the idea that led to centuries of burning women across the fields of Renaissance Europe—we have more recently portrayed her as someone who at worst is led into temptation by men (like the much-discussed working girls who became prostitutes in the early part of the century), and who in normal circumstances plays the minder of manners (as in the Temperance Movement of the turn of the century, where women played a leading role). It is still women who carry the brunt of our moral crusades, like Nancy Reagan in her campaign against drugs (while her husband's contras were trafficking in cocaine), or the feminist antipornographers who harp on the bestial desires of men, or Helen Caldicott in her personal campaign against nuclear power and weaponry.

I do not mean to suggest that these campaigns are of equal importance, or of the same character, except in one way: their moral contents were defined by women. This was likewise the case in the radical movements I studied firsthand—home birth in California, the spiritual movement, the Greens in Germany, and the antiporn movement, all of which grew through the 1970s. Though men often served important political and practical roles in these movements, women were usually at the moral center. For example, they were the majority of the audience at the trial of lay midwife Rosalie Tarpening, arrested for murder when a baby she delivered died at the Madera, California, hospital; and it was a woman doctor whose testimony laid the blame on the hospital's emergency-room crew, a woman lawyer who brought out that testimony and won a dismissal of the murder charge (incidentally, contrary to legend, Tarpening was subsequently convicted of practicing medicine without a license).

When you hear the word "radical," look for the traditional. If women were active in radical movements—if feminism itself seemed such a radical proposition—they were nonetheless, in some way, building from our common sense of what Woman is, what she may be permitted. It could not be otherwise; one cannot overturn one's history by "reversing roles," when the actors remain the same. What feminism and other woman-centered movements did, along with whatever changes they achieved, was to reaffirm women in traditional roles. And one of the most important of those roles was one we associate with Mother: the laying-down of rules to boys.

THE SINNER MAN AND THE HOLY WOMAN

I have known two women who led such movements. Petra Kelly of the Green Party in West Germany, and Nikki Craft of Women Armed for Self-Protection (WASP) in the seventies, and later of the Preying (*sic*) Mantis Women's Brigade (a radical antiporn collective), were at the time I knew them (in the early eighties) driven by identical moral rages. The world they saw around them was corrupt, murderously so: it had killed people close to them (in Kelly's case, a sister whose death from cancer she blamed on chemical pollution). They would neither forgive nor forget that men had made this world, and that *men had broken the promises they had always made to women, to provide and to protect.*

That rage guided every aspect of their activism: if they could sometimes cut deals, with police or politicians or the press, they refused ever to compromise on their demands, breaking the law if the demands were not met, and then going to trial to tell their peers in the jury what they had done and why. (Craft, for example, made a habit of smearing the blood of raped women on the steps of the Santa Cruz Civic Auditorium, where the Miss California Pageant was held each year, in order to dramatize her belief that beauty pageants encourage the hatred of men for women, and thus their proclivity to rape.) And the rage, the purity of their moral anger, likewise guided their personal lives; if anyone in their relationships acted out of expediency, trying to keep their intimacy secret for the sake of public image, it was a man. In a word, these two women possessed a startling integrity; you could differ with their ideas, oppose their demands, but you could not accuse them of being corrupted.

That was part of what gave them an immense authority in their dealings with others, even though they had no power to speak of, except the power to be a terrible nuisance (both had abjured violence against persons, even if they sometimes practiced violence against property), to disrupt the ordinary practices of society. But when I think back to these women, there is the sensation of encountering a power greater than any individual could claim. *There was something archetypal in these women, something superhuman.* They counted on that factor, played with and against it—to shock, to surprise, to convince.

For example, when Kelly went into the hospital for exhaustion in the summer of 1982, a mainstream political party that wanted to recruit her from the Greens sent a huge bouquet of roses to her bedside. As soon as Kelly was discharged, she burned a mock nuclear cruise missile on the lawn of the party's national headquarters. She was, I think, aware of the phallic symbolism of rockets; and she was, I know, both amused and disgusted by the flowers, as if she were merely a little girl who could be wooed so easily.

She showed them otherwise, with her fire. She was no girl-child. She was Kali, the Destroyer, the Hindu goddess; she was Lilith, the first wife whom Adam betrayed, who never forgave. She was Woman, whose cold eye sees the dirt in little boys' clothes, who knows their wiles, who cannot be fooled. Kelly played the part to the hilt.

So did Craft. The first time I saw her, she was working at a fund-raising booth for the Mantis Brigade; a drunken man walked up to her, read her placards, and tried to pat her face. She moved her head. He tried again, and then a man led him away. He was helplessly drunk, helplessly aggressive. He could not control what he felt toward her. And in the two years that I reported on Craft's activities, I saw similar scenes repeated frequently. Men were always poking at her, trying to get her attention. They could not help responding to her. She touched something in them too profound to be ignored, when it suddenly reared up out of their unconscious, and stood before them, incarnated in a living person, a woman.

And mixed with the aggression she aroused in men was shame. The men's auxiliary of the Mantis Brigade was composed of guys who barely dared to raise their eyes, let alone their voices, to Craft ("interrupting a woman," one of them told me, "is a form of rape," and he admitted that he sometimes felt no better than a rapist). They would do a great deal to win her approval— to be reassured by her that they were not just dirty men, but clean New Men.

Once separatism took hold in feminist circles, where it became the dominant philosophy by the late seventies, few men were allowed to remain even at the outer edge of collectives like the Preying Mantis Brigade. These men had certain traits in common. Few of them looked masculine; they were mainly out-of-shape, skinny or plump. Some were gay. All of them, perhaps not coincidentally, were extremely anxious about their personal standards of "good" sexual behavior, in which anything that smacked of aggression was forbidden.

They took it for granted that men, as they were then, did not deserve a place in the hearts (if not the beds), of women. And they believed that the proper role for a feminized male was to do what a woman told him, when she told him, even if it meant denying his own existence. "Why should a women's world without men bother the self-image of a brother opposed to sexist oppression?" wrote one Mantis supporter in a local newspaper.

They thought that this was radical—to allow a woman, always, the final word, when it came to changing relations between the sexes. *But it was old, old.* Not only because voices keep whispering to us that our lives may only be realized in service to a woman; not only because these men were like children trying to earn their mothers' love.

The fact is that when the chips were down, they could behave as badly as any of the men they despised. They were as filled with resentment toward women as the average man, and when the right moment came, they were equally capable of letting their resentments out.

In the fall of 1981, in response to the activism of the Preying Mantis Brigade and such men as this—who had begun walking into local stores that stocked magazines like *Hustler* and *Penthouse,* and tearing the magazines to shreds—a woman friend and I cosponsored a weekend-long conference on erotica and pornography in Santa Cruz. The idea was a community debate, among the Christian and feminist groups who were trying to get pornography out of the county, and those who didn't belong to a group but felt concerned by the issue. My partner and I realized that the event would be controversial; in the course of putting it on, some local feminists tore down our posters, and conservative readers of a local newspaper demanded that our advertisements be canceled, both on the grounds that a Picasso drawing of a woman with a bull that we had used to illustrate our text was obscene. But no one hated the project more than the Santa Cruz Men Against Rape. And one of them went further than anyone else to try to prevent the conference from happening.

One of the first speakers we had lined up was a San Francisco antiporn group called Women Against Violence in Pornography and Media (WAVPM, since disbanded), whose slide show about pornography had generated local and national interest. A few days before the conference, a member of Men Against Rape called them up, and asked to speak with the woman who would be making the presentation at the conference. "I just think you should know," she recalled his words to me shortly afterward, "that there's a lot of controversy about this debate in the community, and there may be trouble." Her response, naturally, was to feel "intimidated," as she told me. ("Isn't that great," I later wrote to a local newspaper, "a man threatening women, in the name of feminism.")

Craft saved the day. She called WAVPM, and in essence gave her personal guarantee, which counted, since she was well-known in the antiporn movement, that the women would be safe in Santa Cruz. She then called the man who had made the threat, and told him: "You can't do this, it's censorship."

Now, I had already called him, and achieved nothing more substantial than an exchange of mutual hatred. But Craft made him apologize. She told him he'd been bad, and he admitted it.

The pathos, for me, was in seeing how a man who had turned his life inside out, like the Men Against Rape (who, I would like to know, can decently be for it?), ended up back where he started: *looking to a woman for approval and justification, and attacking women in revenge against this power to laud or condemn him.*

He acted out that conflict in an extreme way. But the shadow of his gestures fits the outlines of something experienced by many men, in their daily life at home with a woman. *We let our women tell us what we must be to them.*

We leave it to them to tell us what a good man might be. And if we are grateful for their approval, we are no less angry at their power to withhold it.

The pattern parallels and complements our relationship to work, to the world that men make. We work to please our women, and to provide for them, as a good man should.

But no matter how hard we work, we never quite lose the suspicion that we have left something undone, nor our anger at the possibility that a woman may know it.

THE SHAME OF SEX

If Dinnerstein is right, a woman reminds a man of the mother who cleaned his body, his clothing, his language (I too ate soap in my childhood)—who witnessed his inability to care for himself, as his working father did not. She was his first teacher, his first guardian, his first judge and jury. He cannot help loving and hating her; and he cannot grow up to be like her, and soothe his conflict by identifying with her, internalizing her. She remains outside him; he remains the child who fell from her arms.

She is a woman, from whom he receives a care he cannot or does not provide himself; for whom he gives himself in love and labor; and whose powers over him are balanced by her own, parallel dependence, on the fruits of his labor. We can replace her, but it seems that we cannot escape her.

Look at what has happened in our manners, now that aggressive feminine independence ("I can open the door for myself!") is out, and romance is in. Face-to-face with a woman, a man—a decent man, as we currently think of decent men—has an obligation to show her courtesy and respect, if not always obedience; if not, we find *him* that much less worthy of respect. He also has an obligation to make her life easier (the *Ladies' Home Journal* respondents, by a wide majority, liked having doors opened for them). If he does not make that effort, he is not a "good" man—at best, he is a bad boy, okay for fun, but awful for a good woman to live with.

Or even, in some circles, to dance with. Around 1980, when the film *Urban Cowboy* was a hit, a magazine sent me to report on the urban-cowboy bars springing up around San Francisco. One of the aspects of this fad that didn't appear in the movie, where the men treated women the way angry bulls treat their cows and the women liked it, was a code of etiquette that was quite opposed to feminist self-reliance. In those bars, the men in their big hats and high-heeled boots asked women to dance, escorted them to their seats, and paid for the first round of drinks. In a word, *they showed the women deference.* The macho costumes, like the tough-guy songs that the bands onstage were grinding out, were a cover for this deference, this polite submission. If a girl gave a man her heart, he had first to offer his hand, with something in it.

We have been saying lately that this is a sign of a turn backward, toward the kind of relationships men and women had (or were supposed to have had) in the fifties. I think it is less a turning back than an acceptance of what we have always been. There remains a covert comfort for men in staring at the pedestal on which women are placed, as tyrants who can grant us heavenly pleasures, heavenly pardons, and earthly comfort, in exchange for our labors; and for women, in claiming those powers, such as they are.

If men hate women, sometimes, for being better than they are, they are afraid to have women be just as bad as they are. A woman is one thing, but a woman no better than yourself is quite another. If men resent the power women have over them, in the kitchen and the bed, they remain worried about what would happen if women left those places and roles for good. *Then there would be no comfort to be found, no loving bath to wash away a man's sweat and his sins.*

. . .

In Dinnerstein's view, our sexual relationships are likewise part of a lifelong effort to come to terms with the memory of infantile dependence on a woman: for the man, to finally have a woman under his control; for a woman, to take the place of the woman who raised her, to be the object of a man's desire, of his need.

In this they can be separate, yet equal. Her desire, when it is like his own, brings her back to his level (that would be why he says, as I have heard so many men say, with such bullying amazement, "women want it just as much as men do").

And *his conquest is also a submission, once again, to a woman's touch, a confession of his own needs.* She is the symbol of his pride, and of his shame.

It is so common among us: a man desires a woman, and yet he resents her, because his desire confirms his disadvantage in their relations (which in his experience begins in those years when he takes his first job, and makes his first awkward approaches to women). *She can say no at any time*—unless you buy the separatist feminist argument that all sexual relations are mere rape—and unless he is a brute or a fool, he must accept it. *Every time he runs that risk, he knows a certain shame, of needing from her what he cannot provide himself* (unless he wants to be a "jerk-off" all his life), *and which another man cannot provide* (unless he wants to be, worse, a "faggot").

He is ashamed of his desire (as much as women were always supposed to be ashamed of their own), and ashamed of resenting her for what he feels; and the resentment must remain covert, feeding his shame—for how can she be, in any rational sense, to blame? He desires her not for anything she has done, but for what she is—a woman, a particular woman who excites him.

And there is another kind of shame, another reason that his desire confuses him, as it does most pointedly in young men who have never been with a woman in intimacy. I am thinking of a letter from a seventeen-year-old man to his father, in which he recounted how he had repeatedly fled to the boys' room at his high-school prom, to hide from the woman he loved the "monster" he became when he danced with her, and her closeness made him erect. *This is the shame a man feels about his own body, in the presence of a woman;* perhaps (Dinnerstein might say) like the shame a child feels in the presence of the woman who knew him when he made nothing but messes, who knew his helplessness, his dirtiness.

There is a story I have heard from many women, of how one night they turned to a man and said, "Take me"—the first man to whom they had ever said such a thing. And the man said no. It was not that he refused to give her what she wanted; he did not know what he could give her in exchange for her gift, her body.

Her pure body, so unlike his own dirty one. (She is made of "sugar 'n' spice and everything nice," he is made of "snips 'n' snails 'n' puppy-dogs' tails.")

That feeling is behind his sense that her love can redeem his desires, make them part of an act of love, instead of an outburst of pathetic, needy lust. Until she offers him that redemption, he is merely, as the separatists charged with such awful, biological-destiny irony in the seventies, a "dirty prick"—and he knows it. (That is why he washes his hands before leaving the bathroom, when he has touched nothing but his penis. There is a famous joke about this in the Ivy League: "At Yale, we wash our hands when we piss." "At Harvard, we don't piss on our hands.")

It was what I felt, the night I failed in making love, for the first time in my life, the woman willing and ready beside me: *I am taking something from her, more than I can give back.* Only if I had loved her, as I felt she loved me, could I have been worthy of her, her lover, not her defiler. But how could I be, when my love was so corrupted by a mere urge to satisfy myself?

Basketball star Kareem Abdul-Jabbar felt something like the same thing when his first opportunity to make love arrived—and he turned the girl down. And he was equally repelled by himself, and his partner (after the night I described above, I broke off with the woman; not because I had failed to make love with her, but because I was afraid to succeed the next time). "I just didn't want to lose it," he said in his autobiography, *Giant Steps,* "on the ground in the well-traveled darkness of Central Park, to this girl who was hardly a friend." Whom he did not love, as in his "teen dreams and heartfelt fantasies."

"When I finally did make love," said Kareem, "it was warm and affectionate but still bewildering."

And how.

Even when a woman says yes, a man not rarely feels, like a high-school boy begging his date to let him touch her breasts, that *he wants something from her which she does not want from him, and she is right not to want it;* that she can deny it to him, with reason, when she pleases.

That is why some of us say that he "wants only one thing" from her— and that she has the right to make him pay for it, one way or the other.

The idea is both naive and crude, of course. Most of us are far too sophisticated to subscribe to such a cliché these days.

But pay we do. Do we not?

Often enough, we do: He pays. She stays. They make a bargain, as equals of a sort.

The bargain is based on negative gender equality: each falls to the other's level.

The kind of equality we can no longer justify to ourselves, and the one we know best how to live with. The easiest kind there is, and the most painful.

CHAPTER
—— 13 ——

Where the Boys Are... Buried

The running gag of history is that women are in charge of things, that "the hand which rocks the cradle rules the world." Women do have certain powers over men, but ruling the world is not usually the job they have at hand; nor is building it. That is still what men do, and women still take care of the men (and their children) who do it.

But the idea that women are really running the show, that a man works only for his partner's pleasure and at her bidding, keeps its hold on us. It is the bitter subtext under the stress debate—that all the running a man does to impress and support a woman only brings him closer to the grave. This is the reverse image of the Sidney Carton complex—a man whose sacrifice makes him not noble, but contemptible; not a martyr for a great cause, but a mere victim. And yet this image, too, gives men a strange satisfaction, that work helps to provide.

I have suggested that in some ways, the interests of men and women are parallel, when it comes to the family—that *if working for a family is a sacrifice, it is also a pleasurable choice, and a way for a man to feel part of something greater than himself.* It is not, in other words, merely a slavery into which a man is trapped, and which he may brandish to justify his resentment of his mistress, who is also his master. *It is a way for a man to satisfy real and profound needs for his own sake.*

But even back in the contented, placid, mature fifties, the satisfaction was indirect—and bitter. You can sense the bitterness, at a time when divorce was a less casual solution to marital problems, in Vincente Minnelli's 1950 film *Father of the Bride.*

Spencer Tracy, as the father, is told continually by his male friends that his daughter's wedding will bleed his wallet dry. When the big day comes, he is so busy trying to be useful that he misses saying good-bye to his beloved child. It is all played affectionately, and one never doubts the love Tracy and his family feel for each other, but the comedy has a sharp edge. Father pays for the party, but he never gets any fun from it. All he gets is the bills.

And old. The marriage of his daughter is a sign of age, one he fights throughout the film (in one scene, he stuffs himself into a coat he wore in his youth, to prove he hasn't fattened with the years). But it is a lost fight; like everyone around him, as a man sang in the hit fifties musical *Take Me Along,* he is growing old.

And then he would die.

Then everyone would see how hard he had worked. They would be ashamed of themselves for making him do it. *And he would be proved right, morally and practically: he had done it all for their sakes.*

Women are aware of that odd, resentful pleasure in us; the martyr complex is one of the parts of us that women hate and distrust, as often and as much as they appreciate the real sacrifices on which men's families depend. The distrust is particularly pronounced in the daughters of successful men, especially those who ignored their families or divorced their wives (in my observation, a good percentage of feminists came out of such families). What these women saw was a man who used his loved ones to prove to the world that he had a heart, that he was hard but not inhuman, yet gave little to others in a human way. Not surprisingly, the women who witnessed this hypocrisy believe that giving himself to work is just a façade behind which a man can take moral credit for doing what he wants to do.

But men had a reason and defense for making the claim that work was a lethal sacrifice: *behind the rage and nobility men felt in the breadwinner role was an awareness of their greater mortality, relative to women.* And there was an element of reality in this complaint, one available since the fifties to anyone who can read numbers (a talent at which we American men excel). *In demographic terms, the numbers that define a population, men were on the losing side of a revolution.*

Quite simply, as of the 1950 census there were fewer men among us than there were women, for the first time in American history. *Men were no longer the majority, in a society where the majority rules*—a majority that potentially was made up of women, after the Woman Suffrage Movement won them the vote in the 1920s. (If women did not exercise that power for their own interests, as opposed to men's, an awareness of their potential to do so nonetheless showed in the male opposition to the suffragettes, as to the Equal Rights Amendment in the seventies and eighties.)

There were several causes for this demographic shift. One was that, beginning in 1924, when free immigration to the United States was replaced by an ethnic quota system, the massive influx of foreigners to our country was greatly slowed. A majority of the immigrants had always been men— adventurers or desperate fathers, with just enough money to buy themselves a one-way ticket to America.

Another was that by mid-century, large families were becoming a rarity— they are even rarer now—and obstetrics had advanced to a point where the death of a woman in childbirth was unusual. War deaths—the U.S. suffered some 350,000 men killed in World War II, and 40,000 in Korea (and very few women in either)—were also involved. (The ratio of men to women likewise dropped in the 1920 and 1980 censuses, following World War I and the Vietnam war. A recent study of Vietnam veterans showed that their death rates are one-third higher than for other men their age, which may suggest that the effect of war on the life expectancy of men does not end when the guns are put down.)

But taking all that into account, one must still wonder why *the gap that began in 1950, when there were 98.7 men for every 100 women in the population, kept widening through the next three censuses.* By 1980 there were 94.5 males in the U.S. population for every 100 females.

People were not unaware of this trend in the 1950s. Ehrenreich quotes an article from *Today's Health* in 1957: "You men are the weaker sex. Your average lifetime is about four years less than that of women." Moreover, the article continued, "You have a greater chance of dying in each of life's decades than have your womenfolk."

That is still true, except that by 1983, women's lead over men in terms of average lifespan had *widened* to seven years. Men lived to 71, on average, women to 78. Our population was aging, toward a median age of 30 (up from 28 only a decade before); but the survivors were mainly women. "If I were to die tomorrow there would be 20 women or more on my doorstep after my husband the next day," gerontologist Jane Porcino, fifty-eight, told *New York Times* reporter Robert Lindsey in 1981. Behind that shameless behavior, said Porcino, was "the competition for older, unattached men" in a population group where women outnumber men three to two.

It was not merely coincidence, I think, that with a remarkably self-pitying tone, men in the 1950s portrayed their wives as the satisfied dominatrixes of American society—an idea it would take all the fury of the Second Wave of feminism to overturn. In reviewing a half-dozen episodes from the popular 1950s television series *The Honeymooners,* I saw not one in which Alice, the wife of bus driver Ralph Kramden—listen to that name: *crammed in*— does not confront and subdue a rebellion from her silly mate. "I'm the master of this house!" Ralph will shout, while Alice folds her arms, frowns, and waits for him to fall on his face, get up, and admit in a voice half-wheedling, half-proud, "Baby, you're the greatest."

If Alice Kramden always got the last word over Ralph, it was partly because she would still be fixing dinner when he was dead. So would the mother of a Midwest farmgirl whom Kerouac meets on a bus in *On the Road,* whose man has "spent his whole life supporting a woman and her outcroppings and no credit or adoration."

The working stiff and the beatnik had one thing in common: when it was all over, women would take the outcroppings, and men would have the unmarked, unloved, forgotten graves. They would be replaced by the next guy who could do the job, like the embattled homesteader in *Shane* who picks up his rifle to fight off a gunslinger, and tells his wife that "I never thought I'd be saying this, but if I don't come back," then the mysterious stranger, Shane, will do just as well by her as he could. A man will die, doing what he has to do, and someone else will take his place.

This feeling remains strong in us. But it can be broken, if we would take a moment to look death in the face. And it is one that we will have to break, if we are going to get the changes we want in our lives.

The fact is that, *even if by some stretches in our imaginations we are dying for the sake of women, it is mainly women who are keeping us from dying.*

THE DEMOGRAPHY OF DEATH

I would not have thought to count the dead if I had not heard so many women, in the past ten years, complain that "there aren't any good men around." It is not only, as bitter sophisticates say, that "the only good men are gay," nor that the rest of us are "afraid of commitment," nor that women have become impossibly picky. The plainest, simplest, most unanswerable reason that there aren't enough men to go around in the United States is that a lot of the ones who were going around are gone. They are dead; they died young. Yet this is something we take, incredibly, for granted. *We say that there are many more unmarried women than unmarried men, and we do not ask: What happened to the men?*

We can largely rule out one popular explanation: the theory that men are simply the weaker sex, beginning with birth, has only marginal evidence behind it. While it is true that boy children (under 15) are more likely to die than girl children, it is also true that death rates for both have fallen steadily and dramatically since 1960, with the important and scandalous exception of our "inner cities." For example, among infants under one year of age, the overall death rate for boys fell from 3.05 percent in 1960 to 1.23 percent in 1983; for girls, the rate went from 2.32 to 0.92 percent. In absolute and relative terms, the mortality gap between boy and girl babies has largely been closed.

Moreover, that first year of life accounts for some 60 percent of the *total* difference in mortality between boys and girls to age 15. In other words, if boys are biologically weaker, it doesn't show much between the ages of 1 and 15. And *the greater number of boys who die does not efface their numerical advantage in the population, because a slightly higher percentage of live births are boys.* In 1980 there were 104.6 boys under 15 for every 100 girls, and the boys' numerical edge lasted through the next decade of life, though it steadily eroded.

What eroded it—and what was so terribly difficult for me to take account of—were the various forms of what is called "sudden death." It is one thing to be aware that if you are a man under 25, you will pay higher insurance rates on your car than any other category of the population, because insurance-company actuarial tables show that you are the most likely to kill yourself or someone else at the wheel. It is another to attend four funerals of your friends, following fatal crashes, in a span of less than two years, as I did between the ages of 19 and 21. A woman friend reminded me of something I said when I met her at the fourth: "Our friends seem to have a high mortality rate." Our male friends. I said it, and I forgot it, because I could not bear to think about it.

In 1982, a bit less than three men under 25 died in a car for every woman. If you count all forms of sudden death—accidents, homicide, and suicide—the difference between young men and young women is even more striking. The peak year was 1980, when 119.6 young men died suddenly per 100,000 in their demographic group, and 36.3 women. In sum, *relative to women their own age, men are more than three times as likely to meet a sudden end.*

That was true whether you were talking about murder—despite a jump of 121 percent in the homicide rate of young women from 1960 to 1982, which men more than matched—or suicide. Only men over 75 had a higher rate of sudden death than men under 25. And sudden death accounted for more than half of *all* deaths among young men in 1982. *It is the biggest single reason that at the age of 25, there are more women than men in the population.*

What about older men? In 1980, significantly more men than women died of heart disease, respiratory diseases, diseases of the digestive system, cancers; the differences begin to become highly noticeable at the age of 35, when these illnesses pick up the slack for a decline in the number of accidental deaths among men. They balloon at age 45, when men's death rate from all causes is 73 percent higher than women's. Women's death rates do not catch up until after the age of 75—by which time most men are already dead, and the ones who are left are outnumbered two to one by women. The gap in death rates between men and women, even after a decline of 20 percent in the overall death rate since 1950, is still significant: in 1983, the male death rate was still 20 percent higher than the rate for women.

Leaving aside sudden death, when you consider the illnesses that carry mature men off, and the known risk factors for those maladies, you see very quickly that *men are still risking their lives, though in a different way from the ones that got so many of them killed in youth.*

For example, while women are more likely to be moderate drinkers (less than one drink a week) than are men, they are half again as likely not to drink at all as their menfolk—and only about one-third as likely to take a drink three times a week or more. It is hardly coincidental that from the ages of 25 to 75, men are twice as likely to die of cirrhosis of the liver as women. Likewise, respiratory infections accounted for over 120,000 deaths in 1980, 62 percent of them men. By no coincidence, men make up almost exactly the same percentage of those who smoke. They also accounted for about three out of four lung-cancer victims, over 75,000 of them.

When I called Meyer Friedman, coauthor of *Type A Behavior and Your Heart,* in 1981 to discuss his findings about the relation of stress to heart attacks, he admitted that these kinds of risk factors play a role in the Type A's miserable fate. "On the whole," he said in response to a direct question, "they have bad dietary habits." Nor did they exercise much, he noted; as with proper eating, they did not have the time. Both exercise and avoidance of certain kinds of foods—specifically, the kind of fat-rich foods that businessmen consume in restaurants—are known to be good insurance against heart attacks; so is getting enough sleep, another area where the Type A's tend to fall short.

In other words, *you do not need to mention stress in order to explain why these men get heart attacks.* They have already stacked the odds against living to a ripe old age.

What the numbers show, is that from childhood through youth, and all through manhood to old age, *men are shockingly less careful about the risks they run with their health than women are.* It makes you wonder if blaming stress is easier than giving up the right to be careless—*a right that depends, in practice, on the willingness of women to take care of men.*

THE TOUCH THAT RAISES THE DEAD

> *"Sue, darling—you* can't *come in now! Not yet—!"*
> *"But you've been working for* hours—*without food, without rest—I won't* stand *for it!*
> *"You're my* husband *now, Reed Richards! And I want to keep you* healthy!
> *"The world won't come to an end if you take time out for dinner!"*
> *"I wish I could be* sure *of that!"*
> *"Wha-what do you* mean?"

—from "The Coming of Galactus," by Stan Lee

Women are indeed willing to take care of men—especially the women of the powerful among us. The top ranks of American business are not only overwhelmingly male, they are overwhelmingly married. Taking care of an ambitious man who won't take care of himself, or doesn't have the time to do it, is no easy task. And American industry recognizes the fact.

In the case of my friend Peter, his marriage was cause for an immediate promotion; it was an asset that made him "more valuable" in the eyes of the company, as he told me. Indeed he was: he was no longer on his own; he had someone to look after him, to make sure he had clean shirts for meetings with clients, and hot meals when he stumbled home, worn out, as he so often did during a month I spent as a guest in their apartment. He was a more secure investment. He was less likely to fail the company, not to mention his wife.

Peter often said, "the stress is unbelievable," when the subject of his highly paid, high-travel, highly competitive work came up. And when he did, his wife would do something to comfort him—offer a drink, a caress, a word of sympathy. Her attention to him was never less than constant and caring, and if you have ever undertaken such a task, you know that it can be as exhausting as any other. *That is still a woman's job, and a literally vital one.* Had she not been there to do it, he would quickly have reached his limits of exhaustion, emotionally and physically.

I have depended on such comfort, as much as any man; and women have offered it to me, with the expectation that I would need it as much as they needed whatever I could offer. Part of that comfort was to tell me when to stop working, when to put aside the job and take and give pleasure of different kinds—to make love, share a meal, talk about something interesting or amusing to others. And *I found it easier to let a woman give me those choices than to make those decisions for myself;* left on my own, I would work past my capacities.

If my experience is as much like other men's as I think, it indicates a more than personal tendency to let *women bear the responsibility for maintaining a balance in our lives*—literally, a healthy balance.

If so, then the stress debate was *not* only a matter of men saying that they were working themselves to death for women. What remained unspoken in the dialogue of stress (and not by coincidence) was that *men were asking permission and approval from women for not killing themselves. They were asking women to recognize that it is harder to live for someone than to die for her, and to tell men when it had become hard enough.*

They were asking women for the right to change, in a certain way: to put something ahead of work, to get out of the rat race when the stress rose too high. This change involved a revolt against the breadwinner role, as Ehrenreich showed, but it also involved a *reform* of that role—*the negotiating of limits on what could be expected of a breadwinner, limits that men were afraid or incapable of setting for themselves.*

Such a change is still being negotiated. That may be one reason why, despite a drop in overall death rates, and a sharp decline in death rates from stress-related diseases (a decline that did not alter the fact that men still died faster from them), we are still obsessed with stress. Not coincidentally, *we are still negotiating the balance between men's responsibilities to their work and to their loved ones.* And we still find defining a new balance, one more satisfying to both men and women, to be a most difficult task. It demands a change beyond what we have achieved in thirty years of struggling.

Doctors have always known that it is very difficult to get people to change their behavior, even with the threat of illness hanging over them. The change a person makes because of this threat—as we are now learning again, through the AIDS epidemic—is usually directly proportional to how seriously he or she views the danger. In other words, if you think you are merely risking a cold, you may not hesitate to kiss an exciting stranger; if you think the stranger is carrying a fatal AIDS virus in his or her saliva, you may think twice and walk away.

Stress has been used by us to urge women, and especially men, to change, and to justify the changes they are trying to make. But stress is not the "number-one killer" among us, whatever certain doctors tell the public.

What claimed more and more victims over the past thirty years was the violence men did themselves, and each other. That has been the motor of the stress debate, even if we ignored the racket it makes. If we want to shut that motor off—and in the process, to find another source of energy for our intimate lives—we had best take a close look at the violence which fuels it.

CHAPTER
—— 14 ——

All Against All

And be there never so great a Multitude; yet if their actions be directed according to their particular judgements, and particular appetites, they can expect thereby no defence, nor protection, neither against a Common enemy, nor against the injuries of one another. For being distracted in opinions concerning the best use and application of their strength, they do not help, but hinder one another... but also when there is no common enemy, they make warre upon each other, for their particular interests.

—Thomas Hobbes, *Leviathan*

There is something I have never been able to explain to a woman, or to discuss in polite company, for the simple reason that it is obscene—"beyond the customary limits of candor," as the legal definition goes. It concerns the violence men do each other, and which women are, in the main, unable to understand.

In part, I think, this is because women don't like to hear about it. They can't stand the boys-together tone in which the subject comes up, the mix of false modesty and boastfulness that creeps into a man's memories of the time he stood up to a bully, or went to war. (Genuinely modest men will not talk about their heroism until they are asked, as they rarely are, and then they will shrug, as if to say, "You do what you have to do.") And because it is still an exceptional experience (we will look at the relevant statistics in a moment) for a woman to be physically assaulted by someone who is capable of and willing to hurt another person very badly indeed, it is a rare woman who can sense the pain in these memories, the rage and bewilderment and dismay.

And a rare man who can permit himself to admit to it, without feeling far less of a man. One may search through the novels of Ernest Hemingway, Ken Kesey, Jr., Theodore Dreiser, Norman Mailer, or almost anyone else you care to mention, and find nothing that bears directly on the horror a man feels when he realizes, at a very early age, that beating or being beaten on is going to be a more or less constant threat in his life; that it is always going to occupy some shadowy corner of his consciousness, no matter what he does to avoid it. The writers who raise the subject tend to romanticize the experience, to see it as just another test of manhood, to be faced with noble forbearance. The terror of it is something else again—the terror of helplessness, of facing a threat beyond one's powers; of being literally and figuratively emasculated.

(Certain readers may be offended by the terms in which men think about this issue. I apologize to them for the language I am about to use; I know that it is obscene, but it happens to be men's own.)

Stephen King got it right in *The Body,* a novella about four young boys who search the Maine woods for another boy who was struck and killed by a train. At the moment they find the body, they are confronted by a gang of teenagers who want to claim the gruesome prize for themselves. The little kids refuse; one of them, the narrator, tells the leader of the gang, "Suck my fat one, you dime-store hood." (Note the sexual insult, the boast.) At which the older, bigger, tougher boy tells his friends, "I'm gonna break both his fuckin' arms." Writes King:

> I went dead cold. . . . He meant it, you see; the years between then and now have changed my mind about a lot of things, but not about that. When Ace said he was going to break both my arms, he absolutely meant it.

Didn't he, though. I met my own Ace at the age of eleven, a bit younger than the hero of King's novella. I had always fought with my brothers, of course, and sometimes we had hurt each other, in minor ways; but the Preacher, as we called him at the camp where I spent that summer, was something else again. He was about Ace's age, seventeen or so, a big, heavily muscled, frustrated young man, stuck with a pack of kids out in the woods. He needed an outlet for whatever was bothering him, and I provided it. I was the odd boy out in the bunk: a bigmouthed, eggheaded child—an expert at making people dislike me. In other words, I was isolated, visibly weak, without protectors. No one spoke up when the Preacher began, subtly, to pick on me.

He would shove me out of his way, or snarl and move in my direction, just to watch me jump. Then one day he went a little further: he tried to steal a leather halter I was responsible for maintaining at the camp stable, and when I protested, he threw it in my face from a yard away and knocked me down. A few days later, he was waiting by the bathroom door when I went to urinate in the morning, holding a whip. And he used it on me, that day, and every day, warning me not to complain, or worse would happen.

God only knows where he would have stopped. But finally, he was stopped; not by the camp counselors, who left me to my fate, but by a boy of about fifteen, the only boy in the bunk who was tough enough and brave enough to frighten the Preacher. Like the Preacher, he didn't care about me personally, but he had a sense of fairness. And one day he asked me, "Is Preacher pickin' on you?" I just looked at him, and he knew my look. He went over to the Preacher and said, "If you ever lay a finger on that kid again, I'll kill you."

And the Preacher backed down. He left me alone.

Twenty years passed before I brought that story up in company. Around a café table there were my mother (who had never understood why I was so terribly unhappy at that camp), a married couple, and their ten-year-old son. The boy had been raving about something he had seen on the evening news, "an army of cops" who had laid siege to a tenement full of drug dealers in New York City. He was as excited as if he'd seen a war movie. I said, "I don't like stories like that," and his father asked me why. I found myself recounting what had happened that summer.

The little boy stared at me, his mouth open. When I had finished, he said, "You're lying."

"No, I'm not."

"You're lying," he repeated, and then he positively screamed: "Liar!"

Cops killing pushers was the kind of fantasy he could watch on TV, you see. But he knew that what I was talking about could happen to him. In one way or another, it probably had—enough to make the mere mention of it frighten him out of his wits.

Then I knew that what had happened to me was neither strange nor unusual. And that was why, when I interviewed men for this book, I asked every one of them to recall how often, and at what age, they had fought with other boys; if they had ever been seriously injured, or seen someone badly hurt, in a fight; and how they defended themselves from the threat of violence.

Their reponses fit a pattern—a sad and universal model. And that pattern has, I believe, a great deal to do with how we work and love.

Of the men in my sample, only two declared that they had never either been in a fight or witnessed one in which someone was seriously hurt. (By "serious" I mean injured so severely that blood was flowing, bones were broken, physical functioning more than momentarily impaired.) Both denied ever having been physically threatened by other men, either. They were from similar upper-middle-class backgrounds, raised in nice neighborhoods where fighting never went beyond the you-push-me, I-push-you-back stage.

The first time I heard this denial, I let it pass and moved on to other subjects. An hour later the man suddenly recalled, in a raised voice, two occasions when another man had threatened him. On both occasions—at a party, and in a city street on a holiday weekend—he was in the company of a woman, when a guy suddenly stepped up to him and threatened to break his face. He had backed down, away; and though he thought that fighting was "infantile," he trembled with rage to remember the humiliation he had felt. "The fact is," he said, "I don't know how to fight. And I felt like I should," not only for his own sake, but to defend the woman his tormentors had insulted in his presence. And he felt that it could happen again.

The other man who fit this category remembered, under my probing, a time when a car stopped on the road where he was hitchhiking, and a man got out holding a knife; he gave him money, and the man went away. As he saw it, he had lost nothing but a few dollars.

Money meant little enough to him; he had inherited a trust fund that freed him from having to enter into the competition for wealth that most men know. His artistic career was likewise noncompetitive, and so far largely unsuccessful, measured by fame or fortune. He was passive in his relationships with women—his longest affair had lasted less than two years, the others no more than a few months—and apologetic that he had slept with "only fifteen" women in his thirty-five years (which is indeed a low figure for men of his generation in my sample). It seemed to me that he had learned to practice avoidance of conflict and confrontation to an extraordinary degree; it did not seem to me that he had avoided an awareness of the dangers of life.

The rest of my interview subjects had learned different skills. None of them were outright brutes, the kind of men who would as soon hit another human being as look at him or her. But all of them had come up against a man who meant them physical harm—at school, in a bar, in the street. It was a normal part of growing up.

One of them had made a point of refusing to fight. It was a moral stance, and an honorable one, for which he was respected. But he could not have escaped beatings, it turned out, if he had not had a protector, like me in that summer when the Preacher taught me about hell on earth. He was absolved from the interracial war that went on in his Southwest farm community, where the sons of migrant workers fought it out with the Anglos, because his father was head of the local school system, and was known and respected for his work in favor of civil rights. And on the one occasion when a drunken guy from another school slugged him for wandering off his own turf, the other man's older brother stood up for the pacifist, and stopped the massacre on the grounds of fairness. Another protector.

All of the rest of them said, more or less, what a black man raised in a tough neighborhood told me: "I made it plain to people that it wasn't worth the trouble to fuck with me." They defended themselves, or the people they cared about, when they had to, and only then. "I didn't go lookin' for trouble," they said, over and over again, "but I didn't run away from it." They might sometimes back away from it, fists and faces toward their adversaries; but they didn't turn their backs on it.

At the least, like a man who shunned the tough part of the Oklahoma town where he grew up, and the guys who were "just plain crazy," they avoided it. But they never forgot where the violence could be found. When I asked this man, who had kept contact with his childhood friends after moving to New York City, what they talked about at their reunions, he grinned, shook his head, and said: "Those crazies."

My subjects had learned in their bones what I learned, that summer when the Preacher was working me over, lying in wait by the corners where I had to pass: that you must keep a distance between yourself and your enemy, and never put yourself into a position where he can, in the common phrases, "kick your ass," or "fuck you over." If avoidance was to be effective, it nonetheless demanded that they keep the enemy in their field of vision. And when they grew stronger, to be armed and ready, too bad to mess with, able to run and fight another day—to prevail, by force or wit, sooner or later. It was part of the motivation, often enough, that led them toward success, and the power and security it offers. And in the short term, their stance allowed them to keep their honor in two ways: they refused not only to receive, but to inflict violence. They avoided the shame of the victim, and the shame of the bully.

There is a connection here to one of the masculine traits that women have described to me, over and over, with angered wonder: the tendency of men to avoid or minimize emotional confrontation and pain. I became aware of it while speaking with women who had undergone miscarriages—and whose lovers had afterward told them to ignore their pain, and seemed to ignore it themselves. The women could not understand why the men didn't care about their suffering, and they were deeply shocked. I did not meet their partners, but it happened that these conversations followed the same event in my own household, to which I had initially responded like those other men.

And I realized that my own efforts to deal with my wife's pain were not unlike the oblique encouragement—which is what it was—other men had offered me, when I shattered one of my knees on a football field, for example. "Take it easy," they'd said, "it's nothin'." What they were trying to tell me was that to give in to pain was simply and awfully to become helpless before it, and then before whatever came next. The comfort they offered was cold enough, but it was still a kind of comfort—contingent, however, on knowing that the men gathered around me had felt such pain before, and that their silence was the quiet of communion, of shared understanding. And that was the best comfort I or they could hope for, from beings like ourselves. But it is not, I have noticed, the kind of warm and detailed sympathy that women expect from and give to each other—or for that matter, to their men.

Where confrontation arises between men and women, a parallel gap in their responses seems to occur. The gap begins, I think, in the fact that before men learn about intimacy, they have learned to walk away from disputes that arouse their own aggression or another man's, and the possibility of searing hurt that accompanies a fight. As in Selye's theory of stress, a general response to a particular situation is involved; but the response goes deeper than a man's adrenal glands. His sexuality, too, is implicated—one of the domains in which his intimacy with a woman is founded.

Look again at the language of violence: a beating, in some sense, is a negative sexual experience, a cruel fucking, in which anything could happen, and a man could not prevent it from happening. It is, in short, not unlike being raped. That is what the one man in my sample who had been raped told me—a man who had chosen to be homosexual, in part, because he had "never felt physically threatened in a room full of gay men." Generally, men will not admit to such a connection—perhaps, I would argue, for the same reason that women who have been raped hate to remember the experience, so charged with impotent rage and terror.

But the connection is felt, for the simple reason that a man can easily see it acted out, without particularly looking for it. On several occasions in junior high and high school, I saw boys "de-pantsed"—their trousers pulled down around their ankles, binding them, their buttocks and genitals help-lessly exposed. I was kicked, and saw other men kicked in their genitals, and learned to fight hard to keep another guy's hands or feet away from my beltline. And when I read in Lee Iacocca's autobiography that after being fired from the presidency of the Ford Motor Company by Henry Ford II, he "fantasized . . . about kicking him where it hurts," I suspect that behind his fantasy was a perfectly common experience.

If you belong to the half of the human race that does not carry testicles, I doubt that you can easily imagine the sensation of having such a sensitive organ, that is so readily accessible to a swift blow. "Women just don't understand," said a man whose wife had kicked him, more peevishly than viciously, between the legs, "what it feels like." Men, of course, do not have to imagine. They usually learn about their vulnerability by accident, around the age of twelve or thirteen, when puberty occurs.

Until then a boy pays no special attention to the flesh between his legs, which has no special sensitivity. But when his genitals begin to develop, a chance blow—in my case, a football pass that I trapped between my legs—can bring him, nauseated and faint, literally to his knees. From then on, like Huckleberry Finn in a famous scene from Mark Twain's novel, when some-thing drops toward his lap he doesn't open his legs, as if to catch it in a skirt, he closes them, to protect the family jewels.

Of course, along with his genital development goes a new kind of interest in girls. He is equipped now for more than kissing games—at least where his genitals are concerned. His organ will become erect of its own volition, randomly; he cannot ignore it, even if he wishes to. And he is aware that the females around him have noticed the swelling in his pants, that the girls are giggling, turning their eyes away.

The rest of his body is likewise developing; his bones are pushing like early summer corn, the meat on those bones is turning harder and heavier. He suddenly has the weight and strength not only to hit another boy, but to knock him off his feet, maybe to break something. And that is what he sees happening when boys fight, as they have always done. But now they are men. "Boys fight to win," a man who had stabbed another man in a street fight told me, "men fight to live." The days when a fight was merely a matter of honor among boys is over, because he is no longer a boy.

And he is now a man who can work, who can earn his own money. Who can spend that money as he pleases, on himself, or on a girlfriend. He has never been so powerful, or so vulnerable; never had more to gain, or to lose.

These experiences occur more or less simultaneously in a man's life; they are part of the same experience, the same memory. The pleasure that a man's strength can afford, and his awareness of his own vulnerability, arrive together in the same package. He can make love like a man, he can work like a man, he can be hurt like a man.

The worst of the hurt, of course, comes from other men. They are the ones who imprint him with a circuit of response to anger or aggression, one whose opposite poles are horror and murder. To let the current run unchecked between those poles is simply revolting to a decent man. I learned as much by watching the face of one of the gentlest men I have ever known, who recounted to me how a huge drunk had smashed his nose at a party, and how he had "gone crazy," coming back to himself only when he felt his arms pinioned by his friends and saw his aggressor lying unconscious at his feet. But mixed with his self-revulsion was relief: he had not been the one on the ground in the end, helpless before whatever came next.

He had won, but in disgust at what he was capable of doing to another person, and rage at what that person had gratuitously done to him. Yet he had one saving grace—the grace that decent men hold to, when aggression is called for: *he had not wanted to win, he had only been desperately and rightly determined not to lose.*

It is hard to get rid of that feeling, once and for all—that a man must escape being beaten up or down, because he has no choice. And the difficulty does not vanish simply because his opponent is a woman. His response to aggression—his own, or what he takes for hers—is to cut himself out of the situation, to shake his head and walk away. He will back down, or off, and give his opponent the distance he so deeply wants for himself, and with it the implicit promise that victory means less to him than the safety of an honorable truce. It is the best method he knows for modulating a response that has been literally beaten into him.

And it is something that he has had to learn in a way that most women have not. If I have heard many men say that "women are just as cruel to each other emotionally as men are to each other physically," their egalitarianism in this domain nonetheless takes note of a real difference—a difference that is embedded in our intimate manners, that leaves both men and women angry and frustrated.

She wants to "get to the bottom of the problem." He wants to "talk it over later," when he is not so tired, not so full of the aggression that helps him get through the working day, the world of men. She wants him to face up to their conflicts; he wants her to "stop picking on me." She wants, often enough, to gain a sense that he recognizes her moral right to settle the matter on at best mutually agreeable terms, at worst (from his perspective) her terms. And he wants more than anything to get rid of the nagging sense, buried deep in the flesh that is his alone, that this battle, like any other, can end in his literally crushing defeat.

Feminists have raised the issue of masculine violence, of course. But they have tended to talk about violence as if it were something aimed solely at women, by men. The possibility that men learn about violence, not by practicing on women, but on each other, has been left aside by feminist writers, in the main.

The exception is Phyllis Chesler, who in her 1978 book, *About Men,* noted that "most men expect only competition and betrayal from each other." At a time when the mainstream of feminist thinking portrayed all men as belonging from birth to the warmhearted club of masculine beings, as basking in the mantle of "male solidarity," she wrote that "what really exists between men" is the knowledge that other men are enemies, who can be expected to commit "savage acts of betrayal or humiliation of other men." And a man's only real choice, she said, is to learn how "to accept, even embrace, all the suffering and destructiveness that exist, without guilt, without self-pity, without false hope."

This, I think (along with Chesler), is why men, more than women, have a fascination with violence; you need only count the heads and the genders they belong to at a pro football game, or a heavy-metal rock concert, or a showing of *Rambo,* to know as much. Entire industries are built on the power fantasies of adolescent boys, or adolescent men, watching someone else act out the vengeance they would like to express against their enemies.

I cannot believe that this fantasy—or the brutality of our economic competition in the workplace (and brutal is what it is)—reflects merely a thwarted modern desire for the bygone laurels of heroic warriors, as so many New Men have argued. My own experiences, and those of other men, tell me otherwise. We are not merely chasing archetypal ghosts, we are chasing our own pain, the memories that we must live with, of what men did to us that we could not always return to them in kind.

And still do. There has been enormous discussion in our society recently about violence against women. The problem is real, repulsively so. But in practical terms, it seems to me inconceivable that we can solve this problem without taking account of the extent to which violence is likewise a problem for men.

Consider the simple art of murder. In 1960, the homicide rate for men was 3.6 per 100,000 population (among black men, who are more likely to live in the poorest, most violent sector of our society, the homicide rate was *ten times* higher). For women that year, the homicide rate was 1.4 per 100,000, meaning that for every two women who were murdered, five men were killed by another person. Twenty years later, it was true, the homicide rate for women had grown to 3.2 per 100,000, an increase of about 130 percent. But the male homicide rate had grown by over 200 percent, to 10.9. In both absolute and relative terms, an awful lot more men than women were being murdered in our society.

In terms of aggravated assault, the legal term for the most severe kind of interpersonal violence short of murder, a white man is about three times more likely than a white woman to be a victim; for black and Hispanic Americans, men's doleful edge in this category is still on the order of 100 percent.

While it is true that women are far more likely than men to be raped— the incidence of intermale rape, according to available statistics, is virtually insignificant, though it may be underreported—the number of women raped per 100,000 population has remained stable at about two throughout this decade. It is not true, as some feminists have argued, that rape has become the preferred method of keeping a woman in her place, nor that it was the fastest-growing violent crime in our society over the past two decades. That sad distinction belongs to homicide against men.

By men: In every category of violent crime, the person arrested (if an arrest was made) for the act was a male, in at least 85 cases out of 100.

In other words, violence against women has not kept pace with violence against and among men. The chief victims and perpetrators of violence in our society are the people who shave their faces.

It is practically obscene to contend otherwise; the equivalent of saying that violence is a man's due, that he deserves whatever happens to him, simply because he is a man. It is particularly obscene—and shortsighted— coming from the mouths of those who profess to believe in gender equality.

How can anyone imagine that men will cease to inflict violence on women, so long as violence is such a deep part of their experience with other men?

THE VIOLENCE OF A WORKING DAY

In the office of a woman friend who works in my industry, I am introduced to a man—a man my age, who has risen to become editor of a new magazine. We talk a little bit of shop, and he asks me a probing question about a management change at a newspaper I write for. A warning light goes off in my head, and I feel my face changing: this man wants to know something that he could use to hurt me, if ever he cared to name the source of his information to one of my employers who did not like the looseness of my tongue.

And suddenly he changes the subject, his eyes on my face. For no logical reason, he recounts how, in his college days, when he was director of the campus film club, he had the chance to meet a famous filmmaker whom he had worshiped for years. When the meeting took place, the filmmaker was playing chess with a colleague—and he never looked up from the game—while the man telling the story stood there feeling like a shmuck.

He finishes his story, and gives me a gentle, sad look. He has exposed a bit of his own pain to me, and is waiting to see how I will respond. He wants to know what I wanted to know, when he asked his question: whether or not we can trust each other, just a little bit.

There is a rule at work here: in casual encounters, a man is another man's enemy until proven otherwise. He can be counted on to take advantage of your weaknesses, consciously, or reflexively, without quite knowing what he is doing.

Our friendships, in large measure, are an attempt to compensate for the pain in that expectation—to find a relationship in which for once, a man doesn't have to watch his back. But even among friends, there is the constant awareness of the power men hold to hurt each other, to impose themselves by force or guile over other men.

It comes out when there is something at stake, something both men might want. In childhood that might be a toy, or Mommy's attention, which were the major prizes of fights between my brothers and me. A bit later it is a teacher's approval—I have never seen more awful competition than the one which took place in my sixth-grade class for grades that year when we were warned that "everything you do from now on goes on your permanent record" by our guidance counselor.

By the time a boy enters high school, the stakes have expanded dramatically. They now include a place in what my interview subjects called, with a flat laugh, the "pecking order"—which might be defined as the degree of trouble another boy might expect when he tries to pick on you. They also include money—to buy and maintain a car, for example—and thus the jobs available to teenagers, which are limited in number, and thus an object of stiff competition. Academic success is no longer only a matter of pleasing teacher, but of gaining a leg up in the race for admission to a select college (and by extension, a good career); it was at this point that cheating became endemic in the classrooms I sat in (I stopped after being caught in the seventh grade, and didn't cheat again; the men I knew at Harvard sometimes went so far as to destroy other students' laboratory experiments in the highly competitive premed courses). A man has real memories, and real observations, to keep the possibility that someday he will be the victim of another man in his mind.

I believe that our working lives are aimed, in large part, at neutralizing or eliminating such threats. And I know that they are all in a day's work. I have heard too many men warn me, "Cover your ass," or say that they're going to kick someone else's, in order to get on with their jobs, to think otherwise. The language of business is the language of warfare and of violation; in the course of his struggle against the board of Columbia Pictures, Alan Hirschfield alternately declared, "This is war!" and "They're emasculating me." (He even acquired physical wounds, including a broken toe, during the battle of the boardroom.)

In any corporation, some people work as much to damage others' careers as they do to advance their own—just as on any football team, the substitutes do their best to knock the starters off the field in practice, in order to take their place when the big game is played. It is simply ludicrous to contend, as Betty Lehan Harragan did in her Second Wave bestseller, *Games Mother Never Taught You,* that when men enter a corporate environment, "they feel comfortable, part of the organization, one of the fellows," and that they are thereby "bonded in a familiar male camaraderie." The fact of the matter was better expressed by Joseph Heller in *Something Happened:*

In my department, there are six people who are afraid of me, and one secretary who is afraid of all of us. I have one other person working for me who is not afraid of anyone, not even me, and I would fire him quickly, but I'm afraid of him.

That is a fair description of the majority of offices where I have worked. Not one of my working experiences offered an escape from the fear of other men; it was part and parcel of the working life.

Who is afraid of whom? First, the men on your level are afraid that one day you will move past them, and they will be at your mercy. You will be getting more money, more privileges and perquisites; you will have the right and the power to make their lives miserable, if you so choose.

Moreover, the man who hires you is afraid that someday you will take his job. By the time he gets to be a boss, he is old enough to feel tired, and you are probably younger and more energetic than he is. I once thought that when one of my bosses did his best to make my job impossible, by screwing up the deals I made, and changing the organizational chart continually so that no one knew whom he was responsible to, or what for, it was my boss's personal problem. Then I started listening to my friends; to Peter, for example, whose boss did his best to ensure that before every departmental meeting, Peter was in a state of nervous exhaustion. It occurred to me that if there were no such thing as a bottom line to keep bosses honest, no one would ever get any work done; everyone would be too busy trying to keep anyone else from performing his job, to reduce the competition to a helpless state.

The best story I ever heard about this syndrome came from a man who worked as assistant to the managing editor of a travel magazine. His boss had his eye on the top editor's job, which was held by a man whose long and distinguished career in publishing had included virtually no travel writing. So the managing editor persuaded the big boss to travel; with perfect helpfulness, he set up trips that kept his superior out of the office for two weeks of every month. During this time, the managing editor was driving the staff past its customary limits, and cultivating the board of directors, offhandedly and jokingly (oh, yes) complaining about how slack the office had become. Finally, his scheme paid off: the secretaries revolted, and the operation ground to a dead halt while the editor was on the road.

He returned to face a furious group of men, who demanded to know how he could have let things get so far out of hand. The next thing he knew, he was out of a job, and the managing editor had his.

At that point my friend walked into the new head man's office and said, "I want to be the managing editor."

"Absolutely not!" was the reply. "You're too young, and you haven't got the experience."

"No," my friend agreed, "but I'll work hard as hell, and I'll do a good job, and you know it. And what's more, if you give me the job, I'll make you a promise, and I'll keep it: I will *never* do to you what you did to the poor bastard you have just replaced."

He got the job.

MY MENTOR, MY TORMENTOR

Why do you think that the business community became so fascinated, in the late 1970s, with the concept of the "mentor"—the experienced older person who guides and educates his or her protégé in the ways of the workaday world? The idea was especially fascinating to women, whose magazines ran numerous articles on how to find and cultivate such a fellow. The reality was something else again. I have had a mentor, and I can only agree with Iacocca's description of his own: "He has a special niche in my heart—and sometimes I think he was carving it out by hand. He was not only my mentor.... He was my *tor*mentor, but I love him!"

What a mentor tells a protégé is essentially this: "It's a mean old world, and you can get hurt in it. So I'm going to hurt you, a little bit, from time to time, for your own good. I'm going to toughen you up, and someday you'll love me for it."

The bond that is formed in such an exchange is indeed loving—a painful love, but a real one. It is not unlike the love I felt for my protector, in that summer camp over two decades ago, who took pity on me, but whose pity was mixed with contempt. I felt the same thing from the man who taught me to sell, that quintessential American occupation, who alternately offered me a comrade's handshake and the back of his hand. He had told me, when I took a job under him, that it would be hard, but that he would teach me something I could take with me wherever I went. And he did; and I am still grateful to him.

But he could never quite forget that if he taught me everything he knew, I would be his equal—a threat. (On one occasion he unconsciously blew a deal I had set up, for precisely that reason.) Though this was never discussed between us, it was understood; an understanding that in some way we were born enemies, and that it could not be otherwise. We did not make the rules, we only lived with them, as best we could.

We could protect each other from a naked recognition of the competition that was built into our careers, and the loneliness that goes with it. We could forgive each other the hatred one feels for an enemy, and use it as a guilty spur to the gratitude we felt toward one another—for teaching, for understanding, and for putting aside our hostility to work together. We could accomplish more together than either could achieve separately, and take pride in the accomplishment, in our ability to rise above the merely futile enmity that is all too normal in business life. In doing so, we could protect each other from failure, in the competition with other companies, other men.

But we could not change the fact that we were men. And we could not forget that a man is dangerous, in a dangerous world.

I have never loved anyone more than the men who protected me, in one way or another; nor hated anyone more than the men who made their protection necessary. If there is a reality to the tattered, silly concept of male solidarity, it is this, and only this.

Violence is part of our work, and work may well be part of our violence. The former idea is at the center of psychoanalytic theory since Freud: through work we sublimate aggression and hostility, our biopsychological heritage, into socially useful activity. But we are too deeply marked by our own experiences of violence, and the world remains a too violent place, for the sublimation ever to be complete. Mixed with our construction, the worlds we make, are the worlds we break—the worlds of other men. To advance in the world, sooner or later, means stopping another man's advance; to gain something means having to protect it.

To keep violence at bay is still mainly a man's work, and still a way in which men see their work. I am not speaking only of jobs like being a cop, or a soldier, which are the most obvious examples of the protector role. Whatever our jobs, we try to succeed, in part, because with success goes an increased power to resist the violence of other men; and in part because by succeeding, we can offer our loved ones the protection that money can buy, such as it is, from illness or poverty.

We want to be, for someone else, the protector we longed to have for ourselves—on whom we depended, on some occasion still in memory, when the fairness of a more powerful man was all that stood between ourselves and the most frightening defeat—whom we still love in our memory, in our deepest bones. We want to earn that love, and to know that we have earned it—that we are capable enough and brave enough to deserve the gratitude we once felt for another man, *in the eyes of a woman.*

CHAPTER
15

The Iron Fist
in the Velvet Glove

In primitive societies, the exchange of women among men is the cement that holds tribes together, according to anthropologists such as Claude Levi-Strauss. While I am far from certain that our current society represents the peak of civilized development—or any other I can see, for that matter—it seems to me that our women have earned the right to give and take men for themselves. And I have further observed that competition among men is never so unfair or cruel as when its object is a woman.

The race starts early enough: in high school, boys brag or lie about their sexual experiences ("I've forgotten more about getting laid," a guy told me in the seventh grade, "than you'll ever know"). Along with that, they do whatever they can, often enough, to make other guys look bad in front of girls. I recall that a guy who had a car might give a friend and his date a lift to the prom, but he would make certain that the girl knew just how big a favor it was, how pathetic it was for a boy not to have his own wheels. Likewise, beating a guy up was mean enough in itself, but beating him up in front of a girl was a doubly mean pleasure.

And taking a girl away from another boy was the biggest, meanest pleasure of all. Not only had the prize been certified in advance by another man, but winning her made certain that she was yours and yours alone—my gain, your pain. The only possible response the victim could make—since the girl was free to make up her own mind—was to start a fight, in which case he would still look ridiculous, especially if he lost.

And which was out of the question, if the interloper happened to be your friend—which was often the case, then and in my adult life. Where girls were concerned, all was fair, even when the boys were supposedly on the same side. If your best friend wanted your girlfriend, and he could get her away from you, he had the right to try. And often enough, he did, while relying on the friendship for protective covering.

I have ended several friendships with men who pulled this banal trick on me—"You never let me have any fun," pouted one, who hit on every girl he saw me with over a period of a year, after I had warned him not to try it again (he did, and that was that)—and have questioned others. It has come up so many times, even with the few men whom I would die for and vice versa, that I have learned to look out for it even when I don't need to.

I assume, in other words, that if the woman I am with is worth being with, some fool man will try to take her away from me. And one of the reasons I make that assumption is that I have done the same thing to other men. Once learned—as I learned it, for example, the New Year's Eve when one friend told me that another was making love to my date in the next room—the habit is hard to break. If you can't pay back the guy who hurt you in kind, you pass it on to the next man down the line.

At one point in my twenties, when my career entered a particularly difficult phase, my best friend was homosexual, as well as poor. It was an insecure time in my life, and in two crucial respects he posed no threat to me, real or implied: he earned even less money than I did, and he wasn't after the women I wanted. But on one occasion, when we rode the Greyhound together to a neighboring city, he became interested in a pretty redhead. When we got off the bus, and he was taking her to lunch, as he stopped to look around, I moved in and walked off with the girl. And this was the strangest, most compulsive part of my behavior: *I didn't know what I was doing.* I had "not heard" his attentions to the girl, I protested; I didn't know he'd invited her on a lunch date. He had to tell me about it.

And then I remembered, of course, that I *had* heard: I just couldn't stand it. I knew what a good man he was, and I could imagine what a good lover he was, and *I was not about to stand for him becoming part of my competition.*

If a man succeeds in his work in order to be more attractive to women— and success does make a man more attractive, does it not?—part of his success lies in defeating other men, implicitly or explicitly. He must "win" the girl; someone else must "lose" her. And having won her, he must keep her—from other men, who he knows will not hesitate to take advantage of his failure or indecision, to move in on his beloved. *Whether or not she can be trusted, other men cannot.*

His life, his work, his love, are all of a piece. He must work to win, win to work, work to love. Failure in one corner of this triangle will bring the others crashing down, sooner or later—as soon, he suspects and fears, as someone else pushes on his house of cards. And there is always a man, somewhere, who is only too happy to push; who is paying you back for the time someone blew down his own house of cards, or just staying in practice, or not even aware of what he is doing, acting out reflexes hammered into him long ago.

But there must be a limit on this struggle, this terror; or life would be simply unbearable. And men, it seems, are incapable of providing themselves with such limits. They do not feel that they have a choice: life is a struggle, and one must respond. And so they leave that task, of defining how far they must go to defeat their enemies, to their women. They do not only fight to have a woman; they stop fighting when a woman tells them to stop.

It was significant, I think, that the main brake on the fights I saw in high school was applied by girls. It was the girls who stepped between boys who were fighting; the girls who put moral pressure on a man, who warned him that if he beat up another man for no good reason, they would not appreciate it. I saw that scene repeated endlessly at high-school parties, and once in my adult life, when a guy who hung out at one of the rock clubs where I worked as a critic made a point of insulting my lover in front of me. What happened was that my lover passed the word, and every woman regular in the place began to ignore the guy, and any woman they saw in his company. The social pressure wore him down over the next couple of weeks, and he apologized.

The principle here was that *women set the limit on what was acceptable for men.* If men did not always respect those limits—if they took pleasure, at times, in violating them, *just to prove that they were men, after all*— they were nonetheless aware of them. If honor demanded that from time to time they defend a woman, it also demanded that their defense not go beyond what she thought appropriate.

I see that principle operating in other domains of our lives. It is women who tell men to stop smoking, or drinking, or rolling joints when the party gets under way and the boys go into the corner with their drugs (far more often, in my experience, than they order their men to provide them with drugs, behavior exceptional enough to be named with the insult "coke whore" in California during the height of the cocaine craze).

Likewise, it is women who tell a man when he has worked enough. When former Warner Brothers vice-president George Nelson retired, as he wrote for the *New York Times,* he prepared himself a daily schedule that began "at the same time as when I was working," planned to keep him busy until ten P.M., after which "I'd be home in time for the eleven-o'clock news. And then to bed." However, his wife, "thinking I was to begin a new life, turned off the alarm on the clock radio." And then she literally led him through the first, thoroughly pleasant day of his retirement.

"If things keep up this way," joked Nelson, a bit lamely, "my whole retirement will be ruined."

By whom?

Why, by someone who knew what he needed, better than he knew himself; who knew that he needed to oversleep "by three hours," which is what happened when she turned off George's alarm. Who told him, "Don't panic . . . just have a good breakfast." And who apparently made it plain that she would love him just as much if he gave her nothing more than the pleasure of his company.

It is not easy to accept such gifts; in a certain sense, it may even be humiliating, especially for a man who has been brought up to believe that the first rule of life is to be able to take care of himself, as are we all.

Yet how like a man to ask a woman to tell him: Eat this. Do this. Don't do that. Love me, like this.

Not how to be a man, but how to be a human being.

THE BALANCE OF INTIMATE POWER

There is a struggle here, too, and a most unequal one; it came into the open in the seventies, when women announced in startlingly large numbers that they were sick and tired of picking up men's pieces.

If our relationships had remained stable up through the 1960s, that may have been because the breadwinner formula held more or less true in practice: men could feel, and indeed claimed out loud, that women depended on them not for something so intangible as emotional support, but for the very clothes on their backs. And women could feel that whatever their menfolk's achievements in the world, the men still depended on the love they found at home.

But when the inflation spawned by the Vietnam war began to erode men's earning power, encouraging married women into the work force, and a generation of college-educated women began to think that their degrees might be valuable for something besides raising well-rounded kids and keeping their husbands distracted at the end of the day, the equation changed. All of a sudden, men had to face the possibility, and increasingly the reality, that women—the women who had always kept them, literally, from killing themselves; the women who knew their deepest secrets, who had placed their kind, soft hands on the place in a man where the merest blow could lay him low—would be competing with them for the bread they earned.

The goddess came down from her pedestal, holding a terrible, swift sword. A goddess who knew everything about a man he had never told other men; whose hands had fed him, washed him, healed him, when he came home wounded from a day of battering and being battered by other men. She had given him his comfort, his identity, and his life's meaning, and now she could take it away. If her hand were someday raised against a man in the workplace, what a hell the world would be; a hell where the demons knew where to strike a man so that he could never rise again; where *the line he fought to guard, between his lover and his enemies, had been erased, once and for all.*

No wonder that after surveying men in the Army, blue-collar jobs, service occupations, and professional careers, Anthony Astrachan found that

> most of us accept the changing balance of power in our personal lives more easily than we adjust to finding women as peers or bosses at work. . . . We love our wives or lovers, we can be proud of them, admire them, or identify with them. . . . We seldom have positive feelings about women at work, however. . . . subconsciously we see them as combining the power of women with the power of work.

Indeed we do. And the power of a working woman is all the greater when you realize, as I argued above, that the balance of power in our personal lives has not changed nearly so much as we like to think.

In practical and emotional terms, our women—while not yet our equals in terms of the paychecks they bring home—are less dependent on us than they were before. *But we are no less dependent on our women.* They are still raising our children, fixing our meals, comforting us when we need comfort, to a degree that we are not doing the same for them.

They can put on a T-shirt, as women did in the late seventies, that announces, "a woman needs a man like a fish needs a bicycle." The best that men could put on their chests in reply were slogans that put forward the relative sexual merits of truckers (who boasted that they "do it on the road"), scuba divers (who "do it underwater"), and other occupational categories. And women one-upped their sexual boasts with "100 Ways That a Cucumber Is Better than a Man" (for example: it stays hard in the refrigerator, and you can take it out whenever you want).

A man without a woman was a fish out of water; a woman without a man was a fish without a bicycle.

This conflict is not likely to end soon. In fact, men are preparing themselves for a long struggle. That was evident in the fact that every man under forty in my sample was teaching himself to cook and clean—*not for the sake of his intimate partner or partners, but for his own sake.*

"I don't want to depend on a woman to feed me," said one. "You gotta know how to take care of yourself," said another. "I don't want to be like my father—he couldn't even make scrambled eggs," said a third. They thought that acquiring such skills would make them more attractive to women, certainly; but they also agreed with the statement that "a man who can take care of himself is less dependent on a woman," when I put it to them. They saw an inability to care for themselves as a disadvantage in their relationships with women, and they wanted to wipe it off the board.

That is fine, so far as it goes. But if things stop there, I think we will be in trouble. My feeling is that in the longer term, men will have to accept not less, but more dependence on women. They will have to trust women, and not merely strike a bargain with their wives and lovers.

How could it be otherwise—if a man wants to spend part of his life caring for his children; if he wants to take the time to learn about himself and others; if he wants to develop his talent for relationships, and teach that talent to another generation? If that is what he wants, sooner or later he will find himself counting on a woman, to earn the family income, to respect him for taking over tasks that are still not treated as masculine, to be patient while he struggles to find something as valuable, for himself and for her, as the paycheck he might win in the workaday war.

It seems to me that the surfacing of the Gay Liberation Movement at the end of the sixties, and the fact that 10 percent of us are gay, are evidence of just how hard it is for men to place such trust in women—just as my acquaintance and friendships with gay men tell me that for many homosexuals, making love with a man is another way of overcoming one's distrust toward men. (Instead of a blow, a caress; instead of hatred, desire for the enemy with your face.) A lot of gay men, whether they like to admit it or not, are simply more afraid of women than they are of men (one man expressed that fear with the phrase, "Women's pubic bones can really hurt a guy"). They have learned to cope with the powers of men, and to keep a woman's power at bay.

But that is not the alternative chosen—and I do believe it is a choice, not a matter of genetic imperatives—by 90 percent of American men.

While men grow up at war with each other, they will continue to need women to maintain their supply lines, their bloodlines, their thin red line between sanity and hostility. They will need women to prove that there is something more to life than a struggle, until they are capable of proving it to themselves.

In the 1970s, men turned to women for precisely that lesson—but to women who were engaged in a rending struggle of their own. By attaching themselves directly and intimately to the Women's Liberation Movement, men sought escape from a failure to provide a new choice for themselves—a failure, as we will see in Part VI, that terminated the revolt against their fathers that took place in the 1960s. What I want to show now is how the Second Wave offered not only women but also men the vision of a different balance between their intimate and working lives—and how this historic attempt disintegrated under the weight of the opposition it aroused, and also its very success in bringing us to the brink of a fundamental shift. And I want to show how that experience was nonetheless highly useful for men who went through it.

P A R T

———— V ————

NOTES OF A
FEMINIST CONSORT

And whereas some have attributed the Dominion to the man onely, as being of the more excellent Sex; they misreckon in it. For there is not always that difference of strength or prudence between the man and the woman, as that the right can be determined without War.

—Hobbes, *Leviathan*

CHAPTER
16

The Click and the Thud

I am biologically disqualified from ever having a "click," which Jane O' Reilly described, in a famous article for *Ms.* magazine, as

> that parenthesis of truth around a little thing that completes the puzzle of reality in women's minds—the moment that brings a gleam to our eyes and means the revolution has begun.

"Click," in other words, is the epiphanic sound of a woman's consciousness rising—for example, when a dumb guy "kept telling his wife to get up and help Mrs. Jones" serve him his dinner, or sneered, "Ho, ho, my little wife in an executive dining room," to use O'Reilly's examples.

But I am not a woman. I might click my heels, or make a clicking sound with my fingers, but a "housewife's moment of truth," as O'Reilly called it, cannot emerge from my anatomy. In the early 1970s, when her article was written, biology was perhaps not destiny, but neither was it a trumpet that just anyone could play.

So I will not claim that the dozen-odd years I spent in and around the feminist movement, as a lover to an avowed feminist, a campaign worker, and a reporter, ever led up to a click. Instead I will say that I have experienced "thuds"—the kind you hear in the pit of your stomach, as though a soft piece of matter (like the heart) had broken loose from its moorings and crashed onto clenched intestines.

My first was in 1977, when my lover brought me to a party for a women's employment bureau that she was then advising. In the living room of the apartment were gathered the hard-core activists of the bureau, mainly short-haired women (this style was called the "wiffle cut" in lesbian circles) who regarded dealing with men as at best a necessary evil, at worst a sin on the order of carnal intercourse with a wild beast. Such women had become common in feminism around that time, and they presented women like my lover, whose cohabitation with a man stamped her as "male-identified," with a rather cruel dilemma. She was too honest and too brave to deny her connection to me, but my presence at such gatherings exposed her to a great deal of good- and bad-natured ribbing. To spare my lover (not to mention myself) further discomfort, I left the women's room before the excrement could hit the ideological fan, and wandered around the apartment.

Wonder of wonders, in the kitchen I discovered three men drinking beer in silence around the kitchen table, under a wall-size poster of exuberant women with banners and clenched fists which bore the legend "Women United Will Never Be Defeated."

Like me, they could only be feminist consorts. Therefore we had something in common, that I for one was eager to discuss. We could even have as much fun, for a change, as the women in the next room, who always talked so much together about all kinds of neat stuff. Therefore I took a beer from the fridge, turned to them with a big smile, and said, "May I join you?"

All three of them turned their heads. On their faces was a single expression of embarrassed, outraged hostility. In their eyes was the kind of loathing I had sometimes seen in my own mirror, on those evenings when I searched my features to see how deeply I resembled a pig.

All that they knew about me, all that they could have known, was that, like them, I was a man. The enemy of the women united who would never be defeated. The traitor in the bed, the beast with the one-eyed beast between its legs. They could hate me for no other reason than my gender.

As I, like them, had grown to hate and distrust other men, on the basis of my own feminist principles—the principles that led me to cross the street at night, so that I would not pass by a woman, and perhaps frighten her, because a man is a dangerous beast, and I am a man. And thus to the kind of hatred I could read on these men's faces—the hatred of men, of a man—of themselves.

Thud.

I want to answer a question that has been posed to me over and over by men and women to whom I have recounted my experiences in the feminist movement, as a feminist's consort, as her often silent partner, as a man who defended feminism to other men, while defending himself from feminists: "Why did you put yourself through that?"

I must take the blame for allowing that question to be asked. When one talks about this stuff, there is a tendency to exaggerate the bad; it's like being drunk and telling old war stories. And the experience was enough to make you drunk, in a way. It was that heady, that rich, that full of ferment. Drink the wine, take that girl, and get back to the battle.

I am taking up this subject with a curious awareness that no one—outside of a few, still-determined activists—seems to care anymore about what happened during that decade when the personal became political, when bedroom practices and kitchen chores assumed the same importance in American lives as acts of war (and perhaps more than the Equal Rights Amendment). The Second Wave lately seems to be regarded as one of those unfortunate gaffes that decent people forbear mentioning in polite company.

Its real achievements are taken for granted even by rising young women, like the twenty-three-year-old executive I dined with not long ago in New York, who told me with her hardest stare that whatever else she might be, she was most certainly "not a feminist." That she would probably not have the prospect of such a richly paid career before her without the painful sacrifices undertaken by women like the one I loved, in those days when a woman who tried to walk into the executive suite, without a cup of coffee for some guy in a suit in her hand, would have the door slammed on her nose, is what I told her. And she took that as an insult, an assault on her own talents and energies, as have most of the young women from whom I have heard her lines. They are proof of the astonishing success, and the equally astonishing failure, of feminism in our time—just as are the men who get sick thinking about the loving they have no time for, and the women who claim the right to let a man earn their money for them, in the name of the Second Wave.

How quickly we forget. How quickly we deny ourselves—what we were, what we tried to be, what we have become, and why.

But the first, and the hardest, lesson I learned from feminist women was that denial of the self, of what one knows down to the bottom of one's cells to be right and true, is a tragic mistake. And it was a mistake that I made— not only in the self-hatred to which I too gave rein, in those days when I was trying to be the opposite of a male chauvinist pig, but in the silence I kept while a movement that had struggled to overturn the crude dictates of the "biology-is-destiny" formula became that rule's most aggressive champion.

It is not by coincidence, I think, that the way we live now is still largely divided along lines of biology. And that was precisely the destiny I hoped to avoid, not only for my lover, but for myself, when I chose to love a feminist, and thus to politicize my intimate life.

In the concept of gender equality I saw an escape from a destiny that had been marked out for me since I was young enough to know that men's lives resided in their work, and women's in their personal relationships. I saw the possibility of growing up to be something more than the men who walked uncomfortably beside their wives, hands in their pockets, while their children clung to mother's hands, a grouping I saw on every street. I sensed the chance of being a man whose life held something besides work, whose intimate life was more than a deal with a woman as crippled as he.

I saw, in short, *a different way of being a man.* If that vision fell short— so short that we now find ourselves, or so it seems, right back where we started—the fault may not lie with the vision, but with the route we took to arrive at its promise.

THE PORTRAIT OF A FEMINIST LADY

In my journal from 1971 is the record of the first conversation I had with the woman who would become my guide and mentor in the currents of feminism. I met her in an apartment where I had gone to continue my acquaintance with a fellow who was a carpenter, like me at the time, and who I thought might turn out to be a friend.

It was hard to make friends with men, to find a man you could count on; I didn't understand why, but I had discovered, when I dropped out of college the previous fall, that the men I knew at Harvard no longer had time for me. They were busy studying, getting on with their careers in an environment as competitive as any I have ever known, in which the grades one took out of a seminar were usually determined first by how expertly one flattered the professor, second by how subtly one torpedoed the ideas of others, and only then by the originality of one's own thinking.

I had not yet come to see this behavior as typically, pathetically male, but I had taken note of it. And I noted how it coincided with a bizarre syndrome of alternating heat and cold in personal relations, one night when a man I considered a close friend called the apartment where I was living and asked me to come to his dorm and discuss the divorces both sets of our parents were undergoing. When I arrived, he was studying. "I'll be with you in a minute," he called, so I picked up a copy of a magazine and waited for him. Half an hour later he opened his door and said: "Okay, let's make this quick, I've got to get back to my work." I stuttered a few phrases, and left him. We never spoke again, except to say hello. It was as though we had each committed a crime, by admitting that we needed each other; as if we had acquired an indecent power over each other.

Something of that same issue—the need for a man you could trust, and the indecency of needing him—was under the surface of my conversation with the carpenter, as we felt each other out to see exactly why we wanted to be friends. Our talk was in full swing when the woman—call her Sharon— walked into the room, looking for a woman friend who shared the apartment. She was a startling sight: tall, long-haired, her face wrapped around an enormous smile, glowing with energy. I must have stared for a moment, because she laughed before saying, "Don't mind me," and sat down beside us on a piece of tatty furniture.

The carpenter had been telling me about his latest sea voyage, when he and two other men sailed into the middle of a storm, and rode it out for twelve hours, then "lit up a Camel." The woman laughed when he said that. He threw her a look and said, "That's when you find out whether or not you got what it takes."

"Takes for what?" she asked.

"To survive," he said. "It's like Hemingway says, sooner or later you gotta rely on yourself."

"Oh, God," she said, and stood up, "you can't talk to young men about Hemingway." And was gone.

My friendship with the carpenter never went much further than that. He would recount his adventures, and I would listen with an appropriate expression, as I was used to doing when I was with the boys (I always had the feeling, I will admit, that my own brushes with danger were fewer and farther between). But the next time, and the time after that, I remembered what Sharon had said; and it occurred to me that what she had meant was that the carpenter was a phony. And I thought of her the last time I saw him, when he was in pieces after a car crash that occurred when he fell asleep racing home from a canoe trip, not having bothered to take the rest he needed. She had known something about where he was headed that he didn't, something I wanted to know.

I ran into her again, by accident, when I went to visit a guitar player I knew, unannounced. I found him sitting in the corner of his dining room, watching a scene at the dinner table. On one side was his roommate, a handsome, bearded sculptor, and another man whom I recognized with a shock. I had encountered him once before, on a night when my twin brother and I, hearing a woman's screams in the street, had rushed out of our apartment with a screwdriver and a hammer in our hands. There he was, big, heavily muscled, shouting at some girl; the scene was not a rape, just a bad argument. When I told him, "You know, we thought someone was getting killed out here," he turned on me and said, "Come over here and I'll kill *you!*" We went home, and the shouting stopped.

Apparently he hadn't recognized me. He was staring across the table at the woman I'd been thinking of, and her friend. The women wore tense smiles, the men gave them hard stares. No one was speaking. When I pulled out a chair and said hello to the musician, Sharon stood up and said, "Thanks for dinner," took her friend's arm, and walked out of the room. I looked at my friend, who looked away.

What had been going on, I learned weeks later, when Sharon's friend saw me in the street and led me to their new apartment, was that the men had invited the women for dinner, and then, when the meal was finished, had informed them that they couldn't leave until they had been fucked. (A hard word, I know, but appropriate.) That exchange occurred just before my arrival, which by providing a witness made it impossible for the crime to be so coldly undertaken. (I never saw any of those men again; later I learned that the big brute had had his legs broken, walking out of a bar, by three lesbians who had heard him bragging about another rape he had committed.)

It was all a matter of chance, if you believe in chance, that I was in that place at that time. But from that moment on there was a bond between the women and me. In some way we were on the same side. And that is where we stayed.

What drew me to her? Her beauty, of course; not only the beauty of her features, but more important, of her bravery. It was in her shoulders-back walk, the face she kept uplifted in the face of intimidation, the strength of her voice whenever she heard something that went against her principles. I had been associating with men who played it safe, like the Harvard students inching their ways toward tenure in business or academia, or with blind heroes like the carpenter, who sought out danger because they were afraid that they could not be its equal. I had never known anyone with Sharon's moral courage, her refusal to accept less than what she knew to be right. It was, I realized, greater than my own, and I wanted to learn it from her.

Feminism, she knew, as much by instinct as by reason, was dead right. She told me a story, early on in our life together, about what had happened to her in 1968, when she showed up in the office of the committee that was guiding a student strike on her campus. She had helped start the strike, and wanted to keep it going. And while she was standing in the office, one of the men on the all-male committee turned to her and said, "Hey, make us some coffee."

She said, "I don't know how to make coffee."

The other women in the office laughed nervously. The men laughed louder. "She doesn't know how to make coffee?" they shouted, and then, turning to the women, "Somebody show the girl how to make coffee!"

"I don't know how to make coffee," Sharon repeated, "and what's more, I'm damned if I'll learn."

How many times did I see that scene repeated, or hear of one like it from her, in those first years we were together, when she gave up her hobo ex-graduate-student life, and fought her way into the business world? There was the executive who picked on her in the office where she found temporary work as a secretary, responding to her strength as to a provocation. One day he cornered her by the water cooler, in front of the entire secretarial pool, and demanded, "Give me a kiss." When she replied, "Do I get to say where?" he went from office stud to office fool in two seconds flat.

I was back in college, earning my diploma, when she was offered a job in an advertising company, as an assistant account executive—the kind of job women rarely had, only a decade and a half ago, and which they now owe to women like Sharon. The men she worked with—some of them decent guys, some of them not—simply did not know how to deal with her. In the middle of a business meeting, some guy would lean across the table and say, "You're so beautiful, will you have lunch with me?" A client invited her onto a yacht—and canceled the invitation when I suggested that she call him to say I was coming along to test what he had in mind. I remember the disappointment in her face, that her colleague was thinking only of seducing her. She had come to play the game, and the rules kept changing when she entered the room.

She worked harder than any man in her office, where I had the chance to observe her, working part-time in the mail room during and after college. She had to, just to keep her place—in the same way that black professional baseball players, as *Sports Illustrated* discovered in the sixties, must have batting averages thirty points above the usual white players', in order to stay on their teams. And hard as she worked, good as her work was, her bosses would tell her, "You're good, for a girl." On their faces would be a joking smile, and in their eyes (as I saw for myself, more than once) was fear. Years later, after we had separated, she would thank me for telling her, again and again, on those nights when she came home from work worn out and emotionally bruised, that these men were afraid of her, that her success was seen by them as their own failure.

I owed her similar thanks, for being my rock while I struggled to earn my degree, among men whom I could no longer respect in the same way; whom I saw no longer as the best and the brightest, but as the best and the brightest once women were subtracted from their numbers. The arguments she put to me, when we discussed the material I heard in my lectures, could not be found in my textbooks. How was socialism radical, when socialist states were uniformly run by men? What kind of history failed to take into account the women who held men's lives together while they were out building the world? What kind of world was it, anyway, where a woman couldn't walk down the street, or go on a date, or to her job, without wondering what a man might do to her?

She gave me a place in a world still taking shape, and the skills to live in it, by challenging me to be her equal; not just intellectually, but practically, in the most mundane ways. When she came home from work, I cooked for her; I taught myself, and she ate everything but my mistakes. She had to teach me how to clean, how to see what dirty is, and do something about it.

And I wanted to learn, all of it. I had lived like a pig, in my own mess, since leaving my parent's house, and I wanted to live like a human being. Someone had to show me how, and she took on that job. (How many men, trained by feminists, carried those assets into other relationships later on? I still remember the delighted surprise on the face of a woman I slept with years later, when she came home from work, looked around the apartment, and said, "You made the bed!") In doing so, she provided me with a refuge from the breakup of my parents' marriage—whose failure had shocked me, once and for all, out of thinking that I could grow up to be like them—and the outline of a different kind of intimacy, a more profound and honorable exchange, founded not (or so we thought) on mutual maiming and dependence, but on mutual independence.

To her credit, she didn't brag about what she taught me. She made it seem like I did it all myself, on the frequent occasions when feminists came to our home to talk about various projects and ideas. Once, when the founders of a feminist business came over to watch themselves being interviewed on TV—in the early seventies, woman-run businesses still seemed like a startling novelty—and I was the only male in the crowd, passing out the refreshments and taking away the plates, everyone burst out laughing on their way out the door. It was shared laughter, at the absurd appropriateness of having a feminist coffee boy in the women's room. You would never know, to read novels like Marilyn French's *The Women's Room,* that men and women had fun together, changing roles in those days. But that's what it was: fun, and the good clean kind at that.

. . .

For me there was another reward in this apprenticeship, one Sharon might not have been aware of. In her company, and that of the feminists who gathered regularly in our apartment to share experiences and projects, I heard the answer to a question I had been asking myself since junior high school: what do women really think of men?

They thought we were dirty. ("They can't even hit the bowl!" shouted one woman about male bathroom habits.) They thought we were false, that we hid our lusts for other women from our partners, that we thought only of our own pleasures, and expected a woman to provide them. They thought that we could easily be fooled, by any woman who would stoop to conquer, who would flatter our needy egos. In a word, *they thought that we were like children.* It was a terrible thing for a man to hear, but not a bad thing, either, to the extent that it was true.

Yet they thought that men were powerful, that we stood together in "male solidarity"—which was how it looked, when these women were demanding places in the working world that men had kept to themselves. They thought, too, that we used that power to hurt women, whenever we could. The subject came up very often, and it was awfully painful for me to hear.

I had listened to such conversations for two years on the night when Sharon and I dined in a restaurant with two other women. They were repeating the various indictments I listed above—men this, men that. And suddenly I found myself saying: "You know, I feel very hurt when you talk about men that way. I'm a man too. Is that what you think of me?"

One of the women looked away in disgust. Sharon stared at me. The third woman said, "If we feel free to talk like that in front of you, it's because you're different."

"But I'm not different. I'm still a man."

They were quiet for a moment. Then the conversation moved on to other matters. And that was the last time I was obliged to hear it, for as long as Sharon and I lived together.

That was the good part—the sense of being allies together, respecting each other's humanity, in a project that we were defining as we went along. If only it had stayed like that.

CHAPTER

—— 17 ——

The Breaking of the Covenant

Part of the pressure that destroyed this relationship came not from male chauvinist pigs, but from the Women's Movement. That pressure began to grow strong at the precise moment when feminism began to have an impact on the larger society—when men and women both began asking themselves if their personal lives were political, in ways they had never thought of, and if they needed to do something about it.

I doubt that this conjunction of social victory and inner turmoil, which I witnessed in Boston, a stronghold of the Second Wave in the mid-seventies, was merely coincidental. The very success of feminism, like the successes of the antiwar and Civil Rights movements before it, posed a conflict for those whose mission was to guard their ideological purity, and with it their sense of identity. If feminism became no longer a women's movement, but a broad social movement, no one would any longer control its direction—not even, necessarily, women. For those who saw the Women's Movement as the most precious possession women could claim, such an outcome was simply intolerable. It became necessary, in other words, to stop gender equality before it went too far.

At that time the Women's Movement had brought together everyone from businesswomen, like my lover, to wiffle-cut dykes, to ambitious young students; all of these women, and others too numerous to count, were at the gatherings, the parties, the meetings where projects were planned. One of those projects, near the end of 1973, was a "women's restaurant," founded by an ex-nun and a friend of my lover's from a political study group. It was conceived not only as a place to eat but also as a place where women could be themselves—where they could join in a kind of communion, to hear music and poetry, and talk in perfect liberty, over food made *by* women for the profit and support *of* women. Men were not to be excluded, but women would run the show as they saw fit.

The philosophy behind the restaurant was set on a fine, sharp edge—the line that divides women who want to be with women, from women who hate men. It was a line that the Second Wave had been walking, gingerly, since the rage of women began to explode in books like Ingrid Bengis' *Combat in the Erogenous Zone,* which contained an entire chapter on the subject of man-hating.

It had always seemed to me that women had a right to be angry at men— at least as much of a right as men had always claimed to justify their own misogyny. But I could never see how, in the long run, man-hating would benefit either men or women. In the first place, we all shared the same planet, and the same future, like it or not. In the second place, man-hating was no more defensible on moral grounds than any other kind of all-embracing racism. And in the third place, I was hardly disinterested in the outcome of this debate. I wanted a feminism that tolerated men, at least, and heard their concerns, at best—a movement that was building a future where men and women could face each other, finally, without a buffer of rage between them.

That was why I contributed money and housewares to the restaurant, along with Sharon, and why I went with my brother, in his truck, to pick up and deliver the refrigerator that took up one wall of the kitchen. (The scene when we installed it, two strong, embarrassed men trying not to be pushy, working with six women who wanted to show that they were strong, was one of the lovely little comedies of the time.) It was necessary, I thought, to show that men could work for and with women, without expecting anything in return except ordinary thanks—in my view, the minimum that human beings owe each other. And beyond that, I thought of my efforts as an investment in a future when men would have the right to ask women to return a favor—a businesslike way of seeing the matter, certainly, but one I thought would lead to a solidarity, based on what men and women had actually done for each other's sakes.

I began to realize that I was fooling myself when a separatist clique—a group of women dedicated to the construction of a separate women's society, culture, and economy—took over the restaurant. The takeover occurred in stages, as separatists gained control of the collective that owned the place. First, women like Sharon, who brought men to the restaurant, were told that it would be better to leave the boys at home. Sharon explained the change to me one night before leaving the house to eat. She was sorry, she said, but the problem was only temporary, a matter of women exploring their own situation for themselves. But it was the first time I had seen doubt in her face, when it came to a question of feminist principle.

The doubt grew, every time she went to the restaurant and listened to the separatists say, jokingly at first, then insistently, "Women who live with men are male-identified." Identified, you see, with the Enemy, the Other. Finally she stopped going, like some other women in her situation. This particular women's place had become an outpost of the Lesbian Nation.

In other words, the personal was no longer just political; it was a civil war.

That was not what Sharon had signed up for, nor what she was struggling to build. If she sometimes hated specific men, with good reason, she was no man-hater. But she was not male-identified, either; and that was the label against which she had to defend herself, and against which I could not help to defend her, because in the eyes of the women who made that charge, I was the enemy. I was not just a man, I was The Man, at once more and less than human.

This was poison—poisonous for the cooperation of men and women, and for the intimate lives of those who were trying to cooperate. For Sharon, it meant losing the company of women who she had thought were friends. For me, it meant being an encumbrance, an unnecessary evil, whenever Sharon took part in feminist activities. For both of us, it meant being angry with each other over these losses, for reasons that we had hardly the time or energy to debate. The world we were working and loving together to build was under assault on all sides—from men who hated feminism, and women who hated men, both of them filled with an impervious righteousness. And like any newborn, our little world was too fragile to bear the pressure.

Our response was to try, harder than ever, to live out the principles that were at the core of our lives together. But that created another pressure. We had begun to feel that we were in this thing not only together but also alone. In that context, any betrayal carried an extra charge, an extra measure of violation and vengeance.

And betrayal is what we gave each other.

Me first. It happened when I was away on a business trip. I slept with a woman, and then she was my mistress. Now, it was true that I had to spend a lot of lonely time away from home for my work, but beyond that, my motivation for cheating was the same as that of a retired engineer who discussed a similar affair with me, in front of his wife, who had lived out the story with him: "The main reason you cheat," he said, "is that you resent your partner."

His resentment was over taking a job he hated for thirty years, in order to support her (he had offered to change roles with her back in the fifties, and she had been shocked and frightened by the idea). Mine was over the same things that drew me to Sharon: I felt that she was braver, and stronger, than I, though God knows, I couldn't have admitted it. I thought that she was better than I, and I loved and resented her for it.

When Sharon found out what I was up to, she threw me out of the house. When she finally let me come back, she one-upped me: she sought out one of her old lovers, who happened to be a rather macho fellow. After making love (or rather, making hate, in my direction) with him, she told him the story. He offered to break my legs for her. She came home and told me about it; though she had declined the offer, it was apparently still open.

I have never been so blindly, miserably, murderously furious in my life. For a week I moved around in a haze, my mind occupied with where I would obtain the shotgun that would kill first the other man, and then my lover.

I didn't care that she'd slept with another man to get back at me; that was my fault. And I wasn't too disturbed by the irony of the man she'd chosen. I had already noticed that feminists occasionally allied themselves with men who were not only macho, but criminally so; one of Sharon's acquaintances, a dedicated consciousness-raiser, was involved with a drug dealer who treated her the way a pimp treats a whore. I could understand the motivations involved in those choices: it was a matter of deliberately violating the "nice-girl" tenets in which these women had been raised, and of adventuring in worlds that were reserved to men, where violence was the rule: a way of proving that they could be as tough as a man.

But I had never raised the merest suggestion of a physical threat against her; I could not have respected myself if I had. And I expected her to be as good, in that respect, as I was—to protect me from certain threats, as best she could, the same way I protected her (and I had had occasion to protect her in that particular way, in the time we lived together, the times when she stood up to a man who was ready to punch her out, and I stepped in to provide another focus for his anger). She had brought physical violence into our relationship, and I felt that she was holding it over me. The thought made me sick to my stomach.

The illness I felt was compounded of guilt, rage, and a disappointment unlike any I had ever known. I had been counting on her, you see, to help me become a better man—as a man does when he loves a woman, when he looks for a better half. And now I saw that she might consider doing something to me that I would never, in my most vicious moments, have considered doing to her.

But that was exactly what I was now considering. We were still equals, and we had never been lower.

In that moment, we were no longer Mark and Sharon, but man and woman—any man, any woman. With our individuality to each other went our humanity, our ability to see ourselves in each other. It is an essential paradox of ideological thinking, this definition of the Other before one sees the individual; an operation underlying racism, Bolshevism, sexism, and now feminism. In the movement and in our house, the political had crowded out the personal.

We should, in retrospect, have called it quits right then. But we did not. First, because we loved each other, and had a long history of helping each other out; in more ways than one, we needed each other. Second, because we had the common trait of refusing to admit failure.

Unfortunately, we had failed—and not only by the standards of positive gender equality. In fact, one of the key lessons of hindsight in this experience was how little our rhetoric had penetrated us, how beneath our various role reversals we were the same as men and women had always been.

I have told you that men see women as their moral betters. And despite the wounds Sharon and I had inflicted on each other, I still felt that she was my better, that the guilt was mine. The situation was of my creation, and I would have to atone for it.

The way I atoned was by trying to be the man she wanted me to be— by doing what she wanted, when she wanted, in accordance with rules she laid down, like the men I described above, whose feminist activism relieved them of having to define and live by their own moral standards. Sharon went along with me, more from self-protection than any other motive, I think; if she could not trust me, she would rule over me.

At that point feminist principle was reduced between us—as it was in separatist theory—to a power struggle. It was not by coincidence, I think, that Sharon no longer apologized for leaving me at home when she went to "women's" bars to hang out with the girls; my betrayal gave her the right to claim a moral superiority in our relationship, of the kind separatists were claiming in justifying their hatred of men. Nor was it coincidence that our life together, over the next three years, became a struggle not against a world we wanted to change, but against each other.

In that struggle I had ceded her the high moral ground—just as do men who seek to justify their lives through the work they do for the sake of their better halves. But I had not surrendered. In fact, I discovered a whole new set of weapons.

Sharon showed me the way. It came through her, to me, from the articles and books that were then popular in the Women's Movement, all of which I read when Sharon was done with them, and some of which declared what lousy, insensitive lovers men were, how little they knew about pleasing a woman.

Now, it was true that a high-school locker room, which is where most of us learn about sex ("Sometimes," says Al-Jabbar, "it takes years to unload the trash that guys talk to each other"), is hardly where you are likely to find useful information on female sexuality. It is also true that until Masters and Johnson announced it to America in the 1970s, a great many men did not even know that such a thing as a clitoris existed, let alone how to caress it, or with what. It was thus no wonder that "the majority of women have to put up with relatively infrequent orgasms during sexual—at least heterosexual—encounters," as Anselma Dell'Olio wrote in *Ms.*

But it was not necessarily true, as Dell'Olio declared, that all "men are severely troubled by women picking lovers with an awareness of [orgasmic] self-interest." Even Joe Namath had told us, in *Playboy,* that the proof of a real lover was his ability to give a woman orgasms. (I knew that Sharon had that interest, practically from the moment I saw her, and I knew that she therefore recognized my own right to it, to our mutual pleasure.) Nor was it forcibly true, as she continued, that

> The rising chorus of laments about a growing incidence of male impotence probably means that our feeble attempts to correct the situation are going in the right direction. It can't hurt for men to experience a small dose of the medicine women have had to swallow for a century. . . . And if he is turned off, you are well rid of him.

Indeed, pleasure is a woman's right; a right, however, that ought to be claimed in conjunction with her partner's (it was feminists who taught me to view anything else as exploitation).

Moreover, swallowing a dose of that medicine could indeed hurt. In fact, in my case it killed the patient. And I hardly think that my lover, my doctor, was so well and painlessly rid of me.

It is one thing to hear a woman say, "I don't really enjoy making love with you anymore"—hard enough in itself, but a message that can be softened, depending on the woman's tone, and on how she shows you to please her (it is not irrelevant here to note that all women do not take pleasure in precisely the same manner; taking a new lover means, in a very real sense, learning to make love all over again, if the act is worthy of the name). It is another to hear her say, "Do it my way, or I'll get someone who can," in a tone of moral anger like Dell'Olio's.

My response put me smack in the middle of the rising chorus of laments about impotence—or rather, would have, if I had known anyone with whom I could share the problem (it is not the sort of thing you tell another man, who will probably be scared out of his wits by the subject, if he doesn't use it against you to move in on your woman, as some men I took for friends began doing, when the smell of frustration hung heavy in my house). What happened was that as Sharon became more demanding, more commanding, I withdrew from her. I was being hurt, not so much by the demand as the angry way in which it was made; and even if I understood why she was angry, I hated her for it. It is said that hatred is the motivation for rape, but it is nowhere near being adequate support for the act of making love.

My limp response, I later recognized, was an absurd role reversal. By witholding my sex from Sharon, I was doing what women had done for generations when confronted by a man whose incompetence in bed was matched only by his refusal to pay attention to his partner's needs: I went frigid. The most vulnerable part of my body, the one that had taught me about a pain like no other, retreated into its shell of softness and rarely came out.

And this physical withdrawal, this womanlike defense, had an emotional counterpart. I had given up on our future together; no longer had the potency of courage to imagine life with this woman for years to come. I was merely abiding, doing what I had to do, what I was told to do, what I was expected to do.

The same thing happened then to Sharon; we were still equals, still bound together by our essential likeness. When my potency returned, it was her turn to be cold; she understood the meaning of my erectile failures, as she had understood her need to be not just a woman, but a human being, instinctively, irrefutably. For her, as for me, there was no future, just the day to get through.

It lasted another three years like that—desperate years, of watching each other die, of struggling to revive the strongest passion each of us had ever known—and then it was over.

Or so I thought. Five years after I left Sharon, I was still embroiled in debate with feminists, in the California town where I had moved; still asking women—and the wrong women, women who hated men—to acknowledge my viewpoint on these issues, and the humanity behind it. (A dirty job, but no one else would do it for me, the way I needed it done.)

Perhaps, too, this was a way for me of assigning blame on someone besides myself, for the failure of something that might not have failed.

Enough of that. There is plenty of blame to go around, and always has been.

CHAPTER
—— 18 ——

The Political and
the Personal

I
t is now five years since I gave up trying to answer the question posed
with such poignant, telling absurdity by Bertrand B. Pogrebin, the ear-
nestly self-transforming husband of *Ms.* editor Letty Cottin Pogrebin:
"Since the second coming of the Women's Movement, we've known what
to call its enemies," he wrote for that magazine in October 1982. "But what
of its friends, those men who are committed to being the opposite of a male
chauvinist pig?"

Now, I was one of those latter men; I like to think that in some ways I
still am: that I am committed to the principle of equality among human
beings, of all genders, which is precisely what feminism throughout its
centuries-long history (up to the mid-1970s) stood for. But there was no
answer to Bertrand Pogrebin's question, and there could not be.

One can certainly be the opposite of a chauvinist; we might call such
people true democrats, believers in the universality of inalienable human
equality. One may less clearly be the opposite of a pig; a reptile is as much
the contrary of a mammal, as a man's flesh is the opposite of cured ham.

But what is the opposite of a male?

The short answer is: a female.

The short problem with that answer is: if men and women are merely
and only opposites, then how can they be equally human?

They could not, of course—not if their differences were tantamount to
those of separate species. And in that case, feminism could not be based on
the idea of a fundamental commonality among men and women, as human
beings.

On the contrary, feminism would have to start and end with the proposition that never the twain would meet; that biology, if not destiny, was certainly an evolutionary joke—one whose punchline, as it happened, included a feminist literary yearning for, and some experimentation with, novel forms of human insemination. If an identity, not only of the body, but of interests, could not exist between men and women—and what interests, aside from an unknown divine plan, or the brute needs of ecological equilibrium, are shared by lions and lambs?—it would follow that what counted between men and women was not the powers they could discover and encourage in each other, but the powers they could wrest from each other. Feminism would thus be always and only a women's movement, a club for "wimmin," as the wiffle gang liked to call themselves. Women united would never be defeated—not by men, at least.

Which, in fact, happened to be the precise notion of feminism then held to be radically progressive, the key to a better world—of women—within the Women's Movement. As Judith Bat-Ada declared in 1979 (to choose only one of many examples):

> For women, sexual fascism [which Bat-Ada took for the norm in our society] means that men, and in particular a few powerful men, control our behavior, attitudes, fantasies, concepts of love and caring, integrity, that in which we believe and hope, as well as the ways in which we love and to whom and how we make our genitalia available. *In this society we have no choice but to follow these dictates.* [My emphasis.]

Why we should care about the problem, since we "have no choice" in resolving it, is less clear than the sense that for Bat-Ada, love and integrity between men and women were contradictions in terms; our intimate and public lives were the equivalent of sexual fascism, a planned campaign of the extermination of women for men's pleasure. Every man a Nazi, every bedroom a gas chamber.

This was what feminism's voluble "radical" edge had come to, and what it remains in the shriveled collectives that still claim to uphold its radical purity. This was what Adrienne Rich called "a microcosm of the American feminist movement as it stands at the beginning of the 1980s," in which love among equals had been replaced by what Rich called "the enforcement of heterosexuality," to "variations on passivity, torture, rape, mutilation, humiliation." This was the feminism to which Gloria Steinem lent her name, by appearing alongside these advocates of hatred in the anthology *Take*

Back the Night, at the same time that she was urging passage of the Equal Rights Amendment.

But this is what I find most amazing: not just feminists who were trying to hold their movement together kept silent, or spoke out only timidly, when this kind of thing was said and published. *The men who loved feminists and feminism let it be said.* All that Bertrand Pogrebin could reply, with sad self-effacement, was that some women regarded the use of the word "feminist" by men to describe themselves "as a co-optation," explaining with laudable discretion that such women "argue that because of our position in the patriarchal scheme of things, men can be *pro-feminist* but not the thing itself."

He was, after all, not a woman. How could he dare to claim the right to say that a movement which had once sought a better world for women and men both—in which each would be freed of a destiny determined only by what was located between their legs—had allowed itself to be an outlet for a hatred as all-embracing as anything men had ever invented?

And if he did so, would he not be admitting that the ideal to which he had consecrated his life had turned out to be no better, no more kind and human, than those of the "male chauvinist pigs" whose opposite he so desperately hoped to be?

Indeed he would.

Thud.

A CONVERSATION WITH A MAN IN A MIRROR

During the worst of the worst days with Sharon, when I hated myself for becoming exactly the kind of man I had never wanted to be—untrustworthy, weak, frustrated—I found myself staring at my face in the mirror one night before going to bed. "You stink," I told the man in the mirror. "You're no good. A liar, cheat, pig. Just like the guys at the office, the guys on the street."

And then I heard another voice in my head, the kind of voice that a religious person (which, in my way, I admit, I am) would associate with Grace. The voice said, "You know so much about the bad in you. What do you know about the good?"

A feminist Grace, that. A feminist question.

In that long decade of the seventies, women told us what was wrong with men, and many of us listened. They told each other what men had always seen as wrong in women, and celebrated what they took for the good in themselves.

But we—we men, especially the men who took part in that movement—did not do the same. We took it for granted, as men in the main have for some time, that women were better than us; that we were essentially unworthy to be the companions of our betters. We knew that we were bad, but *we did not know if, or how, we were good.*

So we asked our lovers, those brave new women, to tell us.

And they did not know, any more than we did, what a good man might be, what he might become. Like us, they were guessing, improvising their lives as they went along. Sooner or later, they had to guess wrong, because they were only human; neither so much better, nor so much wiser, than men, as we had imagined. They could not save us from ourselves.

When I look back at the attempts women made to tell us how to be good, how to make ourselves over newer than new, and our efforts to toe their line, I hear that awful thud, all over again. I see that in intimacy, as in music, the more one improvises, the more one repeats oneself.

You want to be a good man in the house, for example? Well, make up a contract, said *Ms.*, where feminist consorts looked to see what their women were thinking about. Do what the Shulmans did—Alix Kates and good old whatsis, who was never mentioned by name in the course of a long article about marriage contracts.

The Shulmans divided up every day of the week into neat hourly slots, during which there were "duties" to be fulfilled (what used to be called "conjugal duties," like other pleasures, are significant by their absence from this contract). "As long as all duties are performed," they agreed in writing—you can't leave matters of this import to mere untrustworthy conversation—"each of us may use his/her extra time any way he/she chooses." Paying a servant to do some of these tasks (which, you will recall, is how they were described in the fifties, with a tad less moralistic overtone) was forbidden, because that cost money, and men, of course, tend to make more money than women: "The ability to earn money is a privilege which must not be compounded"—like, say, a fracture, or a felony—"by enabling the larger earner to buy out of his/her duties." (Well, even an executive sometimes has to run off copies when the secretaries go home.)

The Shulmans spelled their duties out in hilarious, ghastly detail: "Wife does home laundry. Husband does dry-cleaning delivery and pickup. Wife strips beds, husband remakes them." But not on weekends, of course: "Husband is free all Saturday, wife is free all Sunday."

Do you know precisely what this marriage sounds like? *A job.*

This was the Achilles' heel in the intimate radicalism of the Second Wave, in the notion that the personal was always and *only* political. Not just the awful distrust, the mania for spelling out every last thing a person *must* do, as if a hostile corporate takeover were being negotiated, instead of a wedding of the soul and body. Worse yet was the idea that treating a relationship like a job could be, in any sense of the term, a radical change.

It may have seemed like some kind of change to oblige men to do more of the housework (assuming that most of it needed to be done at all, which was the opposite of what Friedan argued in *The Feminine Mystique*, where she described how "housewifery expands to fill the time available." Not incidentally, Friedan also noted cases in which men shared housework when they came home from their jobs—yes, even then). But even granting that men should do their share, for their own sake as well as women's, something is more fundamentally old than new here.

The core is this: men and women have treated their relationships like jobs since the dawn of the nuclear family in the hellish days of the Industrial Revolution, right up through the Age of Stress.

Husband makes money. Wife counts, budgets, and saves it.

Husband builds house. Wife feeds him.

Husband spawns kids, wife raises them.

Husband tries to be good. Wife tells him when he is good enough.

How new can you get?

Do you know what would seem really new to me? If men were capable, as Walt Whitman dreamed, of "giving not taking law"—giving, not imposing, what is right, what we can live by. If they did not buy or drudge their way out of their duties, but did what needed to be done, not *for* a woman, but *as a man who loves a woman,* and *whose love raises, not lowers her to his level.*

There are certain things that cannot be negotiated. You cannot negotiate sexual differences, of taste, need, preference, nor the willingness with which people perform duties for each other. You cannot pass a law, or lay down a rule, to make men or women happy, even if you can pass laws that say they are equal. Nor can you negotiate, legislate, or even demand that people love each other.

Love, like the higher law, can only be given. But because we are only human—even when we are wrapped in the purity of an idea—we lose sight of the higher law, the higher dream. We lose our strength, and with it our courage to remember, and thus to imagine, what was good in us, what good we might become. We take, not give, the law. And it will not save us from ourselves, from the crimes we commit in our secret hearts, merely to take that law from a woman.

•   •   •

So here we are, back where we started. A woman wants children, and a man to support herself and her children. The man wants to support someone, and in return, he wants someone to tell him that he has been good. And neither of them is entirely happy with the situation.

It is not that the feminist movement failed. The sign of its success is that we are not happy, that we are each still trying to find what pleasures we can in our own separate-but-equal corners, and finding them to be not enough. We agree—myself, and all the men I spoke with, and even political conservatives who now feel obliged to point out how many women they have appointed to high office—that gender equality is a fact of life; that women have the same rights as men, or should. And we agree that the life one lives ought to be the life one has chosen, regardless of one's gender.

But we do not, most of us, feel that we have a choice to make.

I do not see how feminists can solve this problem—certainly not the misanthropic Furies who jerked feminism back from anything that looked or smelled male, at the precise moment in the seventies when gender equality became the moral law of the land, beyond women's dreams and fears—not as long as they remain within what is only a Women's Movement. And that is where they are; from what I can see, and what feminists tell me, men are still regarded as peripheral to the concerns of feminism (Friedan's *Second Stage,* which essentially argued that this attitude was passé, was simply dismissed by radical feminists with whom I have talked since its publication).

And this fact does not bother feminists—at least, not young feminists like "Priscilla Smith, a 1984 graduate of Yale who now works for the Massachusetts Department of Public Welfare," who told Lydia Chavez of the *New York Times,* on the occasion of NOW's twenty-first annual meeting in 1987, that "talk of the women's movement being over ... makes me angry. The women's culture and communities are alive and well and very strong." Perhaps—but in a world of their own, not the world that men and women share, or could have shared.

I do not see that men or women are listening, as they once listened, to the leaders of the feminist movement. Our lives have moved past the separatist rhetoric of hatred, which dissipated the moral authority that made feminism worth following. The movement still speaks loud and clear—but only for itself, while individual men and women keep trying to invent answers that work in their own lives. I say this not as an attack, but as a report; it is what I have felt, and seen in the lives of others who shared all or part of my experience.

Anger occasionally serves one well in politics; it will not serve in intimacy, unless one wants to found the ties that bind on a sterile hatred (the last bond with men that separatists cling to). The personal is not the political, pure and simple, and never can be. The personal is rooted in the intimate, in the individual; the political is based on the group, and thus on the impersonal. The two domains may overlap at certain points, but *they cannot become identical, without corrupting and impoverishing both.* That is what happened to the Women's Movement, and to the men who shared its adventure. (It is, in another domain, what happened during Ronald Reagan's oh-so-personal presidency.)

If the Women's Movement wants to reclaim a moral leadership, it is certainly not enough for women to claim rights of their own, to move "away from a demand for equality to a recognition of the need for special treatment," as Rita Kramer described the new direction of the Women's Movement recently in the *Los Angeles Times.* Not if that means winning privileges for women that are closed off to men; not if that means that we go on forcing men to make an empty choice between being a bum or a breadwinner. I doubt that this is enough for women, and I know it is not enough for men.

In a crucial respect, we have already tried that special-treatment approach, and for men, as well as for women, it was a tragedy. In the spring of 1982, to give you one example, a feminist group in Santa Cruz advertised for volunteers to prepare a demonstration on abortion rights. The advertisement mentioned only women. I called the group sponsoring the event and asked why men had not been asked to participate. I was told that this was not a men's issue.

To paraphrase Sojourner Truth: Ain't I a man? Didn't I attend an abortion with my lover around that time, and wasn't I shut out at the door, while her woman friend went inside the doors where the operation took place? Didn't my confusion and rage help break up the relationship, as much as my lover's sense that at a crucial moment I had abandoned her, refused the child she wanted to make with me? And didn't many men of my generation, while nodding our heads (like good men) to the proposition that a woman has a right to her own body, feel a similar sense of tragic loss?

I am not arguing that men should have the right to tell women when and how to make babies; nor that abortion is never justified. On the contrary, the right to abortion must remain free. Children who do not have parents who love them are victims before they are aborted, and banning abortion will not change the fact. The current argument against abortion would, all too often, substitute the deaths of women for the deaths of fetuses. And in the most immediate terms, too many antiabortionists would have women keep every child they make, and deny those children food at school, in order to pay for weapons that kill children all over the world, along with the parents who care for them.

I am telling you that even men like myself, who gave the better part of their adult lives to feminism, made an error by more or less passively giving women the right to make life-and-death decisions, for the sake of upholding ideals we believed in. In doing so, we ended up by giving ourselves yet another escape from our own responsibilities, yet another reason to resent women, yet another chance to make an old, tragic error.

Men could not augment the power of women simply by surrendering their own; we have tried that, and it led us into a decade when, as Lois Galgay Rickett, executive vice-president of NOW, told the *New York Times,* "The fact that we have held on to the bulk of the gains" of the Second Wave "during the Reagan administration is a minor miracle." A decade in which men still went off to win the bread, and women kept taking care of the kids; in which both remain, if not angry, frustrated. Some gains.

Men are now in the position that women occupied before the Second Wave took off: isolated, confused by a problem that has no name, and yearning for something better, for some vehicle of the heart and mind that will carry them to a new place, and give them a reason for being there. That yearning is implicit in the gropings of the men's movement, in the stress men claim to feel by the millions.

The Women's Movement, from all the available signs, will not answer that yearning for men. Nor can the paternalistic self-assurance, once again discredited, that helped to make Ronald Reagan the President of the United States.

Somehow, men have to begin to answer those yearnings, those needs, for themselves—and at the same time, to fashion answers to their needs that include *and rely on* women. The tasks to come, it seems to me, will be more difficult for men than for women. For once, we will have to be not just better than ourselves, in order to please women, but better than women—to take more than a subordinate role in the shaping of our own lives, as we did not, when feminism was in flower.

Feminism is dead. Long live feminism.

PART
—— VI ——

CHAMELEONS WITH
A CAUSE

So in America when the sun goes down and I sit on the old broken-down river pier watching the long, long skies over New Jersey and sense all that raw land that rolls in one unbelievable huge bulge over to the West Coast, and all that road going, all the people dreaming in the immensity of it, and in Iowa I know by now the children must be crying in the land where they let the children cry . . . and nobody, nobody knows what's going to happen to anybody besides the forlorn rags of growing old, I think of Dean Moriarty, I even think of Old Dean Moriarty the father we never found . . .

—Jack Kerouac, *On the Road*

What I have told you is that if feminism did not keep its promise to men, it was partly because men failed feminism. If the Second Wave went as far as it did, it was partly because men—not only men like me, but men who tried, one way or another, to change their lives to be the equals of women—wanted and needed a new option in their lives, one they were incapable of providing for themselves, as ultimately they must.

The desire still exists—for men and women both. *But if we are going to fulfill it, we must recognize that it is not merely our invention, but our inheritance*—a gift our parents made us. Before the Second Wave came along, men were struggling with that inheritance—and still are.

The gift that children make their parents is to attempt, consciously and unconsciously, to redeem their parents' mistakes; the gift parents make their children is to provide them with the means of that redemption. *Without such gifts, neither generation can make any progress, achieve a resolution within their lifetimes of the unhappiness that is, like it or not, part and parcel of the human condition.*

More than women, I think, men have refused the inheritance their parents—and in particular, their fathers—have left them. *It is an error as profound, and as tragic, as the error that we made in turning to women during the Second Wave, to save us from ourselves.*

Before we can get on with the task of finding whatever fulfillment is to be found in our lives, *we will be obliged to reconsider what our fathers gave us*—and with something more than the blind hostility to which men of my generation have given rein, when the subject of fatherhood comes up. We are obliged not only for reasons of self-interest, but also of plain human decency. My generation treated its fathers as badly as any generation of men in our country's history treated theirs, and we will go on paying the price of that crime until we acknowledge it, and make amends.

It is especially difficult for Americans to make such an admission, because we are a country that likes to look ahead—in the name of the new, the fresh, the better-than-ever—instead of behind, to whatever old world we came from. It is an essential American illusion that there is always a new start to be had, a break in time between what was and what will be—the kind of illusion, as Alexis de Tocqueville argued, that comes naturally to a people who defined themselves in the heat of revolution, as we did, two brief centuries ago.

But there are no such new starts, any more than there is a new life for a man who denies the old one, simply for the asking.

We are no better than our fathers, any more than we are fundamentally different from them, in what we feel, how we live. And we will not learn from their mistakes merely by denying our commonality with them, which is what I see us trying to do. We will redeem neither them nor ourselves. Their blame, their pain, will remain ours.

Let us be done with blaming, and see what we have to learn from them. In particular, let us recognize that the failure of our fathers to reconcile the demands of work and love was, in equal measure, our own failure. Let us admit that we share this problem, and that we cannot escape sharing its solution.

CHAPTER
—— 19 ——

The Names a Man Calls Himself

Flabby, bald, lobotomized,
he drifted in a sheepish calm,
where no agonizing reappraisal
jarred his concentration on the electric chair—
hanging like an oasis in his air
of lost connections...

—Robert Lowell,
"Memories of West Street and Lepke"

We are aware that our parents grew up through a Depression, but we are little aware that the Depression took place in a different country. From 1890 until 1950, the population of the USA grew by nearly 150 percent, from 62 million to 150 million. Most of that increase took place between 1890 and 1920, when immigration to America was at its peak. The generation of children who passed through the Depression was, among other things, the first truly native generation of these immigrants' offspring.

Their parents or grandparents did not speak American English; in the schools these kids attended, getting them to speak American, and only American, was a priority for teachers. When the kids left school, they went home to ethnically defined neighborhoods, where the language of the Old Country, the shops of the Old Country, the food of the Old Country, and its accent, were on every side. When they grew up, that world would vanish—not only for Afro-Americans who had lost their roots, but for those of European descent, who abandoned the world of their fathers.

One of the first signs I noticed of this was that an awful lot of the fathers of kids in my schools had changed their names. Now, this was an American tradition; "Ellis Island Shorthand," the cutting of syllables from foreign-sounding names, was regularly practiced by officials meeting immigrants at the foot of the Statue of Liberty ("Karpenterovsky, you say? Well, now it's Carpenter").

But it was another thing for a grown man deliberately to change his name—as my father did, and a half-dozen of the fathers of boys I went to school with.

Syllables were dropped, to get a faster, American sound (you know, more like "Smith," "Jones," or "Doe"); in one case I knew of, my friend Blosky's grandfather had changed his name from Bolonovski. Sometimes, as in my father's case, men changed their ethnicity with their names. (Because of my name, and my dark hair and blue eyes, I went through high school, where kids always wanted to know each other's ethnicity, listening to my peers guess that I was Black Irish, a descendant of the Spanish sailors who drifted onto Ireland when the English sank their Armada. In fact I am one-half mixed Italian, and one-half Polish Jew, a not uncommon mix in New York, where I was born; this was the kind of detail in which kids discussed this matter.)

When I first learned that my father had changed his name, and then noticed that the same thing was true for more than a few of my friends, I was shocked. Changing one's name, I knew from my fairy tales, is a magic act that gives new powers to the person who makes the change. Armed with a new name, a tailor who has killed seven flies can become a king, and win a princess. Armed with a secret word, like the ones radio-serial heroes possessed in the days when our fathers were listening to radio, a boy in tough neighborhood streets could become a superman.

But the old name retains a magic power too—a power that can be seized by one's enemies. Criminals understand the principle; it is why they use aliases, go by made-up names. A man's true name tells you where to find him, where he came from, how he can be hurt (or who is protecting him).

My father had claimed, and risked, these powers. Leaving the Navy after the war, he went to college on the GI Bill—like one out of seven veterans, 2.2 million of them in all (not to mention the 7.1 million whose way was paid, back when a dollar went far, through other schooling or job training).

He married a girl he met at college (who dropped out when their first child arrived, in her eighteenth year, as women kept on doing up to the 1980s).

When he graduated from college and got a job teaching, then in an office, he put his wife and three kids into a home bought with a Veterans Administration guaranteed loan (in the peak year of 1956, when both Korean and World War II veterans applied, 607,000 such loans were granted). He had two things his father had not had: his own home and a college education. In American terms, he was already a success. Then he wrote books, and began signing English names to them. Finally he chose one of the names, and kept it.

When I first asked my father why he had changed his name, he did not tell me. Years later, when I had been in the writing business awhile, I asked if he had changed his name because American readers prefer authors with Anglo-Saxon names. He replied, "The primary reason I changed my name was because there was and still is, a lingering prejudice against Italians in the United States.   Indeed I have often wondered what my own life and carreer would have been like if my name were Italian.

I grew up among men who, like my father, came out of big cities where men looked for work, or did the work they could get (when my grandfather's pool hall vanished in 1930, along with spare change, he became and stayed a mail carrier). They went to war and came home heroes: they had saved the world from Fascism, and Russia did not yet have our Bomb. They had made the world safe, if not for democracy, then for themselves and their families.

A grateful society gave them an education and a house. They filled those houses, and those new suburban driveways around the country, with shiny new things made in American factories. They took on new names, or new titles—which amounts to the same thing—in new companies. They had children of their own, who went to bright new schools, where the necessity of teaching children English was now a distant memory.

Part of the price our fathers paid for those achievements, of course, was working—working to sustain a prosperity that they had never known in childhood (what did a man born in 1925 remember from before the Depression?), but which childhood memories of a father's fall had taught them might not last forever. They never forgot those memories—never forgot that what was here today could be gone tomorrow. If they never forgot, it was partly because they had abandoned, with their old names, the places they had come from, the names that went with those places, the people behind the names.

In the old neighborhood, parents and children might have apartments on the same block, in the same building. In the suburbs, the children from such neighborhoods had only each other, and their own little families. Men who had grown up with fathers who worked in the neighborhood now left their homes and went into the city to work, leaving wives and children behind. They were on their own, in a rich new world, carrying within them, like a secret identity, the poverty of the old.

I realized something of that when I went to help my mother pack the house I had grown up in, after my parents' divorce, when she moved to the city to get a job (talk about unsung pioneers of the Second Wave; divorced women with grown, struggling children risked their all to make feminism of the workplace a reality, because they had no choice). It fell to me to clean out the kitchen cupboards. I hadn't thought about it growing up, but those cupboards contained enough canned food to feed six people for a week, without rationing. Then I remembered the massive refrigerators of my friends' homes, always loaded with fresh fruit, vegetables, and milk, their freezers carrying a three-day supply of frozen dinners; and how, alongside all that stuff, my mother kept the merest leftovers until they rotted.

She had never lost the feeling that somehow, someday, there might not be anything to eat. Her parents had not protected her, not completely, from the fear of hunger; there had been too much of it, in that broken decade after the Crash, enough so that even a protected child would see it.

This was the woman who married my father, whom he would try to protect as his own father could not have done. And who would prove to him that he had become a man, the kind of man who could not exist in his father's world.

I asked my father once if it had been as hard for him to break free of his parents' world as it had been for his grandparents to cross the ocean from Italy. He gave me a confused and rather upset look. In many ways he's a modest man, and my question sounded like an invitation to boast. But it was also the first time I put to him, directly, something he hadn't really admitted to himself: he had crossed an ocean of culture.

He, and other men of his generation, had built a new world for themselves, and the old American world had simultaneously been destroyed. They were cut off from it; could not easily go back, to escape, or to understand. Long physical distances, and others of wealth and food and language and dress, the most banal stuff of daily life, separated them from the generation before them.

And this was, in a way their sons' was not, a generation gap of their own making. They had been present at the sacrifice of the fathers who failed; watched and participated in some deeply remembered rite, so that the world might live, the way barbarians killed their kings to placate misfortune. And for bearing that witness, they had been crowned with the good things of life, each a king in his castle.

They had done what they had to do; but they bore the guilt of usurpers. When their own sons rose against them, in the heat of wartime during the 1960s, they would feel it not only as a revolt but also as their crimes, their trials, their condemnation. And they would rage, plead, justify themselves: *how could it have been otherwise?*

THE BEST A MAN COULD DO

The Man in the Gray Flannel Suit added a phrase to our language on its publication in 1955—a phrase we still have in mind when we talk about our fathers. But the phrase quickly became confounded with another, which entered our speech only a year later, through William H. Whyte's warning of the dangers to individualism in our increasingly corporate society, where *The Organization Man* was replacing the Protestant Ethic with the Group Ethic. Whyte's image is the one that stuck; when we hear of "the man in the gray flannel suit," we think of crew-cut drones in shapeless costumes, commuting to jobs where, as Whyte said, "they are not too easily distinguishable from the others in the outward obeisances paid to the good opinions of others."

There he is, the good pluralist liberal hypocrite of the Eisenhower Age, keeping his feelings concealed for the sake of reason, going along with others to be part of the organization, dumb and happy in his lonely crowd. You may recognize the caricature we made of our fathers in the sixties, the bogeymen we are still trying not to become in the eighties. But Whyte's portrait, like Sloan Wilson's, which it complements, is more complex than we recall these days.

Like Ehrenreich's mature husbands, whose home lives had become another grinding job, Whyte's organization man had learned that "the man who keeps his work separate from leisure and the rest of his life . . . wouldn't get very far." Work and leisure had to fit the same pattern, in which work was uppermost. So far, so square.

But the organization man was hardly untroubled by the balance he made:

He believes in leisure, but so does he believe in the Puritan insistence on hard, self-denying work—and there are, alas, only twenty-four hours in a day.... He still works hard, in short, *but now he has to feel somewhat guilty about it.* [My emphasis.]

Why? Because he consumes so much on credit, instead of neither borrower nor lender being, in Poor Richard's formula; because he is trying to prove his good old self-reliance, to "suppress the thought that he was a bureaucrat," one of "those people . . . who preferred safety to adventure." He is no longer the independent, frugal, yet softhearted tough who built America, and he knows it, even if he can't admit it.

But he doesn't feel compelled to admit it, either. For one thing, his wife isn't forcing him to—not the way women began pressuring men to change in the early 1970s. She's happy with the situation: "You don't find as many frustrated women in a place like this," a young woman in a new suburban development told Whyte. "We gals have each other." And when the man came home, Whyte shows, there were community groups, community projects, and so on. The couples he describes have plenty in common, even if they apparently had very little privacy. They may feel, from time to time, that they are missing something, but cannot say exactly what:

They sense that by their immersion in the group they are frustrating other urges, yet they feel that responding to the group is a moral duty— and so they continue, hesitant and unsure, imprisoned in brotherhood.

In *The Man in the Gray Flannel Suit,* Wilson showed a sharper, but still ambivalent, picture of that conflict. Tom Rath (the homonym was deliberate, writes Wilson) was anything but contented in his prison. But his conflict— a somewhat blurred, but strikingly similar conflict to our own contemporary yearnings—was not a matter only of choosing which working unit would swallow him up; he was trying desperately to avoid being swallowed.

The scion of an old Protestant New England family fallen on hard times— not at all incidentally, because his father went down, body and soul, in the Crash—Tom Rath wants to get a job with the United Broadcasting Corporation, because "he thought he might be able to make a lot of money there fast." He doesn't care a bit for work in and of itself, as Wilson shows throughout the book; and he wouldn't really care for money, either, if it weren't for his family. Asked for "the most significant fact" about himself by his future employer, he reflects that "I have children . . . that's probably . . . the only one that will have much importance for long." That, and the fact that during the war he "had killed seventeen men," among them, by accident, his best friend. He is lucky to be alive, but without his kids, it would be empty luck.

Later we learn that before coming home from the war, he had loved a woman in Italy, who bore him a child—and whose existence he has never revealed to his loving but childlike wife, Betsy, the mother of three more children with him. Rath's current problem is not only how and when to tell Betsy the truth, but how he can earn more money for his family without selling his soul to his powerful, lonely boss, Ralph Hopkins, president of the United Broadcasting Corporation.

When Rath makes his way up the corporation's ladder, and becomes a surrogate son to the big boss, he is faced with a moment of truth. Hopkins is dragging his protégé around the country, preparing him for a lifetime of unending work. And Rath, hesitantly, confusedly, turns him down:

"Look, Ralph," he said, using the first name unconsciously, "I don't think I do want to learn the business. I don't think I'm the kind of guy who should try to be a big executive. I'll say it frankly: I don't think I have the willingness to make the sacrifices. I don't want to give up the time. . . . Nobody likes money better than I do. But . . . *I want to be able to look back and figure I spent the time between wars with my family, the way it should have been spent.*" [My emphasis.]

By the end of the book, Rath will have opened his past to his wife, who rushes away into the night, then comes back to him; he has given her the answer, in spades, to her question, "You're going in there [to work] to-morrow and lie to the man if you figure that's what he wants. . . . How long will it be before you decide it isn't necessary to tell the truth to me?" He has been honest beyond the call of duty—a virtue that became a general social and intimate obligation when the gray flannel man's kids grew up, another piece of their inheritance—and Betsy has no choice but to accept his honesty.

Meanwhile, he has been promised a job that will pay well, but will leave him time—as much time as any working man gets—to help his family grow. It is an imperfect solution—we have not yet heard the answer to Betsy's complaint that "we don't seem to have any *fun* anymore"—but he knows only too well that he lives in an imperfect world.

Rath has to see his situation in black-and-white terms, as a choice between boss and family, honesty and selling out, in order to make any kind of choice at all. The book's drama depends on showing how enticing the alternative represented by Hopkins could be; on a business trip, Rath is approached by a lovely young girl who invites him to a party. He turns her away: "I can't." His world is so precarious that if he gives in to temptation for a moment, it will fall apart.

"There are a lot of contradictions in my own thinking," he admits. "I'm still ambitious. I want to get ahead as far as I possibly can without sacrificing my entire personal life."

The note rings false: there is a dissonance in its harmony. A man can sacrifice a lot without giving up his *entire* personal life.

The precise question, then and now, is how much of his personal life, and what kind, a man must give up in order to make his way in the world. That, too, is our inheritance, one of the pawn checks we must re deem.

Rath's answer is tainted. He knows that he's no genius, of business or anything else. "I never will be," he tells Betsy, "and the main reason is, I don't want to be . . . running any big outfit is incredibly hard work." He is a virtuous man, but an average one. And he always will be. To live for his family is not only the best choice he can make, it is the only shot at eternity he is likely to get.

His choice, in other words, is not only a matter of love, but of calculation. The two coexist, in an uneasy balance. The end—his family's happiness, and his own—justifies the means, the compromise Rath makes.

But the price of maintaining the balance is heavy. Not only must Rath admit that he hasn't got what it takes to reach the top. *He must admit that in and of itself, his life is worthless* (even destructive—is he not a proven killer?). Betsy and the kids make his existence worthwhile; which means that *if they denied him, rejected him, he would scarcely exist.* (Is there any wonder that when the sons of America turned a harshly critical eye on our fathers in the 1960s, our fathers reacted as though we were trying to an-nihilate them?) And like the immigrant child who grew up and fled the city, there is no one else behind him, to catch him if he falls.

What glory and shame there is in this compromise; to deny oneself, in order to be resurrected. To sacrifice one's labor, and be given love. How beautiful.

And how awful.

The imbalance between work and love did not begin with my generation. Whyte's organization men, like the man in the gray flannel suit, worried covertly and openly about the way their working lives and their intimate lives affected each other.

But recognizing that a problem exists is far from defining it, let alone finding a solution. My generation defined the problem in Manichean terms: the way our parents lived, and what they lived for, was all wrong. Therefore, if we were different, we would be all right.

My God, were we wrong.

FATHERS, KEEPERS

Were our fathers really like Tom Rath, or was this merely rhetoric, a patina of tender lies over the cold reality of a cold era? My generation, educated in universities where graduate students discovered Karl Marx with the excitement reserved for forbidden fruit—which is what Marxism became and stayed in the USA after World War I—acquired the nasty intellectual habit of seeing history in terms of the neat oppositions of thesis and antithesis, instead of as interpenetrating currents within a river of movement (a habit that the spiritual movement, with its macrobiotic idea that the yin and yang of things are merged degrees of each other, tried hard to overturn). Thus we denied that our fathers could feel, at one and the same time, that they were making a sacrifice for the sake of those they loved, and hated that sacrifice.

But despite the fact that so many of our fathers divorced our mothers, or spent such long hours at work—as do most of their sons—or didn't know quite how to cuddle or change us in our cradles, the fathers I observed over fourteen years of my life, while going through elementary and high schools with the same kids, felt compelled in one way or another to prove their love and pride in their children—to be, in a word, good fathers.

The exceptions stood sharply out from the rest: I am thinking of the men who would hit their kids on the merest pretext, with strangers (like me) in the house to witness; or of the man who competed with his teenage son for the latter's girlfriends, a sort of emotional brutality (not to mention most unfair competition); or those who could not control their drug habits (wealthy executives who lunched on pills were as common in the sixties as cocaine stockbrokers in the eighties), and were as much fun to live with as any junkie. Kids are perfectly capable of judging adults, and the kids I grew up with judged such men as bad fathers, distinct from the majority. Their acts were news to us, fresh events to be thoroughly dissected and analyzed, precisely because they exposed us to events that were out of the norm.

Good fathers did not hit their kids. Good fathers did not stay home drunk, like the father of one of my friends in elementary school. They went to work and came home early enough to have dinner with the kids. Good fathers got along with Mommy, and had nice friends who had nice kids. Good fathers would stand behind you, or if necessary in front of you, if you got into trouble so steep you couldn't handle it.

In short, they would protect their children, in any and every way that they could.

For example, one way in which my father tried to protect the three of his children was to deny the discord between himself and my mother that ultimately led to their divorce. That he and my mother succeeded in this sad and ultimately fruitless task, like so many other parents at this time, could be measured in the complete shock I felt when I was finally informed, at the age of nineteen, of their separation.

And another way, the main way our fathers protected us, was by earning money for us.

It was taken for granted by the kids I grew up with that fathers spent money on their children. Usually, they spent as much as they could. If a kid wanted a toy, and the father could make the money for it, and the kid had been good or would be good while Daddy earned the money, the kid would get it. Some daddies had more money than others, and even we kids considered it a good thing, unless we were ashamed of being rich, to have a daddy who made plenty. We learned early to see what money could buy, and to like it, to want it. Not incidentally, good fathers did not worry their children about money, except to teach them that it counts and you must earn it; *every one of the men I interviewed, whatever his social class, said that his father never discussed money in front of the children.* Compare that to the fact that arguments over money have been the most important source of marital discord in surveys conducted over three generations, and you will realize how much work it took to keep the kids out of those fights.

Our fathers wanted success for us—as much as they had wanted their own, often enough. It would prove something—that they had not sired losers, weak pups, perhaps. Or that they could finally "give my children extravagant Christmases," as my father once told a reporter.

We had made a bargain between us, to do as well as our fathers had, to redeem their struggle on our behalf. We were bonded by pride, in ourselves and each other, for maintaining the bargain; and by resentment, that we had to carry such loads for each other's sakes; and by embarrassment, over what we could not give each other, in spite of all we gave. We were all like children, opening our Christmas presents with the suspicion that we did not deserve them.

That is the truth, about a certain kind of family: the family that our fathers raised, or hoped to raise: a family with a comfortable present, a rich future.

· · ·

But there was a problem with the bargain, and it came out when the sons grew ashamed of having what their fathers gave them. You can hear that shame, from grown-up children who had cleared their plates because "children are starving in Europe," in the *Port Huron Statement,* the radical penmanship of Students for a Democratic Society (SDS) leader Tom Hayden in 1962:

> Many of us began maturing in complacency. As we grew, however, our comfort was penetrated by events too troubling to dismiss.... While two-thirds of mankind suffers undernourishment, our own upper classes

—the same classes from which a high proportion of young radicals came, according to a famous study by Richard E. Peterson, "The Student Left in American Higher Education"—

> revel amidst superfluous abundance ... sapping [the] earth's physical resources.... Some would have us believe that Americans feel contentment amidst prosperity—but might it not better be called a glaze about deeply felt anxieties about their role in the new world?

Our fathers, it seemed, protected us all too well. They fed us the world's cream, and let others starve on the skim. They contained any and every threat that could strike us—"containment" was official U.S. strategic policy, at the same time that Colgate's "invisible shield" was protecting our teeth. They gave us wealth, learning, power.

And we took our own complacency for theirs. We claimed that in making a world for us, they had implicated us in their shame, their greed, their hypocrisy.

The problem, as my generation of men saw it, was that the world of our fathers had betrayed its own values, its own promises. To protect its children, it made war on someone else's children; to make all men equal, it separated the black skins from the whites; to make us adults, it kept us in a state of perpetual childhood.

You hear that angered sense of betrayal echoing through the sixties. "The U.S. government has deceived us," declared the Student Non-Violent Coordinating Committee in 1966, in its claims of concern for the freedom of the Vietnamese people, just as the government has been deceptive in claiming concern for the freedom of colored people . . . in the United States itself. . . . United States law is not being enforced. . . . We maintain that our country's cry of "preserve freedom in the world" is a hypocritical mask. . . .

The hypocritical mask of the father, who promised life—the good life—and then held it down, in the segregated cities of the South, the ghettoes of the North, the terrain of Vietnam. Beneath our rhetoric, we felt betrayed by our fathers: *we had thought that the roles they played for us, as unfailing protectors, were real; and we were infuriated, and frightened, when we learned that all along they had been faking it, to protect us from their own inadequacies.*

If Daddy gave death, it was because his own life—had he not been saying so himself?—was deadly. He lived in "little boxes," like coffins, and that's what he had marked out for his children, as Malvina Reynolds said in a popular folk song of the era. It was easy to use that against him: "People who build gray cities, and wear gray suits, and lead gray lives," says a hippie quoted approvingly by sixties radical Mark Gerzon in *The Whole World Is Watching,* "tell their children that what isn't gray is strange." Junior might be a Freak, but Dad was a Frankenstein.

It was not coincidental that the preferred target of the counterculture and the New Left was the "white liberal"—the poor old organization daddy, "lifeless and dull" in "the formality of the coat-and-tie world," as Gerald Rosenfield of the Free Speech Movement put it with what in yuppie-era retrospect seems like ludicrous self-assurance.

The father who had tried most to be good, and had most succeeded, was the father whose failure was most disgusting.

CHAPTER
—— 20 ——

The Last Time
I Blamed Mother

As 1986 drew to a close, America was once again unhappy with its men. Our beloved President, a straight-shooting, creased fellow in the mold of John Wayne, turned out to be the sort of fool who either can't run his own business or lies to his customers. Our best and brightest on Wall Street and at the Pentagon, when they weren't being arrested for various sorts of multimillion-dollar cheats, were caught in the act of exchanging vital information for drugs, women, or cash.

Plainly, something—or someone—had gone wrong. The general Paul Xavier Kelly, retiring commandant of the Marine Corps, several of whose noncommissioned officers were under investigation for allegedly admitting Russian agents to the most secret chambers of the American embassy in Moscow, blamed working mothers: "Fifty percent of the mothers today work," he told George C. Wilson of the *Washington Post,* "and that means a number of our children are not getting the kind of upbringing in their home that you or I had." By which he meant that "their moral upbringing is being dictated by some nameless, faceless child-care center." There was a problem, and it was a woman's problem; men had other things to do, things that were at least just as important, like defending the right or the duty of women to take care of kids.

Kelly had not chosen a new target: mothers, working or not—in fact, especially when they were not—had been a favorite target of psychologists and filmmakers, to name two popular voices, throughout the fifties, and up through the sixties (when Vietnam made our fathers and leaders look blame-worthy on their own).

If Norman Bates had grown up to be a murdering woman-hater, as he was in Alfred Hitchcock's film *Psycho,* it was because he was still trying hard to please his mother. She had emasculated him, pruned him like you prune a growing tree; Bates's crimes were reenactments of that mutilation (he killed with knives), and a way of claiming his manhood, his primeval power and strength to kill. Something like this construct figured as well in the psychology of homosexuality, where the idea that emasculating mothers produced men who wanted to sleep with each other was dominant, until the Gay Liberation Movement advanced the idea in the late sixties that homosexuality was inherent in human nature.

It had grown so loud, this hatred of mothers, that Friedan felt compelled to take it apart, piece by piece, in *The Feminine Mystique.* By current standards, her defense started on the wrong foot: she conceded the crimes mothers committed against their children. In examining a study of child-beating, she admitted that "the 'parent' with most opportunity to beat that child was, of course, the mother." But Friedan took responsibility for such events off the shoulders of individual women:

> It is time to stop exhorting mothers to 'love' their children more, and face the paradox between the mystique's demand that women devote themselves completely to their home and their children, and the fact that most of the problems now being treated in child-guidance clinics are solved only when the mothers are helped to develop autonomous interests of their own, and no longer need to fill their emotional needs through their children.

Note the repetition of the word "need." Friedan's defense implied—just as Human Potential psychology was doing for men in this decade—that the expressive wife and instrumental husband weren't getting what they needed from each other. And she also made it plain that wives could not morally or practically be blamed for holding up their side of the bargain, any more than for failing to uphold it.

Let me note, having raised the subject, that physical and emotional abuse, among the men with whom I raised this subject, did sometimes come from the mother. It is not true, as current wisdom in the child-abuse reform movement holds, that men do all the abusing of women and children in our families.

The men I spoke with—three of them—who have experienced that abuse had three reasons for hiding it, the second of which does not apply, I think, to women to the same degree. First is that when they expose their experience to others, they must face the question that falls on any victim of sexual abuse: "Didn't you invite it?" The second is that when they are so confronted—as I confronted a man, the first time I heard someone say this—they cannot call on feminist theory, feminist support (which goes, in practice, almost entirely to women) in answering, as they tried to answer, but rarely found words to tell me: "No. I loved my parent, and trusted my parent, and wanted to care for my parent—to become the parent I needed. And so I was trapped. And if I was not helpless, with my parent in front of me, I remembered when I was, and entered into that time again."

And like any children, they did not know better; they did not know that what their parent or parents did to them was beyond human limits. "I didn't realize what was going on," said one, "until I got to high school, and could stay away from home more"—his mother, his abuser, had forbidden him visits until then—"and saw that what was happening to me wasn't normal." Said with a blank face, matter of fact, the shrug that embraces what the world is.

If women were sometimes to blame for the way children turned out, Friedan argued, this was a sign of social illness, of a sick society. She didn't invent the idea—"I am sick!" shouts a Jet in *West Side Story,* the delinquent victim of a "social disease." But she gave it a new twist: the intimate bargain between men and women made women ill, and they passed that illness on to their children: "neither therapy nor love was enough to help these children, if the mother continued to live vicariously through the child," she said.

If men lived through a woman, and felt ill because of it, women lived through their children, and were just as badly damaged. "For women of ability, in America today, I am convinced that there is something about the housewife state that is dangerous," she argued—as much of a danger as that facing "the millions who walked to their own death in the concentration camps." Who would blame the Jew, the Gypsy, the Resister, for what the Nazis did to him or her? And who could deny that

> It is surely as true of women's whole human potential what earlier psycho logical theorists have only deemed true of her sexual potential—that if she is barred from realizing her true nature, she will be sick.

And with her, of course, the children subjected to her sick love, her vicarious need to live through them, her desire to smother the flowers she raised, to keep them clutched to her heart.

Friedan was looking back on a decade in which "delinquency" became a social concern, first among sociologists and journalists watching the urban poor whose malevolent offspring roamed the blackboard jungle, and then among the middle classes (when I was in junior high school, Connecticut state police closed the border with New York to teenagers wanting to go out and get drunk in the latter state's adolescent cowtowns). The kids raised with every advantage an instrumental father and expressive mother could provide were caught in a perpetual "floundering or trial process," as a 1957 opus on *The Psychology of Careers* called it. They were rebels without a cause—after all, what cause did they, could they, have to rebel?

But rebelling they were, even then. And mothers, Friedan announced, were not about to take the blame.

Friedan was one of the few feminist writers who nearly always argued from a belief in the commonality of men and women—which made it sound true when she warned that like men, women were undergoing "progressive dehumanization." As common as the latter term had become—Ortega y Gasset's "The Dehumanization of Art," for example, was a standard text in college literary courses of the sixties and seventies—Friedan's version still has a curious undertone: it suggests that progressivism was precisely what was dehumanizing in our society. And this was indeed curious, in a country that had always identified itself with the triumph of progress, that saw itself as a city on the hill, a beacon for humanity.

But Friedan had picked her moment well: if the notion of progress through science was stronger than ever for Whyte's organization men, some doubt had crept into their confidence. The winning of World War II, as writers like Dinnerstein and Elisabeth Badinter have noted, involved the admission, as well as the commission, of crimes against humanity—crimes carried out on a scientific basis, in keeping with the most up-to-date methods, whether the victims were in concentration camps, or under a hail of fire bombs, or choked by the poison fruit of *Enola Gay*. "If the Japanese had won," remarked Lenny Bruce, "they'd have strung Truman up by the balls" for what he did to Hiroshima and Nagasaki. An obscene truth.

Axis and Allies had made the wiping out of entire societies into the basis of strategic warfare. Generations that followed had a logical reason for tarring them with the same brush, and did. In an unsigned (1963) review of Joseph Heller's bestseller *Catch-22,* a writer in *Daedalus* complained that in the eyes of the book's admirers,

Presumably no distinction exists between the morality of the Nazis, who murdered non-Nordic countrymen because they were non-Nordics, and the morality of the Danes, who rescued non-Nordic country-men because they were human beings—all the morality "of this world" is equally "preposterous." The American effort which Mr. Heller "sat-irizes" was not a crusade, but some Americans who died in it, perhaps even a few colonels, fought as they did because they hated cruelty.

But cruelty had won, in the name of progress. Progress meant efficiency, progress meant rationality, progress meant science; progress could kill. "Think of what science has done for us!" shouts a mad scientist in the 1950s horror film *The Thing from Another World.* "Electricity, atomic energy—" And a soldier cuts him off: "Thanks a lot."

If people forgot it was a dangerous world, they would remember, when Civil Air Defense spotters asked to use their hill as a lookout for Russian bombers (that's from *The Man in the Gray Flannel Suit*), or when their kids came home, bewildered, to tell Mom how their teachers had called a bomb drill, making them lie on their knees in the dusty halls, hands hooked over the backs of their necks. (That memory was what made an anti-nuclear-power poster sell along the California coast in the early eighties: in case of a reactor meltdown, the poster suggested, one should get into just such a position, and "kiss your ass good-bye.")

Women found themselves in a world where what men made was what, at any moment, could smash and burn flat to the ground. Men, it seemed, had broken an essential promise. They could still bring home a paycheck, but they could not protect anyone from annihilation. The best they could do was annihilate someone else.

Progress was not only menacing the home: it had come *into* the home, along with television, convenience food, and washing machines; and in more ways than one, it was making a woman's life miserable.

Depression and war had split up families, forced them to keep moving, to separate; as husbands failed wives and moved along, women took their children on the road or sent them to relatives; and again, when men went into the Army, were killed (like General Kelly's father), or came home to VA housing developments. Women raised in large families, common until the Depression made children a bitter luxury, and who became adults and parents in the postwar era, no longer had their older siblings, their grandparents, their cousins, to show them what to do when baby got a colic, or how to keep up with the diaper drain. Nor did they have a man around to help, not anywhere near as much as help was needed. The men were working, building the richest society the world had ever seen.

But meanwhile, new lives—the very future of the society—were depending on women. Unfortunately, even with a house full of shining machines, the women did not know what they *should* do. "I will tell you," said a woman who gave up her job in 1949, when she married a veteran and moved across the country, and found herself alone with two children every day, "I was desperate." She needed help; it is one thing to improvise for yourself, and another to improvise a child's development.

Fortunately—at least that's how it seemed at the time—science stepped into the gap. Child psychology, pediatrics, and sociology developed guidelines and models of how families functioned—a first step toward defining how they *should* function—only to make things more confusing than ever.

What the young new wives of hardworking, rising men did, when the Baby Boom washed over them, was to use the years (usually one or two) they spent at college or finishing high school before marrying, learning to study, in the service of motherhood. They bought Dr. Benjamin Spock's guidebook to parenting, *The Common-Sense Book of Baby and Child Care,* by the millions, and then the tens of millions. The book was chock-full of "sensible present-day ideas of the care of a child, taking into account his physical and emotional needs," as the doctor introduced it.

The first (1946) edition, like the second, assumed that the primary readers were women. Men, Spock thought, would help, but most of the time they would not be there. You get the idea that he didn't like the assumption; with prescient gender courtesy, he said that "I want to apologize to half the fathers and mothers . . . Everywhere I've called the baby 'him.' " (Is it mere coincidence that girls raised by this book tried to find gender-neutral terms for humans a generation later?) But he knew that women were doing most of the baby-work.

They always had. But now they had to rely first on their own common sense, and not on anyone's experience: "Better to make a few mistakes from being natural than to do everything letter-perfect"—and maybe emasculate "him"—"out of a feeling of worry," said Spock. And when it came down to it, a woman had little else to rely on: "we don't know all the answers yet," admitted Spock (the note of progressive hope: someday we will know all the answers). "Our ideas about how to treat a child have changed a lot in the past and will certainly change in the future."

When had women, married to men, ever been more alone? Not just to play with their appliances, but to figure out how to use them; not just to drive around in a big new car, but to drive to stores, school, playgrounds, over as many hours a day as native women in drought country would spend seeking water? Not just to love the kids, but to save them from whatever happened, armed only with a telephone, a busy pediatrician's phone number, and pages of self-declared transitory wisdom?

Mother deserved credit for raising the kids—an extraordinary act of hope, and perhaps of courage, in a world as uncertain as this. But when you got right down to it, she could not be blamed for how they turned out, and not only because she had the excellent excuse that nobody knew what to do, any more than she did.

If men wanted to keep on making the claim that their own flesh and blood mattered to them, they could not put all the responsibility for the outcome of their spawn on a woman. That would amount to admitting that they had never been around when it counted—an admission that would knock the wind right out of the boast that what a man did, he did for love. If his claim were more than a boast—if, poor sot, he actually believed it— then the failure of his family would be his own. Once again, his sacrifices would have turned out to be a cosmic joke, with him under its heavy butt.

This was a nasty trap, even if men had set it for themselves. Unfortunately, in trying to get out of it, starting in the sixties, men opened its jaws even wider. The Human Potential rhetoric of the "I want a new life" school of divorce gave men the opportunity to believe that since everyone was responsible for his or her own happiness, they were not bound to go on protecting the happiness of their families, if doing so made them miserable. Writes Ehrenreich,

> The male rebels of the '50s had found marriage financially burdensome and sexually repressive; the new psychologists found it, from a scientific point of view, improbable ... the probability that two people's trajectories would overlap or run parallel was about as remote as two meteors coming into alignment ...

The probability that the trajectories could be controlled, of course—that kids would turn out the way the books said they should, among other things—was even more remote. And that made the whole breadwinner equation look like trick arithmetic; if a man couldn't, despite his best efforts, make anyone happy unless he achieved it for himself, why fool himself that he could? Why not just do what a herd of experts was telling him—take the money and run?

Instinct had failed women, because women had been dehumanized, argued Friedan. Instinct would save men, argued the Human Potential gurus. Friedan told women that they needed to be more human, in order to live; men told each other that they needed to live, in order to be more human.

And both sides, in theory, agreed not to condemn the other: if separation and isolation carried a certain price, they also carried a certain dignity, a sense of ultimate responsibility. I do my thing, and you do your thing; if one of us screws up, he or she can't blame me.

In no way was that enough for women. In part that was because, when men flew from commitment, they did indeed blame their wives; "no-fault" divorce was not yet invented, and men trying to hold down alimony judgments had vital legal reasons to save their wealth by painting their women with the filthiest brushes a lawyer could devise.

But if women didn't buy the no-blame theory as much as men did, it was also because women had been taking the blame for so long that even when men were ready to propose a self-serving compromise, their wives and mothers were too angry to listen anymore.

You can see that rage in *The Women's Room,* where Marilyn French savages the notion that mother was ever to blame, dispensing with Friedan's careful defensiveness. Similarly, I remember a conversation around 1980 with a feminist activist who refused to read Dinnerstein, because she thought the book might be "blaming the mother," all over again. If men could claim that women had forced them to work, women could darn well claim that men had forced them to take a bad rap for what happened while Daddy was at the job.

Moreover, before long women were rediscovering motherhood—another idea that the New Men would later adopt for their own uses. Rita Mae Brown's *Rubyfruit Jungle,* a feminist bestseller of the mid-1970s, reached its climax with a rapprochement between a young woman and her grandmother, sitting in her rocker on a porch, talking out her love for life while the granddaughter films her. Nancy Friday's *My Mother, My Self,* another bestseller, operated on the premise that a woman could not deny her mother without denying herself.

The realization that women were not, in crucial ways, fundamentally different from their mothers made it impossible for young women of the Second Wave to blame their mothers for the situation in which they found themselves. If their mothers had merely done the best they could, as Friedan argued, and as young women felt they were doing in their own untidy lives, then no one had the right to call those women names.

And that was why, when Kelly blasted the contemporary working mother, he said, "I know I'm going to walk in a very, very tender area." He knew very well that "a lot of people"—the plural of "person," meaning woman, in current usage—"aren't going to like that remark."

Like casual use of the word "nigger," such terms had become obscene. A good man no longer had the right to blame a woman for the way he had turned out, or the way his children were going to turn out. Women had ruled that tactic out of the game. If the world was a mess—and even men had to agree that things looked that way—it was a mess that men had made, while women were doing their best to clean it up.

So who chopped down the cherry tree, after all, and upset life's bowl? Who would do the time for the crime?

Daddy. The lonely hunter, more alone than ever, in a world changing beyond his wildest dreams. And being a good old sport, he took it. God, how he took it, and is still taking it.

The way one Andrew Merton gave it to him, right in the face in the fall of 1986, was by writing a piece called "Father Hunger," which told readers of *New Age* how "A new generation of men are struggling to become the fathers they never had."

Just what did he mean—"never"? Could it be that instead of being absent on official leave, Daddy had been AWOL? That the general had run out on the juvenile troops—the way we were saying that generals in Vietnam had betrayed their fighting youngsters?

Worse: he had not raised his children—not the boys, anyway—but crippled them. Listen to the drip of saliva off Merton's fangs:

> It is likely that both wimp and macho behavior are different manifes-
> tations of the same underlying psychological problem—the yearning
> for a father who never was.

Psychology got us into this mess, it will get us out. But first you must face the awful truth:

chances are that if you are an adult between twenty and fifty-five, your father was not a big part of your childhood, or big only in a negative way: remote, angry, repressed, vindictive....

And that was what we all turned out to be. Even poor "Terry," who "sought situations and relationships that would be unlike his parents' in any respect," was forced by his broken heart and the helpful but inadequate women's hearts he broke to see that "both his father and himself" could not "develop intimacy while attempting to project an image." Not when the reality was that

> The main business of the father's life was not here with the family; but somewhere else, somewhere outside, where life was played out in a broader sphere, which in his son's imagination was much more fascinating, much more exciting.

And worst of all, "even when a father has enough self-esteem to be honest with his children, father hunger is still possible."

I don't wish to be uncharitable, but men who talk so loosely about their fathers seem to me to be hiding something, even if they're not always weaseling out of something.

They are hiding their own memories of, and responsibilities for, what happened between men and their sons in the 1960s, and kept unfolding like a leaden roll of carpeting over our lives in the 1970s. They are denying that they dealt their fathers blows which, if not quite mortal, struck in vital places.

So let us put aside the question, once and for all, of whether our fathers taught us to love. They taught us to work, and that was no small thing.

Let us ask, instead, the question that all of our ranting about father hunger and distant fathers and Patriarchy has apparently not led us yet to ask: what exactly did *we* do to our fathers, to make us hate them so?

CHAPTER

———— 21 ————

When Father No Longer Knew Best

Writer Richard Trainor, aged thirty-three, told me how at the age of eleven, he was sitting with five friends in a car, and realized that none of them had a father living at home. One of the fathers had died; the rest had divorced, not only from their wives, but from their families.

It was as apocryphal a story as one could want, an illustration of a message men of my generation drank with their school-lunch milk: our parents failed us, left us on our own, as alone as they had become themselves. And men, more than women, failed their children, broke down or cut out. So we felt.

But our fathers did not just leave us in the sixties; some of us drove ours away. The decade that discovered Human Potential, that struck down Freud's fatal complexes and replaced them with infinite hope, was the decade that acted out Oedipus' curse, killed the father, and went blind.

I remember a drunken man, the father of three lovely, smart, nice daughters, one of whom I loved, at whose home I passed New Year's Eve of 1969. In the course of his day, this man—who had been forced by the War Department to take a supervising engineer's job in a shipyard during World War II, instead of being *allowed* to go into combat, to his anger and shame— had heard his older daughters' lovers stand up in church and attack the Vietnam war, suggesting that front-line troops were using just as many drugs as the longhairs in the pews. The subject had been raised—the immorality not only of Vietnam but also of the men who ran our society—and we argued about it right up to the stroke of midnight, when we all collapsed, mother, father, daughters, guests, and feebly wished each other Happy New Year.

The parents went off to bed. And then the father came back into the richly furnished living room where the children were standing, shaking our heads. "I just want you to know," he said in a hazy, trembling voice—they always said, *I just want you to know*—"that Nixon has done everything he said he would. Everything he said he would!"

And a few things he hadn't, as it later turned out. But what we knew then—what made our faces hot and humiliated—was that, whether or not Nixon was trying to end the war, as he'd said he would (it seems to me that he was trying to win it, to be a tougher guy than Johnson or anyone else), this man was identified with Nixon's dilemma, as he saw it: *he had done everything he said he would, and his own children despised him for it.*

One cannot understand this confrontation without realizing that a war was going on—that people were getting killed, and that kids were watching the killing on television. And this war exposed us to our parents' failings, at an early age. In the sixth grade, when I saw a Buddhist monk immolate himself in the streets of Saigon, in a photograph published in *Life* magazine, I asked my parents what it meant. They could not tell me, because no one was telling them (as late as 1964, *Time* magazine was warning that the real stakes in Vietnam were Chinese control of Southeast Asia; since 1978, Vietnam and China have been at war with each other intermittently).

They could thus not explain, when the time came—as so many fathers, tried so desperately to do—why men my age should go into the armed forces during this war. They would shout—and for years, until the truth came home, they shouted, or made pointed jokes, or lectured—that we had to fight for the sake of the country, for the sake of freedom; that we had to save our honor, *to know we had been men.*

As they had been. But they were the kind of men we no longer wanted to be, *any more than they did.* They hated their lives, their stress, their work; they had told us so, it was in the air. That was what they took for honesty, and it was honest enough.

They handed us a platter, and we handed it back with their heads on it.

BEATING A MAN TO JOIN HIM

"What the students" of the Berkeley Free Speech Movement, which kicked off a decade's worth of student revolts in 1964, "were fighting for was the right to participate directly in the world they live in, for the right to confront other men and not catalogs and regulations, forms and procedures, an amplified voice and a televised face," wrote radical veteran Gerald Rosenfield.

A generation raised on televised faces, from Robert Young to Robert Kennedy, wanted to "confront" other men—as equals. From the start, *student radicalism in the sixties was a demand for recognition that the sons of the self-made men be granted manhood, by their fathers.*

That is what made Gerzon's *The Whole World Is Watching* seem like "required reading for the over-30 generation," as *Library Journal* declared in 1969. Gerzon saw his generation as "standing before the closed door of manhood," in the face of "parents [who are] still pushing them to reach the old goals via the old values." He made radicalism into an initiation rite, bemoaning the absence of "a functioning institution marking the transition from childhood to manhood."

As it happens, that was how our fathers saw the military, which during World War II had marked just that passage for them. But Gerzon didn't think of Vietnam as an appropriate rite of passage. And it wasn't the one that mattered for the men who stayed home from the war, as he pointed out:

> The new initiation rite, the real entrance to the adult world, is marriage. . . . Marriage is held out to pre-adults as *the* answer to their problems of sexual and social insecurity . . . liberation from the frustration of unrecognized manhood.

But Gerzon saw through that rite, at least a little (a decade later, he would be proposing marriage and child-rearing as the answer to unmanly frustration): "Marriage is not just holy matrimony but the acceptance of social commitment that irrevocably leads to occupational, financial, and social ties that are difficult to sever." I mean, you can't tie a good man down, can you? "Marriage is, in short, becoming adult." A false initiation, if not a fate worse than death.

Had not Father known that all along? Was that not what he had been telling us himself? And did not Father know best?

Whether he did or not, we hoped he did; just as we hoped, deep down, that he would someday come home again, to protect us, and then to acknowledge us. But we did more than hope: we set out to beat our fathers at their own games.

Running through the rebellion of the sixties, alongside the moral yearning for justice, was an element that I haven't seen discussed anywhere else, and which seems to me to be no small thing: a nasty undertone of sexual one-upmanship. You get a hint of it from writers like Rosenfield, who offhandedly mentions the "long-haired chicks" who filled the crowds (and the speakers' beds, one gathers) at Free Speech rallies. You could feel it in the air, when the Sexual Revolution got under way, and boys started bringing home girls who knew where to obtain the Pill, which hit the mass market in the early sixties, and fathers and mothers began to ask each other, "Are they sleeping together?"

One of my father's novels—entitled, appropriately enough, *Sons*—contains a record of the way the next few scenes unrolled: Wat Tyler brings his lover Dana home from school to the family summer spread, and his father shows him the room where he will sleep alone, on a cot. "He was being very tolerant in his attitude," says Wat,

> including us in his adult world where you offered grown-ups drinks if they didn't want to freshen up first after those tedious Long Island parkways, but he was also making it clear he didn't expect any adult hanky-panky under his roof for the several weeks Dana and I would be there, preferring us to fornicate on the open beach instead, I guessed.

Or not at all. Men raised in an era when nice girls didn't say yes until they were married, and in which antibiotics (that is, the class of drugs that can cure syphilis and gonorrhea, and which we are now breeding resistance to by feeding it to our cattle, which we eat) had not yet been invented, found it hard not to worry for their sons who were leaping into girls' beds ("If she's sleeping with you," said my grandfather, "she's sleeping with other guys, and you don't know what they got." Prescient advice, that).

They also found it hard not to envy their boys (when drunk, there was one man in my parents' circle who would stick his tongue down his sons' girlfriends' throats). The fathers grew up having to earn a woman; the sons, as in everything else, got theirs for the asking.

Moreover, the sons took it as their right to move from woman to woman; they could have as many girls as they wanted. Perhaps we were reading our fathers' minds, acting out the fantasies of men who made *Penthouse,* after *Playboy,* a bestselling magazine in the sixties. Perhaps my father thought he was reading ours in *Sons,* published in 1969, when Wat Tyler hears his father over the phone to his mistress, while Wat is making love with Dana; at which point the young man and woman walk "noisily" out of the house, thinking, "The fucking hypocrite."

Of course, we knew—or could have known, if we paid attention—that our fathers desired other women than our mothers. I doubt that anyone would claim these days that we are any different from or better than they in this regard; not after the days of Serial Monogamy (or serial heartbreak) to which we exposed ourselves in the seventies.

But we did not grant our fathers the right that we were claiming for ourselves: to act out our sexual desires whenever and with whomever we pleased. We demanded that they go on protecting us—that they go on acting as if they loved and would never love anyone but our mothers.

And then we had the nerve—I don't know what else to call it—to tell them that we were morally better (because we loved peace, spelled with an I or an E), bigger studs (and not "possessive" about it, you bet), and more honest people than they were.

And meanwhile, we gave our fathers the privilege of imitating us. I am indeed suggesting that if millions of men separated from their wives, it was in part because they were, for a change, trying to be better, bigger, more honest men than their sons. We changed the rules of the game; and being men who had competed all their lives, they set out to prove that they could keep on playing it, at least as well as we could.

Score one for Dad.

But the game was not yet over.

LOVE AND HATE IN THE NEWER-THAN-NEW WORLD

Daddy had been saying that life wore him down, and we were saying that we feared to be like him. Our self-interest in the matter was evident to all concerned, whether it was called "self-liberation" or "not growing up." But there was another, kinder reason for the revolt of the sons, their rejection of their fathers' lives. *If we accepted what they were, and became like them, we would be colluding not only in our own futile deaths but also in theirs.*

We would be leaving Dad to his fate, to his own blindness—and to the less-than-tender mercies of his sons, who would grow up to be his enemies, as Carl Oglesby of SDS suggested in 1965:

> our proper human struggle is not with Communism or revolutionaries, but with the social desperation that drives good men to violence . . . we have lost that mysterious human social desire for equity that from time to time has given us genuine moral drive. We have become a nation of young, bright-eyed, hard-hearted, slim-waisted, bullet-headed make-out artists.

If there was a hope and kindness underlying Oglesby's radicalism—both of which qualities were soon to vanish—there was also a warning. Our fathers were still young then (my father reached my age of thirty-five in 1961), still bright-eyed, bushy-tailed, and tough-hearted; but time would soften them, and we would take their places. *Their betrayal of us would then be compounded, by ours of them.* We would be helpless to change our situation, and if things went on as they did, that situation would make us into father-killers.

If we were only imagining that, so were our fathers. When *Fortune* magazine polled thirty multimillionaires of the self-made variety in 1986, one of them said, "My kids are going to carve out their own place in this world." A lawyer said that of twenty wills he had drawn up for the self-made men, sixteen of them left at least half their fortunes to charity, instead of to their children.

These were men who made their wealth (such as it is) in the postwar era, by their own sweat, like most of our fathers. (While they believed that they were doing the best thing by keeping their children comfortable but insecure, that was not how America's hereditary upper classes function, as I learned when I got the chance to watch them at Harvard. They made certain that their scions were channeled, endowed, guarded, and set up in life, so that their wealth would have a competent guardian for the next generation.) They wanted their children to sweat just as hard as they had. There was a kind of equality in their philosophy, but a fearful one.

Like their world, our fathers were seemingly self-made. That is what they wanted us to be, as well. But their righteousness on this point contained an element of fear, like the fear a man at work feels toward his colleagues: if they handed us the means, we would become their younger, harder-eyed, even brighter competitors. *They taught us to be afraid of what we could do to them, and we became angry that we felt this fear.*

And we hated them for leaving us afraid, as we hated them for being men that we could neither trust nor grow up to become. This hatred was mixed into our love; and that conflict was behind what we now think of as the failure of the counterculture.

THE THREE STAGES OF RADICALISM

I have wondered why the radical movements I witnessed or took part in followed a similar pattern, which usually took about a decade to unwind— the decade that passes between fifteen and twenty-five in a man's life, when he is learning about love and work. I do not mean only the classic transition from young radical to old conservative, though that is part of the pattern; I mean three distinct stages through which the Civil Rights, antiwar, and spiritual movements passed. They arrived at different times in different movements, and sometimes overlapped; but they kept coming, in movement after movement.

The first stage was one of involvement with a new cause, and a new ideal—not just for society, but for oneself. The white and black students and activists who poured into Mississippi in the Freedom Summer of 1964 tried not only to preach equality, but to live as equals (SNCC leader Bob Moses was so torn by the desire for equality that he preferred licking envelopes to running an office for the movement). The cause provided a mission, and a plan to accomplish it—to register black voters in the South, or for the macrobiotic movement later in that decade, to get the world to eat better. It also provided a code of behavior—from how one spoke, to how one dressed, what one read.

In other words, *the movement, whatever its name, gave people a culture to live in—a culture that was called "counter," but which was invented, just as much as our parents had been obliged to invent theirs.*

In that moment of invention, we became the equal of our parents, in a real sense. That was a real achievement, one that kept people coming into these movements, for a while. It was what a man I interviewed had in mind, looking back on the days when he went from one liberation movement and one commune to another, when he said, halfway between a laugh and a shout, "The sixties were *great.*" In that way, they were.

And still are, in numerous ways: if there is a store in your neighborhood that sells whole-grain foods, the cheapest and most nourishing kind, that is because raggedy hippies and freaks made it their mission to make such foods available, beginning in the sixties, to people who had been raised on the salty, sugared pap of the TV-dinner era. If there is a day-care or abortion-counseling center near your home, you can thank feminist activists who turned away from the less-than-tender care which too many doctors and politicians were providing to women and children in the 1970s. These institutions—and that is what they are—were not just efforts to reclaim "power for the people"; they were attempts to reinvent a culture that had disappeared in the postwar era, when people lost the means and ways of caring for each other, within an extended family, an extended neighborhood. In that way *they were efforts to give back to our children what our grandparents' children had lost; to fulfill, in a concrete and symbolic way, our parents' lives.*

A movement reached the second stage, as Friedan suggested in the case of feminism, when its ideals had been accepted by the wider society, and thus were at once reaffirmed—and altered. At the Democratic party convention of 1964, for example, black radicals from the Mississippi Freedom party found themselves unable to compromise with liberals on seating procedures, and walked out on their own victory: never again was a Democratic convention lily-white. But such a victory was seen as a betrayal, a tempting trap set by the pater, the patriarch, a concession that was conditioned on the movement's eternal childhood.

Concessions, of course, did not come easy. The further a movement went, the greater its opposition from without—it is indeed an historical fact that Richard Nixon did his best to destroy the New Left, and largely succeeded—which is one reason that the counterculture broke down and retreated.

But there was another reason: a conflict that arose within each of these movements, as those who had built the movement struggled to retain its uncompromising moral essence—in a word, its identity—as happened within the Women's Movement. But for the radical young men of the sixties, that identity depended, more than anything else, on not being like our fathers.

That was the unconscious motivation, I believe, for the fact that the radicals became more than ever determined to codify, define, and finalize the principles they were living by—to ensure that whatever they grew up to be, it would not be Dad. And that is ultimately what eroded the moral strength of their movements, which is the strength that counts over the course of a lifetime.

In the third stage, people began to be forced out of those movements, by the guardians of ideological flames. Stokely Carmichael and Charles V. Hamilton warned whites that the Civil Rights Movement had become a purely Black Power movement, and would not welcome them as equals any longer: "we cannot and shall not offer any guarantees that Black Power, if achieved, would be nonracist." This was the first kind of separatism to emerge from the caldron of the sixties (in keeping with the popular idea of national liberation as the ultimate in revolutionary thinking, which history seems to have proven it is not), and not the last.

A similar pattern was followed by antiwar activists, who in frustration at the expansion of the Vietnam war turned increasingly toward violence (in the name of revolutionary humanism), driving pacifist elements out of the movement. Men who marched for peace in the first half of the decade—like Carl Oglesby, who was willing to grant that Lyndon Johnson and his advisers were "honorable men"—were succeeded by the Weathermen, who didn't need a weatherman to tell them whose house to blow down. By the mid-1970s, the Symbionese Liberation Army would be fighting for the self-determination of a "nation" the size of a rural kindergarten class, through tactics that included extorting food for "the people" from that patriarch Hearst, after kidnapping his daughter. The generation gap had become a generational war, of the sons against their fathers, and anything their fathers had made.

Those who stayed in their bitter fighting cells—and there were enough of them to keep the struggle going awhile longer—were caught in a cycle of guilt and rage that drove the radicals further and further away from the moral grounding of love, on the hard rock of what is best for another human being, and into a movement founded on hatred, the thrilling but soft-minded urge to destroy one's enemy. Soft-minded, because there remains a moral truth in history, including our own: what we do to others, we grant others the right to do to us. "The murder is most to the murderer," wrote Whitman, "and comes back most to him."

And I cannot tell you how casually young men—men who knew nothing about killing, from the best families, in the best colleges—talked of the inevitability of murder in the sixties, of the coming war between the establishment and young men. One of my subjects, who had served as a white auxiliary to the Black Panthers in California, noticed this at the time: he had quit his collective, he said, because he "got sick and tired" of hearing "people talk about revolution who didn't have the guts for it"—the guts, he implied, to realize that they were talking about murdering and being murdered, that they had set themselves on a road whose consequences were horrific.

Men who wanted to save from itself the world their fathers had made could ultimately think of no lasting salvation but to destroy it, to "burn the motherfucker down." Like the soldiers led by older men who were burning down Vietnamese villages, they would destroy their fathers, in order to save them.

But no matter how far their radicalism took them, they could not escape becoming the men they wanted so desperately not to be. "It's funny," James Mellen, a former early member of SDS who later joined the Weathermen, told Milton Viorst in *Fire in the Streets,* "you start out being against the war and in favor of world revolution, and you end up in a fistfight on a beach with a motorcycle gangster wearing a Nazi insignia around his neck." The sons of the men who had saved the world from Hitler were still trying to finish their fathers' war.

. . .

What these men, along with the rest of the counterculture, did not take into account was how very hard it is to reinvent oneself—and how impossible it is, if one tries simultaneously to deny a large part of oneself.

Our fathers were, indeed, a large part of us—larger than we care to acknowledge, these days. They had grown into us, even if we were trying not to grow up to be them. You could see how far into us they had grown by what happened in the Spiritual Movement in the fall of 1978.

That fall I was editing a weekly in Santa Cruz, where the first concentrated outburst of what became a national phenomenon was gathering critical mass. Its vehicle was the "Circle of Gold"—a chain letter bearing the New Age legend "Trust-Intention-Integrity-Faith-Mutual Support-Prosperity-Blessings." This was the Boy Scout oath of the counterculture, which in the Spiritual Movement reached its purest form. But it was being recited in a scam as morally bankrupt as anything that happened on Wall Street after the Reagan administration gave a green flag to greed.

The letter had begun circulating among the self-help communities going strong in the Bay Area (like est, Arica, or Actualizations), and moved quickly into the independent spiritual communes, organized around the teachings of a guru, that dotted the Northern California coast. It took off when one of those communities realized the profit-making potential of the scheme, and set its members to proselytizing for it; and among their earliest converts was Baba Ram Dass, whose *Be Here Now* (the title says it all) was a bestseller in the counterculture, and whose buying-in amounted to an impeccable endorsement. (Ram Dass, you see, was the movement's father figure.)

What the Circle of Gold proposed was this: a person would pay $50 to possess the letter, and mail another $50 to the person at the top of a list of twelve names on the letter. He would then make a copy, with his name at the bottom of the list, and sell this copy to someone else for $50. He would also accompany the buyer to the mailbox with a check for the person at the top of the copy, to make sure that Faith was kept with the spirit of the letter.

Now, this amounted to a form of anonymous theft. You do not need a math degree to realize that every time the Circle of Gold changed hands, the number of people involved was multiplied by 2—from 1 to 2, 2 to 4, and so on. If you doubled a grain of rice for every square of a chessboard, by the end of the board's sixty-four spaces you would be piling up an unimaginably huge quantity of the grain. This meant that sooner or later, there would not be enough buyers to support the chain; it would grind to

a halt, and millions of people would lose money—which, the letter promised, could absolutely never happen. Some Integrity.

Listen to the arguments the letter-sellers used to get people to overlook
this fact: "I am forever one with the Infinite Supply of God . . . I disclaim
the idea that I am poor, despondent, broke, crushed, defeated, or dependent.
New opportunities are now opening to me." And the final word: "Let the
Lord be magnified which hath pleasure in the prosperity of his Servant."

A deal with the Devil, our Father who art in Hell. Who had promised us
an infinite supply of whatever we wanted, and left us broke, despondent,
crushed, defeated, and finally, inescapably, dependent. Not only on his wealth,
but on his love, in his ability to take pleasure in the prosperity of his child,
his servant. And that was why, when you spoke with the people busily
promoting the Circle of Gold, you heard the echo of a child, at some long-
ago Christmas, opening package after package in a frenzy of greed and guilt,
trying to please his father by pleasing himself.

The counterculture had killed God, the angry Father; and now it was
reviving him in its own image. It wound up with the God it deserved, the
God it had always wanted, the God it had always had.

THE END OF INNOCENCE

Behind the failure of the radicals was another failure—to invent a place
where men and women could go together, and reasons for being there, that
were better than the places and reasons our parents had known. If more
Americans did not follow the young radicals, the blame lies here. And if
some of the ideas of the counterculture have become mainstream, it is
precisely because they met those criteria.

In general, we were all a lot better at saying what was wrong with our
parents and "their" society than we were at providing more than slogans,
or isolated outposts whose different populations weren't even speaking the
same ideological argot ("When I got to California in 1969," a Dutch woman
told me, "people talked more slang than English"). We could break a world,
but we failed to make the one we were going to build in its place, fast
enough to keep up with our rhetoric, and our needs.

That problem hit me very hard one night in the mountains outside Boul-
der, Colorado, the fall after Woodstock Nation proved that one million
people could live outdoors without killing each other for three days (the
kind of symbolic victory in which the counterculture excelled, at least until
Altamont, where Hell's Angels beat a man to death while the Rolling Stones

played on, replaced Woodstock in our minds). I was camping with a bunch of other kids, in a valley as close to Eden as you might reasonably desire. One of our neighbors was a fellow named White Cloud, who cut his hair like an Indian, and carried a hunting knife. (Whatever turns you on, *do it*.)

White Cloud liked to sing, as did we all (nothing wrong with that). He came to the campfire one night, waited his turn while my guitar was being passed around the circle (share and share alike), and then began a ballad that lasted half an hour. Finally someone said, "Hey, man, why not pass the guitar?"

"Well, okay, mother, if you're gonna be like that," he said. He stood up and walked off with my instrument.

I was stoned, and for a moment I was scared stiff. Then I did the smartest thing I could think of. I turned to two guys I had shared brown rice with the night before, and said, "You gotta come with me. He's got a knife."

They gulped, looked at each other, and stood up.

We went and got the guitar back. But I still wondered what would have happened if White Cloud, instead of handing it over to us—he was mentally ill, but not really mean—had pulled his knife, out there where there was no cop to call, no authority to lay down the law and then enforce it. If, say, he had taken my guitar not absentmindedly, but because he was shooting heroin, like one group camped in the valley, and needed it to sell for his habit.

Then I realized that I was living in a culture where there were no rules; where anarchy was not only the gentle individualism of free beings, but the struggle of the stronger over the weaker. *When the old rules go, there must still be rules; in that way we were no more free than we had ever been, and could never be.*

This was why, I think, we found it so easy, and so reasonable, to complain for the course of a generation that we had been "conditioned" by "society"— a complaint that came out of the Human Potential so prized by our fathers, and that we made our own with a vengeance. We could see that we did not have it all figured out—like the members of one household that practiced group sex, whom I interviewed in 1978, and who kept insisting to me that "we're working it out, day by day." But if we did not have the answers, that was because we were confused by what our parents had taught us, which these sexual revolutionaries also insisted on. The fault was theirs, and theirs alone. If we had infinite choice, they had still trapped us in an eternal childhood. So we said.

Our fathers had, in one way, made possible our effort, and our failure, to be free. They had told us it was a tough world, but they had given us a soft one; and in America of the 1960s, before the Vietnam inflation caught up with us, a young person didn't really have to think too far ahead, because the country was so incredibly rich. As Charles Manson discovered, you could feed and clothe a private army on what our parents threw away. And in the most coldly material terms, the radicals of the sixties were living off that same surplus. (If the harder times of the seventies helped to shut down the radicals, coincidentally or not, the system went through a drawn-out shudder with them; we could not escape our common destinies, then or now.)

There was a contradiction in all this—a contradiction that young men felt, that drove our guilty rage all the harder: if we could experiment with our lives so freely, it was because our fathers, as always, were somewhere off in the distance, paying for us. Young men were still living off the soft machine their fathers had made; and that amounted to acknowledging that we had failed to change our fathers' destinies, or our own.

It was not a new failure—Karl Marx, whose light burned so brightly in the brains of young radicals, had not been able to imagine how to get from the dictatorship of the proletariat to the workers' paradise either (which was a main reason Leninism could march through that hole, and create a dictatorship of the party, with the help of the czarist secret police). But it was still a painful one—when collectives broke down in confusion, when communes dissolved in bills that no one was paying, when free love turned out to be as illusory as the free lunch Dad had provided.

The "alternative society," as it was called, did not merely break down, but gave up. As Stephen Gaskin, who did nothing more or less substantial than found a self-supporting spiritual community of several thousand hippies in Tennessee, put it: "This was the first revolution where the winners went home and played Frisbee." Young people who had made the awful, unrelenting effort of inventing a moral code, and a way of life, decided that they had been mistaken, after all. Breaking a world was the easy part; making a new one was a lifetime job.

When "push came to shove," and they grew up, they had not yet put in place a world of their own; they had been too busy attacking the world their fathers gave them. But in the end, they too had to work for a living—to pay rent, buy food and housewares to cook it in, and someday, even, to feed their children. They were now responsible for themselves, at least, and for others, often enough. Improvisation had taken them only so far. It was time to get to work.

The trap we set for our fathers closed, finally, on us. On all of us: the next time you look at David Stockman's self-serving little opus, *The Triumph of Politics,* ask yourself why it was that even a nice Baby Boom farmboy who had the sense to get out of radical movements before the crash would go into politics with the mission of destroying Social Security, the legislation that had saved our parents from the Crash. Ask yourself why Stockman first idolized Ronald Reagan, then did his best to make the old guy look like a jerk. Ask yourself how he could think that he was doing so in the name of "Conservative" virtues, when conservatism, in its classic and higher sense, means guarding the heritage our fathers (and now, our mothers) left us.

My answer is: to gratify the hatred a man feels for his father, and to expunge the hatred he feels for himself, for what he did to the man he hated. To kill two birds with one heavy stone.

THE RADICALS' ATONEMENT

We cannot bring our fathers back as they were before we attacked them: young, strong, handsome, owners of a world they made for our pleasure (or so they said).

But we can become them. It would not be the first time: Warner Berthoff, that superb teacher, once remarked that Hemingway's revolt against bourgeois American values in the 1920s amounted to being "more bourgeois"—more formally brave and true and honest—"than the bourgeoisie." We are being as importantly earnest as Hemingway, it seems to me, in our rage and yearning for our fathers. We have struck an unconscious bargain with them: we will take up their posts, and do the duty they were not man enough to do, starting with loving up the wife and kids, instead of just being loved.

The main business of our fathers' lives was making money; if you don't mind my saying so, that seems to be the main business of my generation too, not to mention the tough little beasts following our trail. I doubt that this is something we can condemn our fathers for. If they raised us to think that America was "half-factory" (their half) and "half-playground" (our half), as one of my subjects put it, it was always understood that sooner or later, little boys become men and get off the playground.

But the way young men have taken to talking about their fathers, you can tell that they are angry about doing it. And guilty—a guilt no less apparent for being hidden, and projected onto our fathers. We have become artists at refusing guilt—a refusal that shames us, in the part of ourselves that remembers the truth, generating a pain that drives our anger, that leads us to deny and commit our sins all over again.

The denial is taking the form of re-creating our fathers' lives: that is one meaning of the mass of evidence showing that when young people get married and have a child, they live more or less as their parents did, for the first five years of the child's life, at least.

Along with this denial goes a backhanded affirmation, which shows in the numerous couples who are marrying, or living together for years and years, and not having children. My experience of such couples tells me that some of them include at least one partner, and often two, who sincerely doubts his or her worthiness to be a parent. It's as if these people feel that, while they can accept their parents' failure *as parents,* they don't believe that they will be any better in the job.

Our salvation was to be unlike our fathers. But we have turned out to be like them: if our mission in life was to redeem them, in the end we could find no other means than to become them—to kill the king, so that the king might live forever.

CHAPTER

22

The Right Questions, and the Wrong Answers

Has our experience taught us something? Have we changed so much, or not at all? The questions are irrelevant, practically speaking. Our world is changing, and our prospects. Whether we recognize it or not, in these days when the fifties are fashionable (because we want to live there again, or at least look like we do), we have changed with it.

And in the most material terms, we can't go back as far as we might like—back, say, before fathers and sons were at each other's throats and groins. Our standards of living will not be the same as in the rich decades of the sixties and seventies; in most cases, they will fall. But our standards *for* living have not yet fallen—they have grown in the demands we place on love and have remained at least constant in the rewards we expect from work. That is particularly true for the generation following my own.

The currently young cannot repeat—or redeem—all of the mistakes of their elders, because they will not have the chance. But that does not mean they will not try. And from what I can see, at least some are trying, with the most striking hope, strength, and discipline imaginable.

When the Roper Organization surveyed Americans for the *Wall Street Journal* in May 1987, the poll found that the young are the most optimistic about their personal future of any of us. They defined their personal American dream as "freedom to choose how to live" (80 percent), owning their own homes (in nearly the same proportion), and getting a college education (seven out of ten).

The education was apparently seen as a way of achieving the first two goals: that would be why, "in absolute terms," reported the *Journal of Higher Education,* "business is taking many more of the best students" in college for its courses "than it had in the past," which was also the case for computer sciences and communications majors; simultaneously, "only half as great a share of the best students were choosing a social science major in 1983 as were doing so in 1967," and far fewer were studying literature and other liberal arts than had been the case for my generation.

The generation after my own wants to learn how to make a living; they do not want so much to try, and fail, as we did, to invent a way of life.

They want something like what their grandparents had: a home and a family. Unlike my generation, they are willing to wait for it—how long is anybody's guess, but so far they are waiting—and to work for it, right from the start. The younger men and women want freedom (from financial worry), not anarchy; prosperity, not dependence. At least, that is what they seem to be preparing themselves for.

The young are personally confident, but they are also worried about what they see around them, about how little their leaders seem to be able to accomplish in cleaning it up; and not surprisingly, they do not want to take so many chances as my generation did, because they have grown up looking at new, deeper risks.

They have grown into adulthood watching the growing presence of the poor among us, who now count for 15 percent of our expanded population, up from 11 percent before Reagan took office as President—a difference of millions, in absolute terms, enough to notice. They also notice that certain things my generation took for granted have vanished. A ten-year-old boy, riding in his single mother's old car with her and me, said, "You guys had it lucky. I'll never know what it was like when gas was cheap."

They are right to worry. Unfortunately, there is reason to think that all of their preparation will not be enough—for a minority among them, if things work out for the best, but a large minority. Before I tell you what I think we may or must do to achieve a better next stage than that, it may be best to consider where the ax is starting to fall.

THERE'S GONNA BE RENT TO PAY

"For millions of Americans," wrote Steven Greenhouse of the *New York Times* in July 1986, "the American dream is becoming the impossible dream. . . . Americans are now struggling to fight off downward mobility at the end of a century that has stressed upward mobility."

For example, if you consider being middle-class as owning your own home, an awful lot of us are not going to make it into that comfortable, virtuous (which is how Americans and others see it) bracket, as our parents did. I should have known that back in 1970, when I wrote a freshman term paper on housing in America. In researching the subject, I found out what was already common knowledge to many in the field: there would be horrendous shortages of housing in this country within the next decade. It is hardly surprising to learn that home ownership has fallen through the course of the eighties, especially for the so-called Baby Boomers.

As Greenhouse noted, "the rate of home ownership among people under 35 has fallen to 39.7 percent from 43.3 percent in 1981"—nearly a 10-percent drop in just five years. I think one of the dropouts might have been a nice young guy I met in the Minnesota Iron Range in 1984, who was trying to sell the house he had grown up in so that he could afford to establish himself in Arizona, where he had heard that there was work. He had to go where the work was—even though there was a woman in his town who loved him, and whom he loved, who had a job. (He could not let her support him: he had to work, to feel like a man, even if it meant no longer being *her* man.)

When I paid a call on my friend Peter and his wife last year, he was "house-poor," having just put down every dollar he could borrow or mortgage in order to have a home for his wife and daughter, and himself with them. I didn't ask what he paid—I don't like it when people ask me what my rent is, either, or for that matter whether I can "make a living at that," the quintessentially American question—but I can guess from a supplement to the *New York Times* of September 9, 1986, "Residential Property," which said that "single-family houses at the Westchester . . . which have three or four bedrooms, range in price from $120,000 to $140,000," or about four times the average annual income of an average two-earner family. Peter earns something like twice that annually, and probably bought something that cost twice as much. And he was well aware, when he bought the house, that he was signing a contract to work like a dog for the foreseeable future.

That was the deal our fathers made with themselves and their families. What has changed in this picture since our fathers' generation is that we now expect young married couples to work like *two* dogs—or to have one breadwinner who bakes on a double shift.

WHO WILL HAVE A JOB?

Young Americans are willing to work for what they get, which is fine so long as there are ample goods to be earned. But as in the housing market, there is strong evidence to think that there will not be enough of the goods to go around for them.

The latest unemployment figures in the U.S., as of this writing, show that 6.3 percent of those who want to find a job (which is how we define unemployment—those who have given up looking for paid work don't count) are still out of work. That figure is a tad lower than it was before Reagan took office. The U.S. is better off than France, where the figure is 11 percent and rising, or England, where a prosperous middle class coexists with 13-percent unemployment (and, not coincidentally, with a drug and social-violence problem of huge proportions).

But look at our unemployment figure another way. Look at it the way you would when you pass a corner of the street where young men are gathered in a group, passing a bottle and cigarettes and, above all, their time. Look at it the way you would if you came home and your front door swung open because the burglar didn't lock it on his way out. Look at it as one out of every two young black men you pass in the course of an ordinary day, one out of four young white men, one out of thirteen women, one out of sixteen of all of us together. Then add in the people who live on what they find in the street—at least 40,000 of them, and rising, in New York alone, and the hundreds, young and old, on the streets of places as apparently idyllic as Santa Cruz. Literally millions are not counted among the jobless.

One sign of where the job problem is going nearly slipped by me. I had been clipping articles from newspapers every time a factory closed or companies laid off "older managers"—men in their late forties and up, which is not so old in a man's working life—or were merging and firing, and then I stopped. There were too many of them to keep collecting. I did not have room or time for all the stories about people losing jobs.

The U.S. government has a political obligation to put a bright face on that problem. An April 1986 report from the Bureau of Labor Statistics, "Employment Projections for 1995: Data and Methods," declares that through the next decade, unemployment will remain at 7 percent. (Let us note that until 1975, that would have looked like a horror show, instead of optimism; from 1950 through the next quarter-century, unemployment hovered around 5 percent, and went down to 3.5 percent in the sixties, the feast before the debacle.)

The work force, however, is going to grow an awful lot—by about 16 million people, according to the Census Bureau's lowest estimates. Seven percent of 16 million means an additional 1.1 million people who want work, sooner or later, and will not find it. One million people is more than live in the city limits of either Boston or San Francisco. Even spread across a big country like ours, those people will be noticeable, if only as a darker shading on a growing shadow.

The jobs the rest of us will be doing, according to the Bureau of Labor Statistics, are not always going to be the jobs that ambitious young people will want. True, the Bureau foresees a combined total of 29 million executive, managerial, or professional jobs in 1995, an increase of roughly 22 percent. But there will be 16 million more of us, and only 6 million more of those plummy posts to spread among us.

Businessmen, who spend their lives reading numbers, are well aware of those trends. Among other signs, the crunch shows in "the difficulty [of] trying to fill posts with managers" aged fifty or thereabouts, as an executive employment service director told the *New York Times,* noting that "high mortgage payments and children in college" made them more "expensive" than yuppies. The family man, the man who needs more money and benefits for the work he does, is becoming an endangered species.

Even at the top, the plums are no longer always so plummy. Cox found that of the 1,100 executives he surveyed, one-third earned less than $40,000 per year, and about one-half earned less than the mythical Fifty K, which is not much for men who work as many hours as they do, even if it's well over the average. This, of course, may also be one of the reasons that young male executive family heads, as *Fortune* discovered, are complaining about the time they get with their kids: they have reason to feel, watching the pressure mount, that *it will be hard for them to protect the family time they already have, and they will not even get enough money to compensate, in moral and practical terms, for how far their working hours cut into the love and care that they and their women feel a man must give.*

However much they get, they will have to tell themselves that they are lucky just to have a job. As the head of a major television production company told me, "The successful executive today is the guy who fires people." He had reached his present success by doing just that on his previous job, falling in with what he called "a fashion among the executives. You know, they all hang out together. They go to lunch, and they say, 'We're cutting the fat, we're getting lean and mean.'

"So they pass down the orders to the managers, say, to cut five guys," he continued. "And they cut the ones they're afraid will take their jobs away." (In other words, their ablest, most ambitious workers. Are you wondering why we have a productivity problem, let alone what *Fortune* called "The End of Corporate Loyalty"?)

Or the ones who can't fight back: "I'm in a meeting with a guy who's worth a half-billion," he continued, "and his partner, who's worth $150 million, and they're ranting and raving about some secretary who's just making enough to support her family. They're saying, 'We gotta get rid of her.' "

"So what did you say?" asked a woman.

"I said, 'This is unfair, you can't do this,' " he replied.

Then he laughed and shook his head. "What do you *think* I said? I took notes, and I fired her."

Aside from the kind of tasks bright young executives are executing over our dead careers, the only comparable areas of prospective employment growth are sales and services, which already account for 27.5 million jobs, including a large percentage of the lower-paid women's jobs in our society, and which the Bureau believes will absorb 32 million working people's days by 1995. Farm labor will probably decline; factory labor will add 2.5 million paychecks, three-fifths of them for skilled workers.

In all of these areas, wages have been falling in real terms for over a decade, and will probably continue to fall (barring a catastrophic deflation, which no one seems to expect, though "Adam Smith" and others have suggested it might well be coming). Business leaders and economists are indicating that the average American manufacturing wage of some $9 per hour will have to drop part of the way to meet the wages paid in Asia and Latin America. (That is what Reagan led us to when he argued that cutting taxes for corporations and the wealthy would create jobs. It did—ninteenth-century-condition jobs, overseas. American manufacturing jobs have declined throughout the decade.) And already yearly bonuses have replaced annual raises, not only among blue-collar workers but also in executive ranks.

You see what is going on. There will be room and money at the top, but not enough. There will be room and money at the bottom, but relatively little. And the middle is going to be squeezed. Most people will still be able to find a job, but they will not have jobs that will buy much of a dream. *All of us will soon be working harder—in the name of "competitiveness," to use a current buzzword, or just to keep our rank in the army of the employed. But few of us will get more for the work we do.*

The numbers Greenhouse provided here were crunchers: he cited the Bureau of Labor Statistics to show that a man who was thirty in 1959 (my father was then thirty-three) could expect his wages to grow, in real terms, by 49 percent over the next decade. A man who turned thirty in 1983—almost just like me—could expect his earnings to grow by zero over the same time. And on top of that, the wages he would earn (if he were an average man for his age) were already nearly one-fourth less, in constant dollars (that is, once you factor out inflation), than those a thirty-year-old was earning in 1973 (his earnings, incidentally, *dropped* by 1 percent in constant terms over the next decade).

If you think that our reduced prospects may be another reason we're lately so mad at Dad, I won't laugh at you. Our fathers, to their great credit, have not claimed the last laugh. I am thinking of Eric Weissman, the only man I interviewed who asked that I use his real name, and a top entertainment lawyer in Los Angeles, who had told me that the greatest regret of his career was hardly that he had never been head of a major film studio, the ambition that counted most among his Hollywood clientele. What bothered him was that "my daughter will never have a house like mine. She won't be able to live as well as I have lived." That was not his failure—not in any rational sense (if only we were really so rational as we think)—but it was certainly his disappointment.

Disappointment is not what America's best and brightest college students are expecting, according to Casale's surveys. They told him that they wanted children (88 percent—90 percent of the men, compared to 86 percent of the women), and likewise wanted to be "better off financially" than their parents (20 percent), and to have "a good marriage" (30 percent, counting those who wanted to be like their parents, 18 percent of the total, and the 12 percent who did not).

They were strikingly career-oriented, as a group—81 percent had already picked out their careers, and nearly three out of five went on job interviews before graduating. "By March of 1986," wrote Casale, "26 percent of the students in the class of 1986 who intended to work already had accepted job offers." No waiting for maturity on this bus; a person's got to work for a living.

Their education was the means to the payment of a debt; the total costs of a four-year bachelor's program at a private university had hit $50,000 in the early eighties, and in 1987 stood at $75,000 (when people want it, raise the price). College had started to become a luxury, when for two generations it had been close to a birthright.

But here was the shock that awaited them, reported Casale: "Their average weekly salary was $305.77," while they had "expected to make a good deal more. The average salary that college students say they expect to make on their first job is $446.34."

They expected, in short, to earn more than the average thirty-year-old man was earning, and more than he could expect to earn, in absolute terms, ten years from now.

They had a nicely businesslike way of looking at things (not amazingly, since business was their major of choice). But that philosophy, as the numbers above suggest, is going to take them (and the rest of us) only so far.

This much seems plain: business, and the money it generates, will not solve all our problems, as became our main idea of political economy in the eighties, and as our young were and apparently are so willing to believe—not when there is not enough money to buy houses and raise children, and not enough adequate housing or schools to buy with it, and not enough time in a day to make up for the time a man or a woman sells in order to make a living, however "good" a living it may be, and not enough jobs for those who want and need to work. Asking our businessmen to do it is like telling someone to work out a complex equation by making random dents on paper with a hammer.

On paper, or at least some pieces of it, our economy is doing well, according to the Reaganites. But all the papers together say that not just our economy but the world economy is in a delicate, unbalanced state, in which numerous elements—rising world unemployment, conditions of war, the movement of moneys, persons, and goods across borders—could wreck the whole. The problems facing the world economy—massive indebtedness throughout the Americas, the U.S. included, for example—will remain potentially dangerous for some time, everyone agrees. So will mass immigration in search of jobs. These things are happening all over the world, and they are happening in the U.S., because that is the way things go. (Even in the Middle Ages, sick ferrets on the Asian steppes became the Black Plague of Europe, given time. It has always been one world.)

Not surprisingly, for all our confidence in our personal careers, we are asking ourselves what would happen if business could not keep its promises, any more than men could—if it could not provide the conditions for us to be strong and growing. And in at least one domain, we have recognized already that business is not up to the task.

The problem is this: business does not take care of "losers." Business rewards "winners." *Business is an opportunity and in many ways an impersonal one.*

That is business's pride, and in some ways it is worth being proud of. But it is also business's failing—a failing no less profound for all our cheerful efforts in the 1970s to talk up the "game" of business and the "gamesmen" who play it, or for the piteous claims that we "unleash" business (which even Regulatin' Jimmy Carter saw as his master) in this decade.

Our problems are anything but impersonal. We are starting to realize that people are losing in the pursuit of happiness—even good people who are running as fast as they can. The reason: we are playing the wrong game.

The means and the task do not fit each other. What needed rebuilding in America, and still does, was not just the little army, or little factories, or little houses on the prairie. It was—and still is—in large measure a matter of rebuilding the trust that people sensed other people had once felt in each other.

But felt no longer: "You can't trust anyone . . . it's a sickening way to feel," said a wealthy young man (if a tract house and big car makes you wealthy) who was surveyed by the *Washington Post* in early 1987. An apt joke making the rounds at the time was: "In business, how do you say 'Screw you'?"

Answer: "Trust me."

PRESSURE DROP

There is an idea shared by the disappointed fathers of every generation, and in the contrasting straight-ahead ambitions of the best and brightest of our students, that is something new in these United States: the growing sense that there will never be enough of everything to go around for everyone; not enough time, not enough money, not enough to buy with it. A strange idea in a country as rich as ours, but we hear it, along with the young.

I could hear it back in the early seventies, when a reggae tune called "Pressure Drop" ("the pressure gonna drop on you") by Toots and the Maytals was a hit in Cambridge. The pressure was dropping; the days of street battles were over. But just as "bad" meant *good,* the pressure was also rising. The Chicago blues came back, the poor man's music, louder than it had ever been, through amplifiers of a size and power Muddy Waters could only dream of. You couldn't always get what you wanted, sang Mick Jagger, who borrowed that poor man's sound, and you'd have to try hard to get just what you needed. And the clichés sounded profound and new. In a way, they were.

To see just how new this idea could sound in America, look back to the Virginia frontier in the Revolutionary era. A study by Jackson Turner Main found that hardworking men, even those who began as indentured servants, could become landowners within their lifetimes—when land was still the basis of wealth. Listen to Theodore Roosevelt, just after the turn of our century, reminding his listeners at a Kansas campaign stop of Lincoln's words: "I hold that while man exists it is his duty to improve not only his own condition, but to assist in ameliorating mankind." And then when he adds: "In every wise struggle for human betterment, one of the main objects, and often the only object, has been to achieve in large measure equality of opportunity."

This is an American promise—that hard work plus opportunity equals success. But the promise could stay fresh only if there would always be a chicken, a pot, and a kitchen to put them in, for any man (and lately, woman) who would get down and work.

It started to turn sour by 1978 in California, where I lived just after Proposition 13 was passed by direct vote of the population (or rather, of those who took the time to vote; it is humbling for an American to visit West Germany, where 90 percent of the voters go to the polls regularly). This proposition simply said that the taxes on a piece of property could never go above 1 percent of its assessed value, and that this value would remain constant until the property changed hands.

It sounds simple and just enough: the government doesn't have the right to bleed a hardworking person of his or her hard-earned wealth, not in America.

But the new law made no provision for renters. Their monthly payments could be set at any level the proprietor chose. And that level rose precipitously, in part because the new law helped to boost real (as opposed to paper) property values—which were already skyrocketing, as the nation's unemployed and hopeful streamed toward the land of gold. This had the effect of making it harder for renters to become home-owners, of course. Supply and demand then set in with a vengeance; owning something that could be rented had become a legal gold mine. The result was that California's citizens had just divided themselves into two classes, one of them living off the other.

Simultaneously, as I suggested in Part II, we were becoming a class society in another way that we had not been before. In 1970 I surveyed 100 men in Harvard's freshman class, and one of the things I asked them, almost as an afterthought, was: "What social class do you belong to?" Exactly half of them replied, usually with the same phrase scrawled on the survey form, "I don't believe in social classes." If they did choose a class to belong in, they picked "middle." Not even the richest guys in the residential houses would say "upper." They did not want to see themselves as richer or poorer, better or worse than anyone else. But in the post-Vietnam era, to be rich meant living in a big safe house in a big safe country, while poor men died on ground they did not own.

Around the same time that Proposition 13 took effect, Santa Cruz County became embroiled in a savage, no-holds-barred (from libel suits to dirty election tactics) fight over "development"—that is, on how many houses would be built there. The key issue was water, as it now is throughout the United States (someday soon we will realize how stupidly we wasted the priceless Oglalalla Aquifer, the water our Midwest drinks and puts on crops). Opponents of unrestrained "growth" argued that there was not enough water in the county to grow crops, drink, cook, stay clean, and carry off sewage, all of which were vital to the county's life. Developers countered that people had a right to live where they wanted, and to buy houses to live in.

Neither felt that there was any room for compromise—not even in the West, which in Frederick Jackson Turner's classic formulation had "furnish[ed] the forces dominating American character"—among them, "perennial rebirth" (which by then was being desperately sought by a New Age group called Rebirthers, as well as born-again Christians), "new opportunities," a chance of "continually beginning over again."

Instead, we were all locked in a struggle for "scarce resources"—from gasoline (remember the lines at pumps?) to "homes" (which is what Californians call any and every house they own), to jobs and the income that comes from them. My brother told me a story he'd seen on the news: in bloody Boston (son of Bosstown), where neighborhood whites were fighting blacks and "outsiders" (the category I belonged to when I lived there) to stop mandatory busing of their children out of their school districts while black kids came in, going so far as to commit arson and murder to protect (as they saw it) the little they had, so hard to get and keep—this was the context—a little gang of black teenagers doused a white woman in their neighborhood with gasoline and set her afire.

Asked for his motive, one of the boys said, "Only the strong survive." Another line you heard around that time on the radio. The way you heard executives and divorced women saying, "I'm a survivor."

A strange way to boast (cockroaches, we were telling each other, were better survivors than we, because it takes more radiation to kill them). It was especially strange in the richest, strongest country in the world. But it was there, the air whispered and stank of it. *The pressure gonna drop,* said the poor boy a long way from home, *the pressure gonna drop on you.*

It is a statistical fact, as I showed above, that sudden death among young men began to rise sharply in the 1970s, to peak in 1980. Since then the numbers have remained roughly constant, but far higher than they were in the sixties, in absolute and relative terms; more men are dying young, and a higher percentage of men are dying young. The most noticeable increase, of course, was homicide.

In Detroit, "Kids Are Killing Kids," reported the *Washington Post* late in 1986. It told how an eleven-year-old boy "was wearing the new dark-purple silk shirt—the one he had begged his mother to buy—when he and a friend were confronted by two teen-age boys." One of them, aged fourteen, took out a pistol, demanded the shirt, and when he couldn't have it from the brave little man, ruined it with a shot through the stomach that killed his victim.

Detroit was not alone. The *New York Times* reported in early 1987 that New York's state commissioner of mental health had called adolescent violence "a major public health problem." That same month the *Times* profiled twelve teenagers from the borough of Queens, some of whom had allegedly chased two black men through the streets of their neighborhood, Howard Beach, a chase that ended when one of their victims had been badly beaten and the other killed by a car.

The *Times* ran the dirty dozen's pictures; the one that caught my eye was of Jon L. Lester, a seventeen-year-old with the face of a junior-high student, who shortly after being arrested for taking part in the Howard Beach killing found himself in prison serving a one-to-three-year gun-possession charge from an unrelated incident. Even children could now be considered armed and dangerous.

The best his neighbors could tell the *Times* in defense of him and his friends was, "I don't think it was their intention of chasing him out there and getting him hit by a car," as one put it. "They just wanted to chase him and beat him up." *Boys will be boys.* Said another: "Puerto Ricans and colored have no business being here after eight P.M.... The kids had no right to start trouble, but the black men never should have been here." Their mere presence took something away from the white kids, something they were afraid to lose; touched the button that leads to the reflex: *I'll show you how stupid it is to mess with me.*

This rise in violence coexists with a growing struggle in our society for material well-being. I hardly think that this is mere coincidence. The most numerous victims and perpetrators of violence in our society are at or near the bottom of our economic pile; that too is a statistical fact.

It follows that to the extent we let the bottom grow, violence will spread. In a society like ours, which guarantees the free movement of persons, it will spread everywhere. This is a trend just beginning, and we must stop it soon.

Interpersonal violence, of course, has a direct effect on our intimate relations. Just ask couples of whom the woman was raped; ask a man who's too angry over what another man did to him to make love with a woman; ask the women who can't find a man to marry.

But we must recognize that the movement toward violence is taking place in another domain: in our growing militarization as a society. Fish stink, and societies behave from the head down. If the homilies hold, it may be that the rise in interpersonal violence among men and our enormous recent investment in military might as a society are not unrelated phenomena.

Nor, perhaps, is it mere coincidence that these trends have arisen at a time of growing female power. If we are now bankrupting ourselves—as, we were promised, we could bankrupt the Russians—in order to build up our "security" and "strength," our masculine powers, I very much doubt that this has nothing but coincidence to do with the new and greater strengths of women.

When I interviewed Japanese film director Nagisa Oshima, who grew up in World War II, "thinking that I would go away to war and be killed before I was twenty," I asked him if he was aware that in one of his films, *In the Realm of the Senses,* shot in 1975, he had made a curious juxtaposition. While a provincial noble of 1937 is taking a servant girl for his pleasure, and then discovering that her passion and murderous courage far outstrip his own (in the end, she castrates his body, after strangling him), we see repeated images of troops marching off to fight in Manchuria. It looked, I said, as though the troops were fleeing from a female power they could not control.

He wasn't aware of that theme at the time, said Oshima; that came later, when the theme was repeated in other films he made. "What I will say now," he added, "is that women have become stronger than men. And I am very much afraid that men will start a war, in order to run from this power."

We are men; we refuse simply to cut and run, to expose our asses to all kickers. But doing so gives us a reason to say, as men have said throughout the Age of Stress, that we are right to get away from women, from what they can do for or to us, from what they know and think about us. (I think that was part of what Kissinger had in the back of his mind in 1981, when he told the country that a failure to defeat Nicaragua's Sandinistas would expose us as "impotent." Kissinger, like the rest of us, must know in his bones that men are not what they used to be, when it comes to impressing women.)

We are trying to prove to women, if not to ourselves, that we are just as strong as ever we were. But I doubt that our women are fooled, any more than we are fooling ourselves. Women know that we cannot save the world for them—that all our attempts to do so are only getting us in deeper and deeper trouble—which is why substantially more women than men were hostile to the Reagan military buildup, and to his Central American war policy. They know it for the same reason that they doubt our abilities, all on our lonesomes, to buy them little houses on some prairie, and then come home and do an equal share of the parenting. The world is still a threatening place, not to mention a place we can barely afford to pay for, and our women are still unsatisfied. Moreover, unless we take a different approach to the question of what makes us strong, we are going to become even more disappointing in our roles as lovers and providers.

What we can expect from building up our military, and taking more and more of us into its service, was described in detail by economist Lloyd J. Dumas in his recent book, *The Overburdened Economy.* Dumas pointed out that since the Depression, and right through the supply-side Reagan years, an essential assumption of our government's economic thinking is that spending taxes creates jobs. If the Reaganites argued the contrary—that not taxing people lets them create even more jobs—their actions, as in so many domains, were another matter. They spent heavily on acquiring military tools—a 600-ship Navy fleet, tanks, planes, guns, a space defense that worked on costly paper (and was sold to us with drawings done in a child's hand). Making those things indeed created jobs, from Detroit to Silicon Valley and back again. But in the long term, Dumas showed, that investment will take jobs away.

In effect, said Dumas, military production is "distractive," because it siphons talent, resources, and materials out of the economy that could be used "to enhance the material standard of living of the population"—what he called the "contributive" sector of our economy. While tanks and war planes might serve to protect our standard of living, they do not make life better for us in the way that new houses would, for example; and the more military goods we construct, the less of everything else we can construct in their place.

This, suggested Dumas, was the real reason that the Reagan Revolution failed:

> If there is a large distractive sector preempting critical labor and capital from the contributive sector ... no policy which fails to liberate these resources *and* rechannel them into contributive activity can hope to rebuild the nation's productive competence. After all, it is precisely the diversion of these crucial productive resources into noncontributive activity that generated the decay of productive competence in the first place.

In other words, a worker cannot solve two problems at the same time, nor an engineer design two things at the same time—not the kind of things that can be sold in the world economy, which is where America has to sell these days, like everyone else. And since the 1950s, when Dwight Eisenhower warned us that the "military-industrial complex" was gaining unprecedented power in our society, we have put an astonishing percentage of our productive capacity into the making of "goods" that are designed to do nothing more than destroy other people's goods.

For example, wrote Dumas, "in 1982 the Defense Department's investment in plant equipment was *nearly 38 percent* of the [three-year average] combined annual net investment in plant equipment *by all U.S. manufacturing establishments.*" At the same time, the Defense Department held "*more than 46 percent* of the value of the combined stock of physical capital" owned by our manufacturing base in the private sector. (The emphasis in these quotes is Dumas'.) At the same time, two-thirds of our government's investment in research and development—that is, the kind of work that enabled Tokyo to beat the pants off Detroit in the automobile industry—was going into military projects.

In effect, *we are asking our military people to do an impossible job.* We are asking them to keep our standard of living safe, in a dangerous world. But at the same time, *we are asking them to take more out of our economy than they can possibly put back into it—which means slowly wiping out our standard of living.*

Which, as it happens, is still what our men are expected in the main to uphold. In international life, as in our homes, we have come to a point where it is meaningless to promise protection, and to work toward destruction. It is simply no longer an adequate way of responding to the question of what a good man might be, of meeting the expectations we have set ourselves, men and women both.

MEANWHILE, WE ARE FALLING
BEHIND OUR WOMEN

Our recent obsession with our powers of violence has had another, subtler effect on us—especially us men. It has distracted us from questioning the imbalance that arises between men and women when one gender devotes itself to beating the world, and the other to taking care of it. I am referring to the fact, which will apparently remain in force through the next generation, that women provide themselves with a deeper human development than men do, and are thus better equipped to care for themselves and others in ways we have lately come to see as essential for both men and women.

We can see where this trend is taking us by looking at the Soviet Union, our enemy, and our equal (if not our superior, as the Pentagon keeps warning us) in military might. The *New York Times* reported in August of 1985 that "in a country where a rural, traditional way of life had endured much longer than in most Western countries"—and where even more of the gross national product goes to preparing for war than in the U.S.—"the shift from the extended family to the nuclear family is yielding painful results. . . .

Husbands, unable to accept a busy, working wife and unwilling to share her household burdens, are turning to the traditional Russian solace of Vodka.

Or were, until Gorbachev closed off that spigot. Meanwhile,

Wives, whose income is needed to support the family and who are often better educated than their husbands, are holding their families together. . . . The Soviet Union is seeing new phenomena: one-parent families and youngsters who grow up without a male influence either at home or at school, where virtually all teachers are women.

Sound familiar? (The vast majority of American single-parent homes—10.1 million, or about five out of six—are likewise headed by women.)

And the Russians resemble us in other ways too, reported Vladimir Shlapentokh of Michigan State University in 1984:

Male mortality was mounting much faster than female mortality.... Men are losers in competition with women in education.... Of all those with a professional education in 1980, 59 percent were women.

In the U.S., men are likewise less well educated, in general; more women graduate from high school and college. But though more American men than women still go on to graduate or professional schools (and more women drop out of college to get married, even now), like their Russian peers, they are getting less well rounded educations for themselves. "Recent studies," noted Shlapentokh,

> show that female engineers in the Soviet Union devote three times as much of their leisure time to humanitarian and artistic activities as do their male colleagues. Women read more fiction and go to museums, theatres, and concerts much more often.

"There is an absence of fit husbands," he concluded. "Soviet women"— oddly enough, like ours—"more and more value cultural and psychological compatibility with their partners." Failing that, "they would rather stay alone than tie themselves to men whom they cannot help despising."

Strong words; stronger than most American women would use to describe their husbands and lovers. But they could, if they wanted to. In personal terms, the next generation of American women will continue to be superior to men.

Scholastic aptitude tests of college-bound graduates from 1970 to 1984 showed a consistent pattern: men had higher composite scores—for math, natural sciences, social sciences, and English—and women scored higher in English alone. Our young women speak the language we use at the dinner table and in the bedroom; our young men speak the language that helps on a job.

When they grow up, the men leave aside what doesn't help to advance them in the world of work. Nearly three out of five women, and only two out of five men, read books. What they are reading is of interest: 63 percent of women, and only 49 percent of men, read literature. While reading a novel may not be an apparently useful activity, it is indeed a way in which an interested person can learn something about human relations; and men are apparently less interested than women. In fact, what the successful men I have interviewed read in their "spare time" was material related to their careers, which is just one side of human relationships (and not necessarily the nicer one).

Men have their eye on the ball more, though. That was why, I noticed, it was important to belong to a softball team in Santa Cruz; it was where guys made and maintained contacts that helped in business and small-town politics. Women don't care as much for mixing business and pleasure: when the National Parks Service asked Americans how they spend their leisure time in 1982–83, 61 percent of women and 45 percent of men named "walking for pleasure." Among other pleasures, women are more present at performances of classical music, plays, ballet, and art shows.

In short, *women do things because they like doing them, and because doing them helps in understanding themselves and others, to a significantly greater degree than do men.*

For both sexes, the key years for these activities are between sixteen and forty—the years in which we are learning to love, and going to work. In those years, young men make a deal with themselves, to a degree that women do not.

They will cut the superfluous from their lives (like Tom Rath, who gave up playing the mandolin after college, or Iacocca, who never mentions a hobby in his autobiography). They will concentrate the energy they could put into intimate relationships on fitting themselves into the world of work, until their working life is secure enough to allow them the "leisure" of love.

That may be one reason why the Census Bureau reported in 1985 that the median age at which men get married has risen to 25.4 years, "nearing the high estimated for the turn of the century" (when we were emerging from the worst depression we had known until then). You could look at the fact that unmarried couples living together have grown in number by 107,000 per year since 1970, to reach 1.9 million by 1984, and that 70 percent of such couples have no children, as a side effect of putting off marriage until a man is far enough ahead to support the woman, who will stay home with the kids (as our women do, remember). That would seem logical—it can't be proved—given the stagnation of our incomes, which keeps a lot of us waiting.

How long can we expect ourselves, or be expected, to wait?

It is one thing to make a living. It is another to love the life one lives, and live the life one loves, as Mose Allison sang. The latter is what we want to do, men and women both: to take part in the work that makes the world, and to live in the love and trust of others.

You do not need an economics degree and training in calculus to see that if things go on as they are going now, we will have to settle for making a living—at best.

Part of the bargain we will make for that living will be that men, in the main, will go off to earn their livings, however drudgingly, dirtily, or dangerously the earning; and their women will work for a while, or a long while, and then will take care of the children. It is what both of them will know how to do, are trained to do, can be excused for doing.

Thus their lives will remain separate, and unequal. Their satisfactions will be real enough, but not enough to make them happy—no happier than they are now, no less free of "stress." On the contrary, they will probably go on doing their all and getting their less. And they will be more, not less, alone in their struggles—within their families, where each will inhabit a separate domain, and in a society geared to the work of violence, where gain and pain are inextricably linked.

It is a bad bargain, a foolish one. No more than women could in the days of the Second Wave, men cannot do it all: make the world safe for business executives, compete for housing in a market where "creative financing" has become our latest art, hold a job beneath a man who doesn't care how long you work, so long as it matches his own killing hours, and then go home and pretend to be fully, lovingly present.

I do not believe that we have no choice in the matter; nor that the choices we must make are so frightening that it is better to ignore them and grumble about stress; nor that men are better off living short, dying young, and making good-looking corpses, as the Hell's Angels like to say. The bargain we are making is not the only one we could negotiate, and it is not the best we could have—either in material or in moral terms. In the last part of this book, I am bound to ask what might be a better deal, for everyone concerned.

PART
VII

A PLACE TO GO,
A REASON
TO BE THERE

My most important goal in life is to achieve something for myself.... I tend toward the traditional... I want to set up my own business. Maybe I'll find some place really distant and open a restaurant on the beach. I think I'm afraid of getting old and helpless.

> —Antigone Dean, twenty-three,
> quoted in Esprit fashion ad, 1986

What does civilization rest upon—and what object has it, [but] rich, luxuriant, varied personalism?... that Something a man is, (last precious consolation of the drudging poor), standing apart from all else, divine in his own right, and a woman in hers...

> —Walt Whitman,
> *Democratic Vistas,* 1868

CHAPTER

—— 23 ——

A Moral Equivalent of Peace

Great care must be taken not to confound the principle of equality itself with the revolution which finally establishes that principle in the social condition and laws of a nation. Here is the reason for almost all the phenomena that occasion our astonishment.

—Alexis de Tocqueville,
Democracy in America, 1830

It was Karl Marx who proposed that as the economy of a nation advances, it retains within it traces of previous stages of economic development. For example, our so-called postindustrial economy still depends, in large measure, on vast industries; and around its edges, hidden from our daily view, are the near-feudal conditions of migrant labor, the cottage factories of women sewing and assembling garments at home; and beside them, men and women working on word processors, keeping one eye on the kids. In our working lives, thought Marx—it may have been his greatest insight—every act of labor is a reenactment of history.

Carl Jung extended this idea into psychoanalysis: within the consciousness of each individual, he believed, can be found all the varied phases of human development, passed down through the ages like a mythic language of heroic and demonic imagery. The same idea is coming through genetics: even as we set ourselves to making designer genes, we are more and more debating the extent to which subtle portions of our anatomies and characters are passed to us in the moment of conception.

These debates are hardly over. *But we can use them already to see that one of our greatest fears—that the characteristics which enable a man, or a woman, to feel distinct, to say, "This is what I am," are about to be lost—is beside the point.*

We are not about to change so much as that. The Organization Man's regret that he was no longer a frontiersman did not prevent the Corporate Raider from sailing out in the eighties. The sons of the Man in the Gray Flannel Suit have put down their beads and bellbottoms, and put on Father's clothes. People are calling for peace, but soldiers are still making and dying in wars, and "wasting" civilians. Men are still going off to work, and women are raising their children. It is what we are, and what part of us will remain, to the end of the lifetime I see for myself, and in the lives of those I know.

We cannot subtract from ourselves, from what we are and have been. But we can add to it, acquire some new traits; and what we add changes the whole, interpenetrates every level of the beings we have inherited, in our bones, our work, our homes. We remain inside our history, but our history is still alive.

If sharing that history means that we are not entirely distinct from each other—neither as men and women, nor as Americans and the-rest-of-the-world, as we Americans have a tendency to think—we remain *particular.* In our homes and in our workplaces, men and women have, even now, distinct and particular responsibilities and privileges. That is the fact—*not a final, cynical fact, but the first one we must deal with.*

But along with that fact goes a new attitude: we no longer want to know if, but *how* men and women were created equal.

Running underneath the mainstream dialogue of stress, and the counter-culture's wild attempt to invent new identities for men and women whole-sale, and the hopes of young adults to return to the lives they imagine their grandparents had, is a common effort: *We are trying to see which traits belong equally to men and women, and which of them we can only, within our lifetimes, request from and give to each other.*

This effort is part and parcel of men's sometimes grudging and slow efforts to make room for women in public life, and of women's doubts—just as strong as men's—about whether trading a private for a public life is worth the bargain. It is why men have learned to perform new chores, and women new jobs. Inescapably, questions have been raised—*Why should not men and women lead more similar lives? How are they finally, fundamentally, alike or different? What rights and obligations can they therefore claim?*— and they have not gone away.

We are being obliged to find answers to these questions, answers that involve changes in the behavior and standard of living of literally millions of people—not a majority, but enough to affect nearly everyone in our society, to open new choices and decisions. The changes, I have tried to show, though not yet dominant, have nonetheless been steadily coming over the course of three generations. *They involve, most pointedly, an ongoing negotiation about intimate responsibilities, about the appropriate ways that men and women can show their love to and for each other.*

This process, in the language of stress, has been accompanied by an acute sense of "time urgency." Whether or not we still imagine that if we want the world, we can get it now (the boast of the counterculture, and the forlorn cry of contemporary positive thinking), *we apparently believe that we must see who and what we are, and what we can make of ourselves, sooner rather than later.* That was part of what gave the counterculture such desperate energy in the sixties, and the Women's Movement such angry, fearful power in the seventies; and it is part of the reason that we are lately asking businessmen to be "nurturing," and women to be "assertive."

We are worried that we must change again, and it shows. We have stopped whistling while we work. We are finding that we cannot rely only on positive thinking, as first the spiritual movement and then the Reagan revolutionaries proposed over the past decade. The problems—in our society, our politics, our homes—have not been wished or smiled away. The image of fatherly, guiding strength that presided over this country throughout this decade is dissipating beneath jeers, as I write, directed at Wall Street and White House. It's a tough time to be a man, or a woman living in a man's world.

But we are at last coming to see that we need to take our next steps not only from our strengths, real or fantasized; we must also build from our weaknesses. *We are asking—in particular, we are asking men—to act more like a woman would, in certain situations: to be more caring, more present, more attentive to others. And only recently—to some extent, even now—we saw precisely this trait as a lack of ambition, a man's first calling.*

A key theme of the stress debate was the recognition that even the strongest, most successful man has hidden weaknesses; that even a young man's heart is not big enough to hold two worlds together, the parallel worlds of work and love. The most evident and startling fact of the whole debate is this: the world-beating American man broke down and whined. *For the first time, he admitted some kinds of limits to what he was capable of doing in the Real Time world.*

And along with this, he put the essence of his identity in question. Not only because women were attacking him, making new demands, but because he could not live up, in more than a symbolic way, to the demands he placed on himself, to the needs that he could not fulfill within the terms of the choices and exigencies he had accepted for himself. *If there is a single defining difference between my father's generation and mine, it lies in the explicitness with which this conflict has been posed.*

It took immense moral courage to begin to address that problem, for men to wonder what exactly it might be that would make the man in a changing world (and however hard I have been on the New Men, it is for their willingness to take this risk that I admire them). Courage, because no alternatives, no certain resources, were available to the man who asked himself if he must justify himself by more than the work he did in life, and the position it conferred on him; and because, while seeking alternatives, he remained bound by the savage laws of competition with other men— to win the wealth that women still in the main depend on men to provide, and the sense of safety that he could only provide for himself.

But beyond those conditions, men, in particular, find it difficult to face their weaknesses, because a man is expected to be unfailingly strong, to look past failure to his next success; and an American man, especially, wants to start over fresh from failure, to begin a new life in his New World. Yet one lesson of the Age of Stress—one we seem, slowly, to be absorbing— is that we cannot simply start anew, whenever the fancy strikes us. Our fathers could not; their sons could not; and the generation behind us will not be able to, either.

The implications of that lesson are both personal and political. We have seen how men who wanted to be New found themselves bound by old desires, old realities; and at the same time, we see that radicalism, whether couched in the psychological language of stress or the ideological terms of conservatism, feminism, and Marxism alike, has failed us. It could not help but fail, because mixed with the affirmation of the new was a recklessly naive denial of the old—of what we are, and have continued to be. *Men and women made a choice, but they defined that choice in terms that defied a successful resolution.*

The Age of Stress has been a time in which Americans, and in particular ways American men, gave themselves immense choices, in such profusion that none of them could be fully realized. We tried to make war, and enjoy the prosperity of peace; to work as much as a body can stand, and then be matchless lovers and parents; to be as eager for change as human beings ever have been, and afraid of the changes we set in motion.

Perhaps we do not need to be afraid of our choices, or of ourselves. We *do* need to accept the consequences of the choices and changes before us, and the limits of what we can accomplish within our lifetimes.

The greatest of those limits is at once practical and moral. It is a practical fact that men's work, or the work that men do, is more highly remunerated in our society than the work women do; and that in exchange for this higher remuneration, men make a proportionately greater sacrifice of the time that they could spend with those they care about and for. But it is also a moral fact—and this part of the burden is shared by both men and women—that we find a kind of comfort in this situation. Our burdens are heavy, but familiar; men and women alike feel capable of assuming them. And both of us wonder if we can add new burdens, new responsibilities, to the equation without falling apart.

Assume for a moment, even if you do not agree that intimacy and paid labor ought to be more equally divided among men and women, that allowing men and women to enter further into each other's domains is within our grasp. What comes next, practically speaking?

I want to make my own bias clear: I think that work alone will not get us out of the Age of Stress, and that left to our current devices, work is the solution we—and most heavily, we men—will choose. That solution is seemingly being forced upon us, men and women alike—hard work, and not the kind that will make us happier.

We cannot get away from work, of one kind or another, and I wouldn't want us to; mere idleness, forced or chosen, is a curse. *But work alone is not going to make us happy, nor richer and safer than we are now*—and we are already, and still, the richest, safest society in the history of the world, so far as material well-being goes—*if working continues to impoverish our characters.*

Men, more than women, have voiced just such a sense of impoverishment throughout the Age of Stress—a sense that they have been denied the rewards of their labors, that all their efforts, all their changes, are unavailing. Not only in the eyes of women, at a time of overt female rage, but in their own eyes.

We—especially, but not only, we men—do not respect ourselves; that is what we have been hinting throughout the Age of Stress. That is what Dr. Norman Shealey recognized, back when I talked with him in 1981, in saying that "a lack of self-esteem is the root of all illness"—a problem of crisis proportions in California, where a politician named John Vasconcellos recently started a committee on self-esteem in the state assembly. It is what Totman recognized: men and women who don't like themselves, and who can't think of or find reasons for being as they are, are weakened physically and spiritually.

It is not coincidence, I have argued, that this time of longing for self-esteem is also the era of a neverending military buildup. When one recalls that this was when sudden death rose so quickly among us—that is, us men—it seems that we are no longer rebels without a cause, but martyrs looking for a cross, for ultimate proofs of our manhood, in an age of growing female power.

It is so much simpler to be a hero: to be struck down, hammer in hand, like Thor at Ragnarok; to take the blade in the neck, like Sidney Carton did, and ask death to be the witness of one's goodness. Far simpler, really, than to take one's good with one's bad, and try to keep the good in sight, and to keep to it. But neither men nor women can well afford such simplicities now. *We have become aware of their mortal cost.*

But how do we earn each other's respect, and beyond that, trust, when the old promises no longer hold, and will not again? What sacrifices can we honorably ask each other to make? What must we give in return? *They are not new questions, but they are being posed with the expectation of new answers.*

Among contemporary men the responses have been phrased first in silence, then in mutters, then in the outraged protests of young men against their fathers, and finally in bitter dreams of better-than-ever fatherhood, accompanied by symptoms of stress. One fundamental point remains unaddressed: we still do not know or agree if a good man should be willing to work himself to death for a woman and children, if he should defy the dictates of "society," the "traditions" and "conditioning" he inherited, or go along with them, wrapped in his gray flannel uniform; if he is at best a lover or a fighter, a maker or a breaker of the world.

THE JUGGLER'S SHOES

For me and most of the men I know, these are not abstract questions, even if they are not often spoken aloud. Decent men do ask themselves what they owe to others, what acts and convictions can be considered worthy, if not always or entirely noble. In talking to my subjects, I felt that most were doing their best to "keep three balls—money, work, and love—in the air at the same time," as one man described his practical philosophy of life to me. If they sometimes dropped one of the balls, they sooner or later went back and picked it up. They were trying to perform a difficult act gracefully.

The flying objects that they concentrated on hardest, of course, were work and money. By my lights, they should not be faulted for that. For one thing, in nearly every case these men were the principal family earners, in keeping with the pattern I described in Part I, still the norm in middle- or upper-class society. That was true, for example, of a television news editor who informed his wife, a full-time mother of three and a part-time graphic artist, that he was moving the family to another city to take a better job—the same money, but less pressure, slightly shorter hours.

She didn't like it—she was happy where she was, and he had not fully consulted her or heeded her wishes in making the decision—but she had to accept part of his reasoning: namely, that his current job was killing him ("What I would like most," he said about his career, "would be the right to take a nap in the afternoon"), and that she could not earn enough money to support the family on a middle-class level. Beyond that, I think, she understood that if he wanted more time with his children than occasional exhausted dinners and Sundays at the municipal pool, he would have to make his move, and take them along.

I had asked him what happiness meant to him, and he said: "I think what you get is moments of happiness—like when you're just walking along, and you see the front of a building in a different way, and for some reason, you're contented." In effect, these moments were all that he had time for, all that his present life would afford him. He was trying, among other things, to increase his chance of finding them, of having more hours to fit them into.

His life was not outwardly, as he described it, greatly different from that of his father, a businessman who died of a heart attack while the son was in college. *But the kind of happiness the son wanted and believed that he could attain was different:* as traditional as it seemed, the career pattern he had chosen was taking him, if slowly, closer to his family than his father had been.

In another family in which a man had changed his life for the sake of a woman and given up the goal, for more than a decade, that mattered most to him in order to care for her and their children, I saw the same exigencies—that someone has to earn the money, and that someone will probably be the man; and that in accepting this, he must learn the art of a juggler while standing in a painfully tight space.

He had wanted, from his adolescence on, to be a successful musician. He had the talent, and he had the discipline. But one night in our early twenties, when we were discussing the notion that an artistic career—well he knew how long it takes to build one, how much travel and nightwork is demanded of a player—might preclude lifelong intimate relations, he said, "If I had to choose between my art and love, I'd take the love." And in a way, that is what he did.

He met his wife while playing in a nightclub, with a band that never went anywhere. For four years after they married, he attempted the impossible: to make a successful career in music without going on the road ("You know," a musician who stayed that route told me, "it's like being a business executive, because that's who you sit next to in the planes"), without leaving the woman he loved for days, then weeks, then months at a time. And finally he called around and found a job in the computer industry. His stepchildren were in school, and someone would have to put them through college.

They stayed in the house that was his wife's, by a previous marriage— an hour and a half in bus time from his office. He left the house at six-thirty A.M. every day, and came home a bit over twelve hours later. Then he did some physical exercises—at least after the second winter on this routine, past the age of thirty, when he caught pneumonia—and practiced his instruments. He was a one-dish-wonder of a cook when he got married, and ten years later he still was—one of the missed opportunities, as he said in a letter, of "trying to fit a size 12 life into a size 10 shoe."

All the same, he kept his art alive—with the unwavering support of his wife, who sat in the audience on the occasional nights when he played with a band, and never groaned over the money he invested, always frugally, in recording sessions and instruments. She realized that if this passion of his life was allowed to be entirely put aside, something vital would go out of him—something that had been part of the man who charmed her from a stage, that was more than mere show. And she recognized and respected the fact that he had accepted the consequences of the choice he had already made, before he was married—that he would take love over ambition, if and when he had to.

It seems old in a way, doesn't it; he sounds like Tom Rath. And like Rath, he is sometimes angry. People have blamed his wife for not working— though taking care of him and the kids, as she goes about it, is certainly a full-time job well done—but that is not what he is angry about. I don't believe that he resents the choice he has made, or his wife for being the occasion of his choice, either. *He is angry because, quite simply, that is the way things are.*

He said it well: the immediate problem is how to fit a size 12 life into a size 10 shoe. The apparent parameters of the problem—at least the problem that individuals are in a position to solve for themselves—are money and time.

But there is another factor that I saw at work here, and in the other couples who were dealing successfully with these constraints: *the man and woman had accepted that their situation was common, that they were in it together. Their mutual dependence was seen as an essential strength; they recognized that neither of them could make it through the hard times alone.*

INTERDEPENDENCE AND FIDELITY

In these relationships I saw one of the saving graces of our fears about the entry of women into work. *I saw that women who have worked*—as all of these men's wives had, at one time or another—*had learned to respect their men more, not less, for the work their men performed.* If they wanted more, not less, tenderness and intimacy from these men, *they had come to understand why it was so difficult for the men to provide it.*

These are not perfect men, any more than you and I are. *But they were good enough to live for themselves and others, and their women were good enough to recognize the fact.*

In a way, we always have been; we have simply raised our standards of what is good. I am certain that men do not want those standards to fall again, any more than women do. And that is why, finally, I think that men and women can trust each other, more than they have during the Age of Stress. Their interests, in the long run, are the same: they cannot get what they want without each other. There will be deviations, perversions, set-backs to achieving those interests, as there always have been. Yet men and women will keep each other more or less honest, more or less turned in the right direction, the direction they choose together.

But in order to get that "more," we will all have to sacrifice our most cherished, and narrow, definition of independence—that there can be only one of anything in the world, and the One, that Number One, can be us—or at the least, to see it in a new way, as *an equal interdependence. We must recognize our mutual dependence on each other, our need for each other*—a need we have kept on denying, and returning to, throughout the Age of Stress.

We cannot escape that dependence, for which we should be grateful. It is what makes our equality possible; it is what makes us human, in a human world. *But what makes recognizing our interdependence so difficult is that neither men nor women can do the job of fully working and loving, alone.* We can never address each other from a position of complete strength; we must therefore accept the at times humiliating necessity of turning to others in times of weakness.

It remains a fact, for example, that men who do not have the respect of women are more likely to break or fail—unless you happen to think it a coincidence that the highest percentages of divorced or perpetually single men in our society can be found within our prisons. Likewise, I suspect that men who are forced (or force themselves) to seek their respect away from women, or by simply and merely fooling women, are men who will go on trying to break and ruin others. (That is the truth in the as yet ambiguous demand of New Men that every last guy be a fully involved family man.)

If being a man comes to mean loving a world, and not just building it, then men who need women will need a woman's respect on terms far beyond those demanded by either the Man in the Gray Flannel Suit or the Second Stage postfeminists. This, too, is behind the silence and stress of the New Men; *they are aware that they are going to be in the position of asking women for more, not less, admiration and esteem, love and tolerance; and being students of feminism (it is what has made them new), they are likewise aware that women are not about to compromise on their own demands.*

Suppose, for example, that it became more and more common in our society—it is already, as I have shown, a minority case—for women to assume the primary burden of breadwinning in our families, as Lillian Clary did when she and Mike conceived their first child. Such a movement would inevitably place women in a position of great material power within these families—the same power that certain men have wielded, consciously or unconsciously, for so long.

We—especially, once again, we men—have been worried to give women such power. That is one of the reasons that so few of us have even proposed such an arrangement to women. *But beyond the practical aspect, there is the question of how a man would feel when he was more than ever dependent on a woman—more than Tom Rath, more than Lee Iacocca, more than his father—to affirm his worth.*

A man who does not make more money than a woman—and I have been in this position, from time to time—still needs her to treat him like a man (that is why poor men work so hard—and believe me, they do—at being studs). If he does not need her to do his dishes, he needs to feel, when he is standing at the sink, that she is not thinking, "I could get anyone to do that"—just as much as she does, as her frustrated Second Wave mother and older sister did. If he is not entitled to thanks every time he does something that needs doing, *he still needs to know that he is not being taken for granted.*

This, I think, is the positive note in our longing for romance. The young men I interviewed were indeed romantic; they believed that they owed a woman the best that they could provide, do, or be. Even the men who were going from woman to woman, like a musician I met in Boston, shared this standard: "I wouldn't marry a woman," he said, "because I respect women too much." (A year later—ho, ho—I met his wife, who looked happy enough.) *A man gives a woman his best, or he'd best give her nothing, and stay away;* that is what they believed. *And they believed that they would have the right to expect love and respect in return for their best efforts—a respect that included tolerance for their own attempts, however awkward, to change.*

I think that this is a fair enough expectation. But alongside it was another, which I heard nearly as often, and found troubling: a startling precision, on the part of both men and women, about what they were looking for in their future partners. They wanted intimate partners who would not take them for granted—*but they posed this expectation in terms of a conflict that they must always be prepared to win.*

It was most marked in the young business people. A rising banker said that his future marital "partner" had to be just as smart, sociable, and hardworking as himself, and as sexually desirous as his numerous adventures had made him (otherwise, he said, "I might as well just keep screwing around"). A young woman who thought that "taking a year out of my life" to do something she had never done, like travel abroad, would be fatal to her career, and who was due to inherit several million dollars, said that the man she wanted to marry would be older and richer than herself (that is, no longer spending his time and his vital fluids at the young banker's pace). Both of them had a shopping list; and while waiting for someone to answer to it, they occupied themselves in relationships with people who came, at times, to love them, and whom they allowed to love them, always knowing that in the end they would break off the relationship.

When I met the banker, he had just ended one of these relationships, with a woman whose sexual charms did not compensate his nagging doubts that he might have to explain her lack of business savvy to his colleagues, whose wives, unlike his bedmate, were accomplished professionals. And he had broken it off painfully, without understanding his own motives, vaguely aware that he had come to love the woman he rejected. Like many men who divorced their wives during the sixties and seventies, he could not confront the weakness he sensed in his own needs, the implications of the terms he had set for his intimate life.

And like the young postfeminist woman executive, he wanted to cut an intimate deal, on the best terms possible. *They did not want to make an investment in another person; they saw their relationships as the just return on the investments they had already made in themselves.* Their marriages would be traditional in the most startling sense, if they followed their convictions through: they would exchange their privileges and domains as calculatedly as medieval princes in search of feudal rents.

Part of what bothered me in this little dance was the ironic twist it performed on the feminist idea of gender equality—a twist closer to the hostility of separatism than to the dream of free and equal beings that began the Second Wave. But worse was the underlying notion—the same notion we apply to our careers—that a given man or woman is replaceable. Someone else can be found who is just as good-looking, just as successful, just as talkative and socially presentable. Someone else can do the intimate job, according to a neat short list of characteristics.

No: a given man or woman—a person so like, yet so unlike us, or anyone else—can never be replaced. The experiences a man and woman share in intimacy, in a life together, may never become entirely new lives, but will never be the same lives they could have with someone else. We are not walking lists of powers and assets, to be traded in deals. That concept will not serve our needs in an age when men and women want more and better, as they are perfectly right to do.

Perhaps the return of such attitudes is a natural, if regrettable, legacy of our parents' generation, in which mutual reliance degenerated into the mutual recrimination of the divorce court. If we cannot count on each other, we must count on ourselves; it is a seemingly inevitable fact. Certainly, this young man and woman took themselves for relentlessly modern: intimacy, they implied, was an armed truce between equally self-reliant powers. They saw this as being tough—they dressed, by the way, in accord with the "tough look" that was so prominent in their urban habitat through the early eighties—but also as a realistic romanticism, not unlike the kind of gruff but loving combat of 1930s screwball comedies, when Cary Grant and Irene Dunne would battle their way toward the nuptial bed.

But they had failed to take note of the saving grace in those comedies— that at the end, Cary and Irene would admit to their failures, their mistakes, their need for each other. And the young toughs seemed to me, finally, to be expressing not confidence in their own strengths, but a deep underlying fear of what might happen if ever they surrendered their powers. *They were looking not for someone they could trust, but for someone they could afford to trust, whose strength would never overcome their own.*

We can see the same theme emerging from New Age wise boys like one Justin Sterling, who in 1984 was telling his public that "a man's job is to control his woman, when she needs it . . . but only when she gives him permission." The woman who reported those ideas remarked, "His words echoed a gutsy honesty that I could find no argument with . . . . I admired Justin's sense of vision."

Some gutsy vision. Men cannot control women—they cannot even control each other.

And why should men control women, when you think of it? Are women so dangerous?

Were the stress doctors and the separatists right—have we nothing to offer each other but sudden or grinding death?

Are we condemned to a mere brutal honesty—don't mess with, tread on, screw with me, I'm more trouble than I'm worth—*or can we trust each other for something better?*

We can, of course, survive without each other, to some extent; single mothers have proven it, along with the workaholic boys. *But we know that something is lacking here, that even in our hardest-won solitude we are as incomplete as ever we have been together, in intimate worlds that no longer meet our expectations.* If we do not, thanks to progress of some kind, need each other to conceive, or to make a living, *we still need each other to live—to do the work that needs to be done, to love each other and feel loved.*

In order to accept that final reality, we are beginning to ask ourselves what would happen if each and all of us sacrificed certain powers and privileges—if men gave more of their time to the personal, and women to the impersonal domains of our lives. But in the short run, I believe, *men will have a greater moral sacrifice to make than will women.* Not only will we have to accept a more heightened emotional and material dependence on our partners, *but we must simultaneously claim the responsibility for our intimate acts, in a way that we have not over three generations.*

I am thinking that we must extend our notion of *fidelity* in our intimate lives—and certainly not in a vain attempt to assure ourselves that our politicians sleep with no women but the ones they marry, or that when men or women say, "I gotta work late tonight, honey," working is what they'll be up to, or that we will not run the risk of exposing ourselves and our loved ones to herpes or AIDS. We are too obsessed with fidelity, narrowly defined by the specter of intimate betrayal; we have downgraded fidelity in the broadest sense, as *a constancy of men and women to each other throughout life.*

I am thinking of a man who wrote to me that he wanted to live, and have children, with several women at once. *Yet when a woman he loved, who loved him, gave him a written, signed promise that she would live with him on his own terms, he refused.*

The situation had something ludicrous in it, but there was something serious beneath the farce. Was he still caught in the moral rule that we applied to our fathers—that when a man makes a mother of a woman, he belongs to her, and only her? I think so; but more important, *he may have been avoiding the moral weight of his dream.*

If he had accepted the woman's words, plighted that particular troth, he would have had to give up a fantasy, and take the reality; as much as a man who would trade all the one-night stands he could ever have, in order to make love with one woman, his lawful wedded wife. He would have to make a promise, to return a woman's extraordinary gifts. He knew that she would keep her word, but he wondered if he could keep his own. He was uncertain that however things turned out, whatever family he invented, he could remain present and responsible. If he was no longer bound by his father's rules of conduct, he held himself to something like the rules our fathers tried and failed to live by.

In this sense, at least, our fathers' painful experience has something to teach us: *if intimacy is to have any meaning, it lies in continuity.* We already sense this—it is why one of the unwritten rules of the monogamous serialists was to "stay friends" with the partners they loved and left; it is why spiritual communes, voluntary extended families rooted in some variety of traditional scriptures and looking forward to a New Age of love, flourished throughout the 1970s. *We have emerged from a moment in our history in which first our parents, in the havoc of Depression, war, and divorce, and then ourselves, found ourselves cut off from our families' pasts. And we have concluded that if a family*—whatever families we choose to found, whether man and wife or "loving friends," in the phrase of a woman who told me, "my family is my friends"—*cannot be said to have a past, it must nonetheless have a future.*

Here, however confused by messages of vengeance and cries of pain, is the great insight of the New Men: *if a man can be defined by nothing else, they seem to be saying, he can be defined by the ties he binds himself with, and by the other people he is tied to throughout his life.* They have proposed that the real wealth of life lies in relationships, as strongly as men have ever proposed it. If they have not resolved Tom Rath's awful paradox—that a man is Something, alone at last, but that alone, he is nothing—they have declared themselves willing, if not yet entirely able, to live with it. And they have at last denied that a man who gives himself to loving is not, somehow, quite as much a man as the one who holds only the power to make or break a world. They have argued, in fact, that the love a man feels in others, and feels toward himself from others, is the center of what would otherwise be a hollow, whimpering world.

But they have not yet fully addressed the burdens, as opposed to the pleasures, that await them when they reach that core. The burdens I have in mind are not mysterious: they are the ones that are still carried by women, at a five-to-one ratio over men, in single-parent families; and which are carried in the same or greater proportion by working wives and mothers in average families: not just taking care of business, but taking care of homes, and most vitally, the emotional needs of the people who live in them.

Part of the reason that men can avoid those burdens on a lifelong basis is so obvious that it has escaped our notice, the way a mustache only rarely protrudes into a man's field of vision. As I argued in Part IV, there are not enough men to go around. A self-supporting man of reasonable decency is a relatively rare commodity in our society, compared to the numbers of self-accomplished women. He can therefore trade partners, when the need arises, more easily than a woman can. And that is, on the evidence, what millions of men have done, and were doing even before no-fault, no-alimony divorce removed a critical legal barrier to dissolving marriages.

If a man does less of the work of caring in most families than a woman does, it is partly because he does not have to do as much as she must, in order to seem of equal value in the marriage market. It sounds cold, I know, but it is the flip side of the fact that, just as she is still the final bulwark against a vacuum in child care, he is in most cases the family's best hope of attaining a decent standard of living.

Yet men must recognize that the power afforded them by their numerical shortage and their fiscal weight has carried a steep price, when measured against their hope to lead richer lives. It has given women reason to claim that their concern for, involvement with, and final responsibility for families is greater than that of men; and thus to entrench themselves in the home, at precisely the moment when men most need them to accept a greater share of the work we pay people to do. That is perhaps not the way things have to be, but according to current evidence, it is still the fact of our intimate matters—and I do not see how the fact will change, unless men make a certain sacrifice.

Not all marriages are happy; not all divorces are futile or brutal. *But it nonetheless seems that there is a clause on the intimate contract that men wish to negotiate with women, in larger than fine print: to accept, as much as women have, the responsibility for ensuring that intimacy in its various forms endures over the course of a lifetime.* It is a failure to accept that responsibility, in part, that keeps abortion a woman's issue; that makes men fear their ability to care for their children, and children doubt the destinies their fathers are working to provide for them.

In a blunt word: *if men have recently gained the freedom to act according to their own impulses, they should not be astonished that those subject to the consequences of their impulses find it difficult to rely on them.* And if they want to be loved and trusted—as it seems they do—I doubt that they will achieve those gains without giving up what has been a precious, but on the record rather dubious share of their freedom.

WOMEN AND MEN UNITED

In Part IV I argued that if men carry a burden of silence about their deepest dreams and needs, it is partly due to the fact that *we must still live in a world where other men make use of our weaknesses, of the emotions we try to hide so that they cannot be used against us.*

It is a natural fear, for men like us. And not a stupid one, not at all— because the New Man who wants a well-paying job, for his own sake and his loved ones, is still up against the workaday wolves; just as the gay man is up against the forces of intolerance, the black man and woman against the forces of racism, the working woman against her all-male board of directors, even now. We are afraid to be under another's control—in particular, we men are—because we have learned to be.

For that reason, I think it is all to the good that women, who do not in the main experience violence as men do, are taking a larger role in our public life. We do not know how far that effect will reach yet; whether it will become possible for men and women to cooperate, in every sphere, with the same energy and power they are now bringing to competition in the working world. We do not know what it would be like to inhabit a world where beating the other guy isn't everything, but remains the only thing better than getting beaten.

But in the meanwhile, *when men leave the world of work and move toward the home, we will*—it is what we sense, what we feel—*be not only under the vastly heightened power of a woman, but the equally terrifying power of other men, to laugh at, attack, and perhaps break the little worlds of love to which we will seem, in part even to ourselves, to be retreating.*

If men are not making two-thirds of the family income—the money that provides for a home, for the kids' schooling, the doctor bills, the cars—who will? And who will provide the margin of safety, such as it is, in a family's fortunes, in a world where a working woman earns less than 60 cents to her working man's dollar?

If the New Men cried so loud in the eighties, I think it was in large part precisely because they felt that awful and reasonable fear. Their new expectations came up against the crunch I described in Part VI—as the earning power of men declined, relative to the cost of housing, and as the public sector's schools, transportation systems, medical services, and family aid programs declined in quality and rose in cost. *They were being asked, as individuals, to reconcile their heightened goals for themselves and those they loved, with a hostile social environment.*

One of the staggering ironies of our time is that this environment was created by an administration that claimed, always and foremost, to act in the name of "family values." Somehow, cutting budgets for school lunches, and federal aid for public education, and benefits to veterans and the elderly on Social Security, and other programs too numerous to mention was presented—and accepted, for years, by the public—as a tribute to the family's limitless capacity to earn and buy what it needed for itself. It was not. As numerous observers have commented, what took place under President Reagan was a net transfer of our society's wealth from the lower and middle classes to the upper classes. The average family was hit hard by Reaganomics, and has not yet come near recovering.

And along with this transfer went a further widening of the gap that John Kenneth Galbraith identified so eloquently in *The Affluent Society,* between the private wealth that individuals may gain, and a poverty of the resources we give to the public domain:

In recent years, the papers of any major city—those of New York are an excellent example—tell daily of the shortcomings in the elementary municipal and metropolitan services. The schools are old and over-crowded. The police force is under strength. The parks and play-grounds are insufficient. Streets and empty lots are filfthy, and the sanitation staff is underequipped and in need of men. Access to the city by those who work there is uncertain and painful and becoming more so.

And so on. Those words were written at the beginning of the Age of Stress, in 1958, and they are not yet dated. Nor is Galbraith's prescription: *that the route to greater economic security in our society, as a whole and for individuals, lies not in cutting, but in expanding the share of our resources that are devoted to public services.*

Look at it this way: a working couple in New York, two nice young professionals with school-age children, would be happy to cut back somewhat on their working time and spend more with the kids. But in the short and long terms, that would mean a reduction in income. They would not be able to afford to send the kids to a private school, as middle-class people in New York and many other American cities are wont to do, for the simple reason that public schools are in an awful state. And when the rent on their apartment rose, as rents do these days, they might not be able to afford the increase and might be obliged to take a new apartment—assuming they could find one—entailing an even longer commute on terrible transportation to and from their jobs and even less time at home. They might even have to cut back on their medical insurance, and hope that no one was hit by a car that spun out over a pothole.

I have deliberately chosen a relatively privileged case to make my point: *in our society, private individuals are expected to make up, through their own efforts, for a societal unwillingness to invest in necessary goods and services.* And I must tell you: it is a humbling shock for an American to see that in France, West Germany, and other countries whose development is comparable to ours, the public services that support families—health insurance, transportation, schooling, housing subsidies, and so on—are vastly more sweeping and high-calibered than back home. Moreover, it is difficult to avoid the conclusion that one of the reasons that French families, to take an example with which I am familiar, have vastly greater amounts of time to spend with each other than do Americans, is that the parents are not always out making money in order to pay from their own pockets for the services that government could more effectively provide.

Public priorities *do* have an impact on private lives. Our public priorities are not now, in any sense of the term, aimed at housing, feeding, educating, or otherwise supporting family life, to anything like the extent to which such support is required. It is not the point of this book to describe in detail how such programs might work. *But it seems plain that without some such shift in our values and goals as a society, no more than a few individuals will be able to make greater progress toward the values that millions of people have come to expect.*

And frankly, I shudder to think of the rage—especially from those Americans now in their childhoods, who have had the chance to witness the tail end of the Reaganite binge, and will no doubt wonder why they have been left to pay for it and to get along with the crumbled ruins of our public sector—if political and social leaders do not take account of such needs. I strongly suspect that it would make the generational conflict of the sixties look like bingo night at the neighborhood church. At the very least, I am sure, *we are not now preparing for ourselves the sort of society in which men and women are free to develop their intimate wealth in anything like comfort and security.* And I think I can promise you that most of us will not be very happy to live in it.

If there is a common political project in which our male-dominated parties and feminist interest groups can unite, it may well be this: to ensure that both men and women start and end their lives in America as *inheritors of a common wealth.* This, as it happens, is precisely the classical meaning of conservatism—to conserve, and build upon, just such a common wealth; a meaning that was pushed aside in the eighties by self-declared conservatives. One hopes that this will prove to be only a temporary aberration.

In gender terms, classical conservatism parallels the concept of "husbandry"—one who guards, protects, and adds to necessary resources of the home economy. If we have turned away, in recent years, from both the essence of conservatism and of husbanding, that may be a vengeful continuation of the masculine sense that if a world is worth making, it is all the same being made only for the sake of women. But this is another of the promises that no longer hold.

The promises that men and women made to each other before were perhaps equal, but exclusive: if women have always promised to clean up men's messes, men have always promised not to leave them too much of a mess to clean up. But one of the messages of the environmental scandals of the 1970s, like the Love Canal fiasco (in which it was learned that chemical dumping by the Hooker Corporation had poisoned an entire neighborhood), was that the mess men make has gotten out of hand.

And behind men's abdication of responsibility—which is, inevitably, also an abdication of power, because power belongs to those who exercise it— is our separation between the making of things and the keeping of them: a gender separation. A man makes the outbuildings, said Kerouac, and gets the unmarked grave. Someone else will inherit his achievements, and it will be her job to see that they are kept up. He is a creator, and a procreator; she is the loving servant, charged with his maintenance when work is done. The idea that it might be otherwise sounds so comic to us that in 1978, performance artist Rob Brezsny, a part-time janitor, made audiences laugh at his Janitorial Arts Collective, as he sternly warned them, "Clean up your own mess!"

The joke, once again, is on men. That is partly why women have lately found it so easy to laugh at us.

We have already recognized this problem, in part; that is why, as I said above, men want to learn how to cook and clean for themselves, to reclaim some power vis-à-vis women. But there is also a desire for moral self-respect in these acts, founded on a new contract: *that men and women will make, and keep, the same promises to each other.* This was among the demands that came through the feminist movement: that what men put into the world, they are just as responsible as women for maintaining. But once again, the idea is becoming men's own—slowly, but I think surely.

It may not be coincidence that as this idea takes hold, services are becoming the dominant growth sector of our economy. It is here, of course, that most of our newly employed women, and growing numbers of men, are working—a fact that has troubled many commentators, because service jobs tend to be relatively low-paid. That is unfortunately true, for the women and men working long hours for insufficient wages; it would be less unfortunate, as I suggested above, if wages were not the sole means of access to a good life in our society. But even now, we can see that *as services become more important to our economy, the barriers between our work and our love will come down.* They will come down because *the kind of work that men and women are doing is less harshly divided between those who make, and those who serve the makers.*

We have begun to see that the kind of labor we most need now is the labor that goes into caring for oneself, and others—of attending to the consequences of our acts, and of those who depend on their outcome. It is the labor that makes this country livable, that maintains our way of life. And behind this revaluation of what has always been seen as women's work, on the part of men, is not only the hope that men could rely on themselves to do what women have always done for them—that much, men see already—but that in so doing, *they can regain the sense that others can rely on them.*

THE BALANCE OF OUR LIVES

One day I made a list of all the things that I am personally responsible for maintaining. It included: my apartment, my business and off-time clothes, my food stocks and kitchen utensils; my relationships with my wife, my family, my friends, my business colleagues; my working tools and supplies (library, files, computer, typewriter, pencils and pens, and so on); my health; my correspondence; my income; my music and language skills . . .

What this little exercise showed me is that I have plenty of things to do with my time, but that *I cannot do much more with the time I have.* And neither, I would bet, can you—not if you, too, have to work for a living, to support a life, and the lives you share in intimacy. There are certain tasks that must be left aside, certain pleasures that must be forgone.

The choices we make among them are partly conscious, and partly not. And that is inescapable, because if we were compelled to choose what we were to do next, every moment of every day, we would soon go mad. There must be a core principle among the welter of these choices, a reflex that tells us that what we have decided to do, in this moment and the moments that follow, is right.

That is part of what women mean when they say—and I hear women saying it, more than men—that intimacy is a day-to-day affair, a kind of habit one lives by. They mean that if intimacy is what matters most to a person, it will show in the effort that a person makes to support it, day in and day out. They mean that there are certain aspects of life that cannot simply be put aside, but that must be woven into the multitude of acts that make up a day. Where our relations to others are concerned, we have to make do with the time we have, and we have to find that time, every day.

Yet the fact is that we do not all have time, even over the course of a lifetime, to become as different as we may want to be. That is our excuse— though not an excuse for avoiding the work we must still do—but it is also a kind of grace. Some things take a long time in the doing, longer than any person's lifetime. Even if men and women do their best, right now, and for as long as they live, those following us will still have plenty left to do. We thus do not have to blame ourselves for leaving some things undone, as each and all of us inevitably will.

This is not only a moral principle, but a good home remedy. There is nothing quite so helpful, I have found, in getting rid of "stress" than repeating the American mantra: "So what." Things didn't go quite the way I wanted today? So what. I went through a hard time with a woman? So what. I may never be all the man I want to be?

Guess what? I care about it, and I care for the men and women who are trying to do and make things right; but I do not care, to the point of despairing about when or if everything will be *all* right, *all* the time. I can't afford to, and I doubt that everyone else can, either.

If each of us gets *something* right, and enough of those somethings contribute to the *same* thing—namely, *the good of each and all of us,* and not just the greatest good of the greatest number—then that would be more than most of us can claim, at the moment.

It would, in a way, be less than the rewards we promise to those few among us who are willing and able to stand the terrible stress of what we call "success." But what a relief: *to stop pursuing happiness, and consider the happiness we already possess; to measure ourselves from the inside out, instead of the other way around; to find our wealth, as individuals and as a society, not only in what we have gained from, but in what we have given to each other.*

There is enough time urgency in our lives without adding to it. And I do not want to add to your urgency by telling you, once again, that you must change, now, in accordance with someone's more or less expert opinion. What I have tried to show, instead, is that *we are already, and still, changing. If the motion we are making is slow—slower than some of us like to admit—it nonetheless continues, and has continued over three generations.*

In some ways it seems that this motion and the "stress" it causes are being imposed on us—by changes in our economy, by women making new demands on men, by the breakdown of old balances between work and intimacy, man and woman. *But the major part of this shift—and that is the extraordinary thing—is voluntary.* No one has ever passed a law to demand that men do more housework, but a few men are actually doing a woman's share of it. Millions of others are doing more than they used to. No major corporation, to my knowledge, has eagerly hired candidates who refuse flat out to move when and where the company wants, whatever his family would prefer—but that is what some men are doing. And not only because women have forced them, either—no more than that women went to work solely for the money during the last few recessions. On the evidence, *it is because they both believe that this will make them happier.*

Our struggle to integrate these new values into our daily lives is the consequence of a choice made by millions of people, and one that seems attractive to millions more. And it seems to me that if people stick by these choices—if they refuse to give up the emotional wealth that we are coming to see as the supreme goal and value of life—then *over the course of our lifetimes, if not tomorrow, our culture will bend further to accommodate them.* We can already see the effects of this trend—in the demands that this or that corporation make "flex-time" available to certain workers; in the efforts we are making to define the care that must be provided to children of working parents, and by whom; and in a renascent debate over what government owes to the people, in order to meet basic social needs.

The material, practical obstacles to this shift remain real and heavy enough. But it seems to me that the ultimate obstacle remains one posed by the ongoing feminist debate in our society—ongoing, because we are still dealing with a question posed explicitly, in force, for the first time by feminists. It is this: *whether or not what men gain, women must lose, and vice versa.*

That dilemma comes down to two further questions: *Must men gain the time to learn the art of relationships at the expense of their families' futures, or the love and respect of others by sacrificing their chances for success in the world? Must women give up their primacy in the family, and take on even more of the work men do?*

Yes—and no. Yes, because neither men nor women, we are saying more and more clearly, can be considered complete if their only claim to humanity is the job they do. Yes, because no one, we are finally admitting, has a natural right to a monopoly on the intimate domains of our lives. And a thousand times no—because *we have finally begun to recognize that men have become cut off from the bedrock of their lives, and that they cannot find their ground without learning from women; and that women are cut off from the world, and cannot merely reject it to the hands of men.*

And because, most simply and finally, *we have recognized that the choice is ours to make, whatever its costs, whatever its risks.* Some individuals have proven the point—people no more heroic or unique than the rest of us, whose lives are no better or worse, after making their choices, than the ones we now lead.

Part of what drives most of us to stay in the circles we have made for ourselves is that we are afraid of what would happen if we did not. We are afraid of letting down the kids who want new toys; or of never being able to afford a house to put our families in; or that if a woman goes to work, her children will never really be hers.

We are afraid that if we try something different, our world will fall apart. It is as though we can't really afford to go on living in our present stress, but we are afraid that we can't afford not to bear it.

And men, in particular, are afraid: afraid that they will not be able to pay the price, in time and money, that defines a man, even now. Just as, throughout the Age of Stress, we did not know if we could afford to love, or not to love; to work, or not to work.

We have forced ourselves, radicals and conservatives alike, toward an either-or choice, sensing all the while that both options were incomplete. We have left ourselves little room in between—as if life had not been ever and always an in-between proposition, between birth and death, love and labor, behind and ahead. We have avoided measuring the weight and value of these domains, yet struggled to give them a final, satisfying measure.

Where will we set the balance? As we can—as in one way or another, we must, and will?

It is inconceivable that we must go on forcing men and women to choose between making a living, and making a life—inconceivable that we cannot find ways and means of caring for each other, beyond the care we already give.

It is inconceivable that men and women cannot find in the love that they may offer each other and the lives they can live together a greater richness than we now possess; that they cannot offer this wealth to their children, and that their children would not, in the end, accept it, such as it is.

It is inconceivable, because *that is what we already know.* That is what we have lived and what we have tried to tell each other, so often yet so indirectly. It is no longer merely an abstract vision. It is where we are going, and we know the reasons for going there.

Notes on Method

I would call the method of this book "subjective journalism." It is not a new method: the essence of journalism has always been a debate between the objective and the subjective, between the fact and the interpretation one may justifiably place on it.

In "objective" journalism, speculation is limited, and always proceeds from a fact, which is considered as having an existence independent of its reporter (assuming the reporter is trustworthy). In subjective journalism, the observer's experience, as well as the perspective based on it, is taken as the first fact; and the first speculation is to ask how closely this fact corresponds to others' "facts," seeing those facts as observations rooted in the experience of differing people and their different perspectives.

This means, for example, asking what different people have in mind—as I asked my subjects—what they think "stress" stands for, and what it feels like to them. It means noting their dialogue even when it makes no apparent sense, when it hesitates or switches to another subject by reflex. It means asking what allows a person to subscribe to a given notion, at a given time, and not taking those notions as concrete facts. And it involves using the writer's experience as an explicit point of comparison, without assuming that what happened to the writer is an indisputable personal truth.

Much of my research was used to corroborate or disprove what were, at the outset, my subjective impressions and intuitions about the lives covered by the period I wrote about. A good part of it was directed at statistical sources—for example, in order to see how typical it is for a young man to lose several friends to automobile crashes at a given moment in their lives.

Another part of the evidence was culled from newspapers, films, novels, periodicals. Here I was looking for trends in popular thinking—some of which I had already covered for various magazines. A working writer knows that editors follow fashions, and those fashions respond to readers' changing interests. Pop culture isn't worth all the time we give it, much less its current glory, but it does have something to say about what people respond to in the images and ideas they subscribe to.

Research for this book began in 1981 with telephone or in-person inteviews with numerous doctors and other practitioners who were using psychosomatic diagnoses or treatments, or researchers studying psychological correlates of illness. Since 1975 I had been covering the so-called holistic health movement for various magazines, and these interviews were compiled for one such article, "How Your Personality Affects Your Health." But when my research was done, I could not write the story: the pieces did not add up. Too much of what I had been told did not make solid sense. There was a story behind the story, to which I returned four years later, this time putting aside the latest developments and concentrating on the evolution of the theory of stress. What I then did was to compare this evolution to the patterns by which other movements I knew of firsthand had evolved, and then to compare these patterns to other firsthand accounts and to available statistical data.

This research was constantly checked and expanded through interviewing and follow-up conversations (when possible) with a sample of forty men, aged seventeen to seventy-three, several of whom were interviewed in the presence of their wives. Supplemental conversations or events from personal journals were sometimes used. Where anonymity was requested, or material was taken from noninterview situations, identifying details have been altered or omitted. All quotes remain accurate.

Certain questions were asked in each interview—employment history, experiences of violence, sexual history, marital record, nuclear family history. Income and age were recorded. Other matters covered depended on the age of the subject—for example, a twenty-five-year-old man would not be likely to have the same military experience as a man who was of draft age in World War II—on the subject's willingness to answer certain questions, and on the particular areas of employment or personal relations best represented in the individual's experience.

The material was not uniform, but it was pointed. Interviews were structured to uncover as many variations or likenesses in the subjects' experience as possible, in accord with the themes emerging from previous research. Again, this is basically a journalistic method, to cover a complex story as it unfolds, gathering, comparing, and adding up pieces of it until a pattern can be identified and documented.

One overall criticism that can be leveled at this approach is that it lacks a rigorously scientific base, if not a system of analysis. In a certain sense, yes: an analysis that emerges from current and recent events is hardly likely to follow the model of scientific or literary structuralism, to take one example. There are too many variables in the equation; it is not like analyzing tribal myths or the Bible. What is lost in the science, one hopes, is gained in scope, in the wealth of connections that can be found in different faces of a long moment.

Part of the point of the "new journalists"—the invention of Tom Wolfe, as far as the label goes—was that subjective and objective methods can be usefully mixed, and that by mixing them journalism can be a form of literature, something you keep instead of throwing out the fish in it. Whether this is good or bad for American writing is for readers to decide. Part of what I tried to do in writing this book was to extend one side of this debate, and, I hope, not on swampy ground.

ACKNOWLEDGMENTS, CONTINUED

Gambit: *The Fourteenth Chronicle: Letters and Diaries of John Dos Passos.* Copyright © 1973 by Gambit.

Harper & Row: *The Mermaid and the Minotaur: Sexual Arrangements and Human Malaise* by Dorothy Dinnerstein. Copyright © 1976 by Dorothy Dinnerstein.

Houghton Mifflin Company: *A Mother's Work* by Deborah Fallows. Copyright © 1985 by Deborah Fallows. Reprinted with permission of Houghton Mifflin Company. *The Affluent Society* by John Kenneth Galbraith, fourth edition. Copyright © 1984 by John Kenneth Galbraith.

International Herald Tribune: "Victories Bring New, More Difficult Battles for Us Feminists" by Lydia Chavez. Appeared in the *International Herald Tribune* July 16–17, 1987. Copyright © *The New York Times.* "Placing the Older Manager" by Elizabeth Fowler. Appeared in the *International Herald Tribune* September 17, 1986. Copyright © 1986 *The New York Times.* "In U.S., Millions Face Downward Mobility" by Steven Greenhouse. Appeared in the *International Herald Tribune* July 19–20, 1986. Copyright © *The New York Times.* "Men at a Premium in U.S. Homes" by Robert Lindsey. Appeared in the *International Herald Tribune* June 25, 1981. Copyright © *The New York Times.* "Workers Fail to Save Hyatt Clark" by Thomas Luceck. Appeared in the *International Herald Tribune* May 9–10, 1987. Copyright © 1987 *The New York Times.* "In the Soviet Union, A Modern Society is Beset by a Host of Modern Problems" by Seth Mydans. Appeared in the *International Herald Tribune* August 27, 1986. Copyright © 1987 *The New York Times.* "On Your Mark, Get Set—Retire! That Was the Idea" by George Nelson. Appeared in the *International Herald Tribune* May 13, 1986. Copyright © 1986 *The New York Times.* "Hooked on Money: Treatment Is Needed" by Jay B. Rohrlich. Appeared in the *International Herald Tribune* May 8, 1987. Copyright © 1987 *The New York Times.* "By Soviet Evidence, Women Seem Superior" by Vladimir Shlapentokh. Appeared in the *International Herald Tribune* February 9, 1984. Copyright © 1984 *The New York Times.*

Ladies' Home Journal: "The Men in Your Life" by J. Clive Enos, Ph.D., and Sondra Forsyth Enos, *Ladies' Home Journal*, March 1985. Copyright © 1985, Meredith Corporation. All rights reserved. Reprinted from *Ladies' Home Journal* magazine with permission of the authors.

The Los Angeles Times–Washington Post Service: "Feminism: Full Circle Back to Special Treatment" by Rita Kramer. Copyright © 1986 *The Los Angeles Times.*

The McCall Publishing Company: "Stress—And How to Live with It" by William A. Nolen, *McCall's*, April 1975. Reprinted with permission from *McCall's* magazine. Copyright © 1975 by The McCall Publishing Group. "Stress: Why Women Suffer More" by Maureen Smith. Reprinted with permission from *McCall's* magazine. Copyright © 1976 by The McCall Publishing Group.

Nation's Business: "How to Survive Burnout" by Herbert Freudenberger and Geraldine Richardson. Reprinted by permission, *Nation's Business*, December 1980. Copyright © 1980, U.S. Chamber of Commerce.

New Directions Publishing Corporation: F. Scott Fitzgerald. *The Crack-Up*. Copyright © 1945 by New Directions Publishing Corporation. Reprinted by permission of New Directions.

New York Academy of Sciences: "An Emotional Life-History Pattern Associated with Neoplastic Disease" by Lawrence LeShan. Reprinted from *Annals of the New York Academy of Sciences*, v. 125, 1966.

The New York Times: "As Sex Roles Change, Men Turn to Therapy to Cope with Stress" by Daniel Goleman, August 21, 1984. Copyright © 1984 *The New York Times*. "For Some Executives, Success Has a Terrible Price" by Daniel Goleman, August 24, 1986. Copyright © 1986 *The New York Times*. "Markets for New and Old Houses are on the Rise" by Alan Oser, *Residential Property*, a supplement to the Sunday *New York Times*, September 9, 1986. Copyright © 1986 *The New York Times*. "Youths' Neighbors Stunned by the Charges in Attack on Blacks" by Richard Meislin, and "Howard Beach: A Mood of Ambivalent Display" by Nick Ravo, February 12, 1987. Copyright © 1987 *The New York Times*. "The American Wife" by Ann Taylor Fleming, *The New York Times Magazine*, October 26, 1986. Copyright © 1986 *The New York Times*.

Newsweek Inc.: "No Baby on Board" by Barbara Kantrowitz, September 1, 1986. Copyright © 1986 by Newsweek Inc.

Pantheon Books: *Social Causes of Illness* by Richard Totman. Copyright © 1979 by Richard Totman. *Working* by Studs Terkel. Copyright © 1974 by Studs Terkel. Reprinted with permission of Pantheon books, a Division of Random House, Inc.

Pergamon Press, Inc.: "The Social Adjustment Rating Scale" by T. H. Holmes and R. H. Rahe. Reprinted with permission from *The Journal of Psychosomatic Research*. Copyright © 1967, Pergamon Journals, Ltd.

Random House, Inc.: *Power! How to Get It, How to Use It* by Michael Korda and Paul Gitlin. Copyright © 1975 by Michael Korda and Paul Gitlin. Reprinted with permission of Random House, Inc.

Sage Publications, Inc.: *At Home and at Work: The Family's Allocation of Labor* by Michael Geerken and Walter Cove. Copyright © 1986 by Sage Publications, Inc. Reprinted by permission of Sage Publications, Inc.

St. Martin's Press Incorporated: *Inside Corporate America* by Allan Cox. Copyright © 1982 by Allan Cox. St. Martin's Press, Inc., New York.

Science Digest: "Do You Have a Cancer Personality?" by Dava Sobel. *Science Digest*, July 1976.

Simon & Schuster, Inc.: *The Second Stage* by Betty Friedan. Copyright © 1981 by Betty Friedan. Reprinted with permission of Summit, a division of Simon & Schuster, Inc. *Fire in the Streets: America in the 1960's* by Milton Viorst. Copyright © 1979 by Milton Viorst; *The Organization Man* by William Whyte Jr. Copyright © 1956 by William Whyte. *Some American Men* by Gloria Emerson. Copyright © 1985 by Gloria Emerson. Reprinted with permission of Simon & Schuster.

Time Inc.: "The No. 1 Cause of Executive Guilt: Who's Taking Care of the Children—And How Will They Turn Out?" by Fern Schumer Chapman, *Fortune*, February 16, 1987. Copyright © 1987 by Time Inc.

U.S. News & World Report: "Interview with Expert on Job Stress Cary Cherniss," *U.S. News & World Report*, February 18, 1980. Copyright © 1980 by *U.S. News & World Report*.

The University of California Press: *The Overburdened Economy* by Lloyd J. Dumas. Publisher: The Regents of The University of California. Copyright © 1986 by Lloyd J. Dumas. Reprinted with permission of the publisher. All rights reserved.

The University of North Carolina Press: *From Working Girl to Working Mother: The Female Labor Force in the United States, 1820–1980* by Lynn Y. Weiner. Copyright © 1985 by The University of North Carolina Press.

Viking Penguin Inc.: *The Whole World Is Watching* by Mark Gerzon. Copyright © 1969 by Mark Gerzon; *On the Road* by Jack Kerouac. Copyright © 1957 by Jack Kerouac. Renewed © 1985 by Stella Kerouac and Jan Kerouac; *Ambitious Men: Their Drives, Dreams, and Delusions* by Srully Blotnick. Copyright © 1987 by Srully Blotnick. All rights reserved. Reprinted by permission of Viking Penguin Inc.

Vintage Books: *The New Radicals: A Report with Documents* by Paul Jacobs and Saul Landau. Copyright © 1966 by Paul Jacobs and Saul Landau. Reprinted with permission of Random House, Inc.

The Wall Street Journal: "Labor Letter" column. Reprinted by permission of *The Wall Street Journal*. Copyright © Dow Jones & Company, Inc. All rights reserved.

The Washington Post: "In Middle America, a Mood of Despair" by David S. Broder, Haynes Johnson, and Paul Taylor, April 22, 1987. Copyright ©

1987 *The Washington Post.* "In Detroit, the Murder Capital, Kids Are Killing Kids" by Bill McAllister, December 4, 1986. Copyright © 1986 *The Washington Post.*

William Morrow & Company: "Afterword." From *Take Back The Night.* Copyright © 1980 by Adrienne Rich. Reprinted with permission of William Morrow & Company.

Index